GETTING RESULTS THROUGH COLLABORATION

Networks and Network Structures for
Public Policy and Management

edited by
Myrna P. Mandell

Q

QUORUM BOOKS
Westport, Connecticut • London

Library of Congress Cataloging-in-Publication Data

Getting results through collaboration : networks and network structures for public policy and management / edited by Myrna P. Mandell.

    p. cm.

    Includes bibliographical references and index.

    ISBN 1-56720-455-4 (alk. paper)

    1. Policy networks. I. Mandell, Myrna P.

  H97.7 .G48 2001

  352.3'7—dc21   2001016130

British Library Cataloguing in Publication Data is available.

Library of Congress Catalog Card Number: 2001016130
ISBN: 1-56720-455-4

First published in 2001

Quorum Books, 88 Post Road West, Westport, CT 06881
An imprint of Greenwood Publishing Group, Inc.
www.quorumbooks.com

Printed in the United States of America

∞™ The paper used in this book complies with the Permanent Paper Standard issued by the National Information Standards Organization (Z39.48-1984).

10 9 8 7 6 5 4 3 2 1

Contents

Contents

Figures and Tables

Preface

This book reflects two important trends in the field of public administration. One is the move toward the growing use of networks and network structures as unique types of collaborative efforts. The second is the important realization that networks and network structures have a dramatic impact on our ability to effectively develop and manage public policy. These trends demonstrate not only the growing importance of networks and network structures, but also the need to better understand these concepts and how they can make a difference in the way we will handle our complex public programs in the future. I am therefore struck by the importance of putting together a book on networks and network structures that examines concepts that have relevance not only today, but for the future as well. Indeed, I feel strongly that this should not just be another book on networks and network structures. To ensure this, every effort has been made to take the many diverse themes on networks and network structures and pull them together into a coherent whole.

In addition, theoretical concepts and ideas from academics have been meshed with insights from practitioners not only to provide the reader with cutting-edge concepts and theories, but also to add the dimension of what these concepts and theories can mean at the "ground level." There is also a recognition that networks and network structures are not constrained by geographical boundaries, but occur throughout the world and across borders. The impact of what these international and cross-country settings will mean to future collaborations is also explored. And finally, organization behavior concerns at the micro level (motivation, change, interpersonal relations) are coupled with organization theory concerns at the macro level (structural, political, contextual, and managerial).

Although the idea for this book was originally based on a special symposium, "The Impact of Collaborative Efforts," published in *Policy Studies Review* (16[1], spring 1999), this book goes well beyond the symposium in a number of ways. First of all, it presents the latest thinking and research on networks and network structures that will have an impact on the development of future public policy. This can be seen particularly around the discussions of what is meant by collaboration and the different ways it can be operationalized. The concept of networks and network structures has moved us from a focus on only one organization to a focus on interactions among many organizations. Here we add to this the impact of these types of interactions within different countries, as well as interactions of actors across country borders.

As a result of this broader perspective, a second area of importance is also covered in this book. That is, that instead of a one-sided emphasis on the opportunities and promises of collaborations through networks and network structures, this book takes a hard look at some of the pitfalls and constraints surrounding these types of collaborations. Included are issues of power; conflicts between individual and organizational commitments; the dichotomy between the need for flexibility and the need for rules and procedures; the difference between the needs and expectations of a "national public" and a "local public"; and accountability issues resulting from the need to satisfy outside regulators and foundations, and the need to satisfy the goals of the network.

Third is an emphasis on the difference between what is referred to as collaborations through networks in the business-management literature, and collaborations through networks and network structures for public policy and management. The literature on collaborations through networks in the private sector emphasizes the move toward collaborations through alliances or other types of partnerships meant to improve the operations of a particular business. They therefore bring together a number of organizations within a network-type structure, but all with a view of the interests of the core business that basically controls the relations. In essence, the organizations involved in the network remain intact and can go about their business with relatively few changes required. The collaborations discussed in this book are concerned with networks of individuals and/or organizations that are not in the same business and cannot control each other. What holds them together is a sometimes strong and sometimes weak concern about an issue or problem area that requires these very diverse entities to try to work together. In order to accomplish this, they must first see themselves as part of a total system requiring individual adaptations in order to form a new whole. As a result, the management techniques discussed in the business literature cannot be applied indiscriminately in these endeavors. Instead, a revised perspective of management that incorporates insights "into the completeness, interconnection, implementability, and functioning of networks" (see chapter 2 by Agranoff and McGuire) is needed and is developed in this book.

Fourth, although much has been written on networks and network structures, this literature emphasizes issues primarily at the macro (structural) level. This book also deals with these issues but adds the important, and often overlooked, behavioral issues, so prevalent in these networks and network structures. In this regard, a number of issues around motivation, change, and communication are addressed.

Fifth, the incorporation of a number of international collaborations highlights the importance that the culture of a country plays in these types of collaborations. Culture refers to the attitudes and values of the people, as well as the political and economic systems of the country. Rather than seeing networks and network structures only as tools to foster solutions through innovative, collaborative methods, depending on the cultural foundations of the country involved, they are also seen as tools to reduce the level of services offered by government. The point is that networks and network structures "have become a commodity that is traded politically to suit those in power in their pursuit of cost saving and further control. In other words, networks [and network structures] are factored in as part of the solution without adequate funding or voice" (see chapter 17 by Walker and Goodyear).

Finally, throughout this book, there is an emphasis on innovations currently being developed in these collaborations that will have an impact on their use for the future. For example, the use of computer programs to build a knowledge base among participants is seen as a means to encourage the formation of multidisciplinary projects. Instead of a view of separate individuals working alone at their computers, the use of computers is seen as a means to enhance participants' understanding of each other's perspectives and through this understanding to foster the commitment for individuals with diverse backgrounds and affiliations to work together (see chapter 18 by Allen, Bosch, and Kilvington). This type of innovative thinking is also reflected in the way lessons learned in an African country are applied successfully to communities in the United States, instead of the more usual emphasis of applying U.S. techniques to other countries.

In the future, although much will surely remain the same, much will also be new. This book is therefore presented as a means to deal with what will be. In the process, it is hoped that this book will be seen as a means not only to meet the future, but also to be in the forefront of shaping that future.

Getting Results Through

COLLABORATION

1

Overview of the Book

Myrna P. Mandell

T HIS BOOK IS DIVIDED INTO FOUR PARTS. Part One develops theoretical themes at the macro level. Part Two moves from the macro level to the micro level and deals with a variety of behavioral issues. Part Three provides an in-depth look at networks and network structures based on field analyses, from both the United States and the international arena. Part Four rounds out the perspectives in the book with the experiences and insights of practitioners worldwide. Detailed descriptions of each of these parts are given below.

Part One

Part One, "Models and Typologies for Understanding the Nature and Management of Networks," begins with chapter 2, "After the Network Is Formed: Process, Power, and Performance," by Robert Agranoff and Michael McGuire. In order to improve our knowledge of networks and to develop the capacity of managers operating in such settings, more research into the process, or the "black box," of networks is needed. Although the authors cannot answer all the questions that need answers, they selectively raise some core questions and suggest preliminary answers, derived from their own and others' research, to those questions that would contribute to framing any potential theory of network and collaborative management. Four issues or basic operating questions related to network management are covered:

- Whether there are functional equivalents to traditional management procedures, and whether there is a POSDCORB equivalent in network management

- Whether group decision approaches in network management are the same as those derived from applied behavioral science, or other collaborative learning and deciding processes are at work
- How power comes into play, and what effects it has on group problem resolution
- Whether public management networks produce results that otherwise would not have occurred.

The light shed on these issues may begin a dialogue concerning network management.

Chapter 3, "From Subnet to Supranet: A Proposal for a Comparative Network Framework to Examine Network Interactions Across Borders," by Matthew Mingus, looks at the Comparative Network Framework (CNF) Typology developed for cross-border network relations. Cross-border forms of public organizations, such as the Pacific Salmon Commission, are increasingly utilized to help manage complex policy and implementation issues. This research suggests that knowledge of the existing subnational, regional, and/or national networks (subnets) might eventually help nations design more effective and efficient cross-border networks (supranets) to assist in or even provide joint public management.

In chapter 4, "Assessing and Modeling Determinants of Capacity for Action in Networked Public Programs," by Glenn Rainey and Terry Busson, the authors compare three types of programs that depend on multijurisdictional cooperative arrangements for implementation. They use the comparison to refine modeling of causal relationships and performance dimensions in networked programs, using five key attributes: infrastructure, environmental constraints and munificence, goals, cultural values, and technological options and opportunities. Based on this analysis, they draw some conclusions for public policy.

Chapter 5, "Multiorganizational, Multisector, and Multicommunity Organizations: Setting the Research Agenda," by Beverly Cigler, examines aspects of the organizing and managing dimensions of multicommunity collaboration. Previously published research, including an article in the symposium "The Impact of Collaborative Efforts" (*Policy Studies Review*, spring 1999), reported that collaborations can vary along a continuum involving simple information sharing, cooperative, coordinative, and truly collaborative interaction in which actors recognize a "shared identity." This chapter explains the continuum of partnerships tested by the research, summarizes the set of "preconditions" for the emergence of multiorganizational, multisector, and multicommunity organizations, and focuses on the development of research questions that flow from the findings.

Part Two

Part Two, "Behavioral Implications of Networks," begins with chapter 6, "Environmental Networks: Relying on Process or Outcome for Motivation," by Lisa Nelson. Organization and network leaders must attend to the dynamics of the network and to the relationship between the network and the organizations represented in it, and they must assess what is necessary to maintain the motivation of the individual participants in this context. To help leaders do this, this chapter explores four elements of motivation in environmental networks: differences between organizational and participant preferences; accountability and changing goals; coercion and trust; and the risks and benefits of expanding participation.

Chapter 7, "Bringing about Change in a Public School System: An Interorganizational Network Approach," by Rupert Chisholm, looks at a successful effort to mobilize various groups and individuals in a rural community to bring about change. The effort grew from three workshops sponsored by an interorganizational network for social concerns. Included are the concepts and theory underlying work to trigger and facilitate change, details of the strategy and action steps, dynamics of the change process, lessons from engaging in the change process, and continuing work to make the change a permanent part of the community.

Part Three

Part Three, "Lessons from the Field: Extending Analytical Findings," begins with chapter 8, "The Impact of Network Structures on Community-Building Efforts: The Los Angeles Roundtable for Children Community Studies," by Myrna Mandell. This chapter is based on a study of five community-building efforts conducted by the Los Angeles Roundtable for Children. It was found that the effectiveness of community-building efforts in this study depended on the extent to which they operated as network structures. The discussion centers on two broad areas of concern: the need to rethink and reshape our perceptions of what is meant by community collaborations; and the need to adapt to the realities of community collaborations. This applies to practitioners and community members alike and raises issues involving the development of new roles and capacities. The chapter concludes with some thoughts on the development of future community-building efforts.

Chapter 9, "Creating Networks for Interorganizational Settings: A Two-Year Follow-up Study on Determinants," by Renu Khator and Nicole Ayers Brunson, extends the work presented in the symposium "The Impact of Collaborative Efforts" (*Policy Studies Review*, spring 1999). This chapter analyzes results of a survey of the participants in the Tampa Bay National Estuary Program two years after completing the project. Participants reflect on what they thought the results were; why they participated in the project; key achievements; and whether they feel their network is still a viable alternative.

Chapter 10, "Cross-Sectoral Policy Networks: Lessons from Developing and Transitioning Countries," by Derick Brinkerhoff and Jennifer Brinkerhoff, covers three cases of policy networks in developing and transitioning countries. The preliminary lessons relate to situational variables that constrain or facilitate cross-sectoral networks for policy reform, and mechanisms and processes for bringing together diverse groups to cooperate around a policy issue. The authors present an overview of critical issues related to managing such policy networks, highlighting the particular challenges for networks in developing and transitioning countries. These challenges include a multiplicity of actors, power differentials among actors, changing contexts and agendas, vague understandings of sectoral roles and responsibilities, and capacity building.

Chapter 11, "Will the People Really Speak? A Networking Perspective on Hong Kong as It Attempts to Build a Democratic Political Infrastructure," by Robert Gage, looks at the changes in the electoral system since the former British colony returned to Chinese sovereignty. The new electoral system initially frustrates the expression of a public mandate through universal suffrage. The institutional framework of social, cultural, economic, and political networks, established or already in place when Chinese sovereignty was established on July 1, 1997, will thus be built only partially on a democratic foundation. The new political culture, including particularly the political networks, will predictably be thwarted from development. These networks are constrained, as they had been under the British system, from assuming their full roles in the fabric of Hong Kong's regional system of influence in the South China area. This is a very cautious approach to political reform at best.

Chapter 12, "The New South Wales Demonstration Projects in Integrated Community Care," by Michael Fine, examines the collaborative approach to linking community support services that developed as part of these projects in New South Wales, Australia. Project development is outlined from the time of the original call for expressions of interest to the implementation of the planned initiatives, considering the limited options available to service providers to enhance the way the different agencies worked together. The author discusses their main outcomes at the formal completion of the program, reviews the conditions that assisted or impeded the achievement of collaborative project goals, and presents recommendations on the future development of community care in New South Wales.

Part Four

Part Four, "Lessons from the Field: Views of Practitioners," begins with chapter 13, "Neighborhood Networks in Worcester: Partnerships That Work," by Richard Ford, Laurie Ross, and Mardia Coleman. Here, the authors document the growth of building partnerships in urban Worcester (the second-largest urban area in New England) and ways in which tools developed in Africa have been adapted to fit domestic U.S. needs. As a result of their work on joint or collaborative action in Kenya, the authors secured funds to bring Kenyans to Worcester to run training courses on community-based planning and action. As a result, very productive partnerships are now working that involve a number of different kinds of groups.

Chapter 14, "Reaching Consensus on the Tampa Bay Estuary Program Interlocal Agreement: A Perspective," by Richard Eckenrod, gives a practitioner's view of the Tampa Bay Estuary Program in Florida. The author discusses his perceptions of the factors contributing to the success in reaching consensus in this project, as well as the methods used to overcome barriers to consensus.

In chapter 15, "Thoughts on Motivational Problems in Networks," by Nina Burkardt, the author comments on the questions raised in Lisa Nelson's chapter (chapter 6) on how to maintain motivation in interorganizational networks and delineates several means used to do so. More important, she raises the concern that although many networks work well together, many others fall apart. She calls for further research on which conflicts are amenable to solutions by networks; the problems of identification and involvement of a full range of actors; and linking network processes with network products.

Chapter 16, "Empowering Communities Through the Use of Place Management," by Illana Halliday, looks at the implementation of place management in Fairfield City, Australia. "Place management" is a unique type of collaborative effort that involves coordinating the efforts of a number of government agencies and community groups around a specific location, rather than around a functional area. Several different forms of place management have been introduced, with a wide variety of boundaries and outcomes that best suit each place. The author discusses several challenges facing the city council in terms of implementing place management. Key issues around the definition of place, role clarification and resource decisions, working with the politics, and developing partnerships with the community are explored. For a country where the government provides all services through separate functional organizations and agencies, it has been a challenging experiment for those involved. As such, this chapter offers invaluable insights into the impact of political and social constraints on the ability to collaborate through the formation of networks.

Chapter 17, "Getting Things Done Through Networks," by Shayne Walker and Catherine Goodyear, examines joint projects both across cultural lines and within the same indigenous cultures in New Zealand. Collaboration and cooperation and looking out for one another have not only remained core values, but have been and still contribute a valid and necessary survival and development strategy to which groups of people have remained committed. In spite of this, however, the authors find that networks can be used to empower and disempower. The use of networks to prop up a reduction in the provision of core services has meant that they themselves have become commodities that are traded politically to suit those in power in their pursuit of cost saving and further control.

And finally, in chapter 18, "Integrated Systems for Knowledge Management: A Participatory Framework to Help Communities Identify and Adopt More Sustainable Resource-Management Practices," by Will Allen, Ockie Bosch, and Margaret Kilvington, the authors examine the ISKM framework, which strengthens and enhances the application of methods to promote participation and self-help in natural resource-management projects. This encourages the formation of multidisciplinary projects, which involve not only technical experts, but also personnel with complementary skills in the management of participation and conflict, and the integration of biophysical and social aspects of problem solving. The need for participatory or collaborative approaches to meet environmental challenges is especially important in communities where human and financial resources may be limited. By focusing on improving information use within a collaborative approach, people can broaden the scope of their actions and solve problems previously beyond their capacity.

PART ONE

Models and Typologies for Understanding
the Nature and Management of Networks

2

After the Network Is Formed
Process, Power, and Performance

Robert Agranoff & Michael McGuire

T HE PRIMACY OF NETWORK MANAGEMENT is now clear, although public sector scholars are just beginning to recognize it as a distinctive endeavor. If it is indeed a distinct function from that of hierarchical management (Kettl, 1996; Milward, 1994; O'Toole, 1997a), then focused research and improved conceptualization on this core public activity need to be accelerated. Indeed, as the use of networks in public management increases, more and more questions regarding this research arena are being developed. The authors' view is that network management is in search of an equivalent to the hierarchical organizational authority paradigm of bureaucratic management. Weiner (1990) predicts that organizational management and transorganizational (network) management will become two parallel but overlapping streams within administrative theory, relying heavily on both behavioral science and management science research and practice. Clearly, the authors' research on managing within inter-local economic development networks (Agranoff and McGuire, 1998; 1999a; 1999b) raises numerous questions regarding network management. In order to improve our knowledge of networks and to develop the capacity of managers operating in such settings, more research into the process, or the "black box," of networks is needed.

What is known is that managers operate in networks through various forms of collaborative problem solving (Agranoff, 1996; Radin et al., 1996), but managing networks should not be confused with managing hierarchies. The classical

management approach, which has informed both public and business administration for more than a century, is mostly intraorganizational and based primarily
on the activities of planning (establishing organizational goals), organizing
(structuring and designing the organization), and leading (achieving the goals).
This approach is based on coordination through hierarchies, strict chains of
command, and management that takes place within the confines of separate organizational entities (Mandell, 1988). In contrast, network settings are not based in
a central authority and cannot be guided by a single organizational goal. The
primary activities of the network manager involve selecting the appropriate
actors and resources, shaping the operating context of the network, and developing ways to cope with strategic and operational complexity (Kickert et al., 1997).
While networks coordinate and facilitate, rarely is real authority granted to a
manager across the network of organizations as a whole. Nor is such a move possible or feasible. Each organization representative brings and keeps his or her
authority, managing together.

Networks are key elements of public and public–private management
because of the involved and multisector nature of public organizing. An increasing number of organizations can no longer be "structured like medieval king-
doms, walled off and protected from hostile forces" (Powell, 1990, p. 298). The
hallmark of the postbureaucratic or post-Fordist mode of organizing is flexibility
and capacity for innovation. Clegg (1990) concludes that whereas bureaucratic
or modern organization was premised on mass forms, what he identifies as postmodern organizing is premised on niches, and whereas jobs were once highly
differentiated, they are now dedifferentiated, demarcated, and multiskilled. The
old determinism of size as a contingency variable in organizing is giving way to
more complex and fragmentary relational forms. Networking is more prevalent
also because of the general diffusion of information among several organized
entities and disciplines, increasing cultures of trust as diverse organizational representatives learn to work together, increasing education requirements and levels
of cognitive complexity brought to bear on problems, expanding knowledge
bases that complicate abilities to reach solutions, and rapid shift and replacement
of technologies (Alter and Hage, 1993). Lipnack and Stamps (1994, p. 3) conclude that "the network is emerging as the signature form of organization in the
information age, just as bureaucracy stamped the industrial age, hierarchy controlled in the agricultural era, and the small group roamed in the nomadic era."

As a result, there are many more questions than answers in network management. Not all of them can be covered in a few pages. But we can selectively
raise some core questions and suggest preliminary answers, derived from our
own and others' research, to those questions that would contribute to framing any
potential theory of network and collaborative management. In this chapter, we
have chosen four issues or basic operating questions related to network management. First, we raise the issue of whether there are functional equivalents to traditional management procedures. Is there a POSDCORB equivalent in network
management? Second, we investigate the group decision approaches in network
management. Are they the same as those derived from applied behavioral science

or are other collaborative learning and decision processes at work? Third, we examine the issue of power in networks, which is often neglected, particularly its effect on the synergistic creativity that reciprocal relationships hope to produce. How does power come into play, and what is its effect on group problem resolution? Fourth, we pursue the issue of network results or network productivity. Do public-management networks produce results that otherwise would not have occurred? The light we shed on these issues may begin a dialogue concerning network management.

What Are the Critical Functional Equivalents to Traditional Management Processes? Is There a POSDCORB Equivalent Set of Tasks?

When a public- or private-sector manager is observed operating in his or her "home" organization, one can clearly describe, in the most general sense, what activities are being performed at any given time and, for the most part, why they are being performed. A vocabulary or nomenclature that has developed and been refined for many decades is available to us to help elucidate the manager's daily activities within a single organization's bureaucratic structure. For example, many textbook descriptions of management include tasks such as planning, organizing, and leading, and for more than sixty years the field has relied, to varying degrees, on a simple acronym—POSDCORB—to distill management activities into seven basic tasks. Furthermore, managers have certain remedies to fix single organizational problems. If an organization appears to lack direction, planning may be the answer; if communication and coordination are poor across departments within an organization, a restructuring may be in order; if absenteeism is unusually high and production in some departments is falling, stronger leadership may be needed. Scholars have identified many behaviors used in managing networks and when it is best to use them, but a similar functional and conceptual equivalent of traditional management processes has not yet been developed (Hanf and O'Toole, 1992). We open the chapter with a purely suggestive grouping of network management behaviors as a way to summarize the literature in a substantive way.

One general class of behaviors specifically addressed in the literature involves the general tasks of *activation*. Activating includes identifying participants for (Lipnack and Stamps, 1994) as well as stakeholders to (Gray, 1989) the network and tapping the skills, knowledge, and resources of these persons (Agranoff and McGuire, 1999a). All interests should be included in network processes (Innes and Booher, 1999). Network managers arrange (Klijn and Teisman, 1997), stabilize as much as possible (Stone, 1999), nurture (O'Toole, 1988), and integrate (Lipnack and Stamps, 1994) the network structure. Activation is a critical component of network management because resources like money, information, and expertise are the integrating mechanisms of networks. According to Scharpf (1978), selective activation of potential participants to the network is "an essential prerequisite for successful interorganizational policy formation and policy implementation" and, if performed correctly, is based on "the correct identification of 'necessary participants' in policy-congruent networks," as well as the willingness of these potential participants to devote resources to the network and not be influenced by actors who may have other interests at stake (p. 364). We know from the urban regime literature (Stoker and Mossberger, 1994; Stone, 1989; Stone, 1999) that governing coalitions in cities must "bring together resources that are adequate to address the identifying agenda," or the arrangements will not be effective (Stone, 1999, p. 3). Such regimes operate according to network principles, but do so informally, usually through fabricated nongovernmental organizations on mutually arrived at agendas. Activating the right players with the right resources is the crucial task of governing in cities through coalitions of public and nongovernmental organizations. Since the probability of activating a weak link in the chain—involving the wrong player or the wrong set of resources—is greater than zero (see Landau, 1991), this task is of crucial importance to network effectiveness. Deactivation also appears to be an important component of network management. For this task, network structures are rearranged and shifted if not performing as desired. The most common prescription in this regard is to introduce new actors as a means to change the network dynamic, shift the influence of existing actors, and facilitate fluid leadership roles (Klijn, 1996; Klijn and Teisman, 1997; O'Toole, 1988; Termeer and Koppenjan, 1997).

Other management behaviors identified in the literature are consistent with the general task of *framing*. Like activation, framing is used both during the formation of the network and as a management tool when network effectiveness diminishes or is suboptimal. Unlike activation, framing is a more subtle task— no network participants are replaced—but many argue that it is just as necessary. Framing involves establishing and influencing the operating rules of the network (Gray, 1989; Klijn, 1996; Mandell, 1990), influencing its prevailing values and norms (Kickert and Koppenjan, 1997; O'Toole, 1997b), and altering the perceptions of the network participants (Termeer and Koppenjan, 1997). A manager can frame the network context by introducing new ideas to the network (Kickert et al., 1997) and thereby create (or celebrate) a shared purpose or vision (Gray, 1989; Lipnack and Stamps, 1994; Mandell, 1988; O'Toole, 1997b). An explicit shared purpose or program rationale (Mandell, 1990; Porter, 1981) can be framed and championed by the manager, providing the glue that holds the network together. The rules of interaction among participants and the perception of that interaction are malleable, and conscious change in the latter through framing can jump-start an unproductive network. In this regard, the manager might offer suggestions for looking at a problem differently or recommend an alternative decision-making mechanism. Although not a simple or straightforward managerial task, framing "gives shape to purposes, and . . . has great influence in the alignment of various forms of engagement" (Stone, 1999, p. 7). Framing helps set the stage for network formation.

In addition to activating the network and framing the interaction of network participants, the literature indicates that network managers need to induce individuals to make a commitment to the joint undertaking—and to keep that commitment. A manager must often sell an idea to potential network participants to secure commitment; support for the network and its purposes must be built (Gray, 1989; Innes and Booher, 1999; Mandell, 1990). *Mobilizing* "requires a view of the strategic whole and an ability to develop and achieve a set of common objectives based on this whole" (Mandell, 1988, p. 33). Managers build support for the network by mobilizing organizations (Mossberger and Hale, 1999) and coalitions (Kickert and Koppenjan, 1997) and forging an agreement on the role and scope of network operations (see Benson, 1975). Additionally, the ability to manage networks is related to the internal support and cooperation of the manager's primary organization. A manager in city government, for example, should have the cooperation of a city council and his or her chief executive as a means to more confidently engage in networking and achieve the strategic purpose at hand (Agranoff and McGuire, 1999a).

Research on network management also addresses *synthesizing* the network by creating the environment and enhancing the conditions for favorable, productive interaction among network participants. Managers must find a way to blend the various participants—each with conflicting goals or different perceptions or dissimilar values—to fulfill the strategic purpose of the network. The network manager seeks to achieve cooperation among actors while preventing, minimizing, or removing obstacles to the cooperation. This steering of network processes is tantamount to game management in the sense that the result of the network process "derives from the interaction between the strategies of all actors involved" (Klijn and Teisman, 1997, p. 99). The strategies of each network participant and the outcomes of those strategies are influenced by the patterns of relations and interactions that have developed in the network. Relationships and interactions that result in achieving the network purpose—synthesis—are the aim of the network manager, and important management behaviors include facilitating and furthering interaction among participants (Agranoff and McGuire, 1999a; Kickert and Koppenjan, 1997), reducing complexity and uncertainty by promoting information exchange (Innes and Booher, 1999; Mossberger and Hale, 1999; O'Toole, 1988, 1997b), changing incentives to cooperation (Kickert et al., 1997), developing new rules and procedures of interaction (Klijn, 1996; Termeer and Koppenjan, 1997), changing positions, relations, and roles of participants (Kickert et al., 1997; Klijn, 1996), helping the network to be self-organizing (Innes and Booher, 1999), and engendering effective communication among participants (Kickert et al., 1997; Mandell, 1990). Synthesizing seeks to lower the cost of interaction, which can be substantial in network settings.

The management tasks discussed in the rapidly growing literature in network management are nearly seamless in their applicability. That is, just as a manager in a single organization may lead, plan, and organize simultaneously within the context of a particular goal, so too are multiple behaviors utilized in network settings. Synthesizing and activating are management tasks often used in conjunction. For example, the removal of a network participant can have myriad effects on the network. Alternatively, if the attitudes and behaviors of some participants are stifling productive interaction, the manager might try to create an environment within which greater interaction can take place by changing (improving) the incentives of participation or "reassigning" (facilitating the reassignment of) various roles within the network. Similarly, synthesizing the network is often accompanied by reframing, or a conscious attempt to change the network participants' perception of the interaction changes. After or during deactivation or reframing, managers must mobilize support for the changes, reestablish the purpose of the network, and make sure all participants are "onboard."

Are the Approaches to "Groupware" Substantively Different from Those Derived From the Applied Behavioral Science Approaches That Emanate From Human Relations Research?

This is a core issue in network management. "Groupware," or group development that reaches a mutual understanding and transcends the more immediate and interactive bases of coordination and communication through hierarchy, describes interagency task group development for reaching jointly arrived at solutions. It leads to results that are qualitatively different from those of interorganizational coordination and/or mutual adjustment. Groupware requires that multiple cultures, procedures, and divisions of labor be incorporated into the network (Clegg and Hardy, 1996). Decisions are deliberative, creative, and group-based, as organization representatives shed some of their ideology and forge redefined problems, a mutual course of action, a multiorganizational implementation technology, diversified methods of resource acquisition, and so on. Limited empirical research of network process suggests that strong emphasis must be placed on multiorganizational problem-solving techniques for values clarification and role negotiations within action planning, collaborative capacity building, and intense team building and process consultation within survey feedback.

Groupware leads to synergistic products. Operating by groupware clearly requires the application of standard applied behavioral-science techniques, but is more required? Myron Weiner (1990, p. 456) suggests that in transorganizational (network) management, techniques similar to organization management are normally employed: group problem solving, force-field analysis, action planning, team building, process consultation, and others. However, the two domains are distinctive in at least two ways: In network management, empowerment is based on *information* rather than authority, and existing organizational structures are *dependent* variables for network systems. The several organizations working together can be fashioned into new systems, using the flow of information to link the transorganizational system.

One possible ingredient in the interorganizational information flows that are necessary for developing groupware is social capital. Fountain (1998, p. 104) refers to social capital as the "stock" that is created when a group of organizations develops the ability to work together for mutual productive gain (for related definitions, see Coleman, 1990; Putnam, 1993). Social capital is essential for groups of disparate representatives to work toward sharing resources held by individual organizations:

> Like physical capital and human capital—tools and training that enhance individual productivity—"social capital" refers to features of social organization, such as networks, norms, and trust, that facilitate coordination and cooperation for mutual benefit. The notion of social capital extends our understanding of "cooperation" or "collaboration" in two significant ways. First, linking cooperation to the economic concept "capital" signals the investment or growth potential of a group's ability to work jointly. Second, the concept identifies the structure created from collaborative effort as capital. (p. 105)

Fountain argues that the important elements of social capital are trust, norms, and operations of the network, which are closely related to the values and objectives of the actors. Social capital has been associated with increased innovation and economic growth within the biotechnology and information industries, as well as revitalization in manufacturing. As a result, Fountain suggests that tools that enhance the creation of social capital need to be part of policies promoting innovation and productivity growth (p. 113).

Shared learning is a fundamental component of groupware. Collaborative processes among organizational representatives can be characterized as joint learning systems. Innes and Booher (1999, p. 3) suggest that a new mindset is needed to overcome traditional notions of producing specific agreements and actions. The idea is similar to Senge's (1990, p. 3) learning organization, "where people continually expand their capacity to create the results they truly desire, where new and expansive patterns of thinking are nurtured, where collective aspiration is set free, and where people are continually learning how to learn together." To Innes and Booher, the most important consequences occur not at the end, but during the discussion process itself. An environment conducive to learning is created when network members follow principles of civil discourse, where all are listened to and where conditions of sincerity, comprehensibility, accuracy, and legitimacy are met. Collaborative discussions involve creating shared meaning, pursuing mechanisms other than arguing and debating, bringing out added knowledge, and formulating ideas and processes of joint action, which can result in "good answers through process" (p. 5). Senge suggests that learning organizations require five core disciplines: personal mastery, mental models, shared vision, team learning, and systems thinking. Like learning organizations, networks require similar collective "cognitive capabilities" since "the intelligence of a network lies in the patterns of relationships among its members" (Lipnack and Stamps, 1994, p. 210).

Groupware is also developed through negotiation. Bardach (1998, p. 232) refers to a "culture of joint problem solving" that includes an "ethos that values equality, adaptability, discretion and results." Part of this ethos is to overcome bureaucratic tendencies (hierarchy, stability, obedience, procedures) through a lively sense of value creating possibilities. Nevertheless, Bardach (p. 238) also suggests that "collaboration is a matter of exhortation, explication, persuasion, give and take. To collaborate is to negotiate." Negotiations have to take into account all interests—personal, organizational, partner organizations, and the collective (Galaskiewicz and Zaheer, 1999). Bardach (pp. 245–246) suggests that there may be stages in network negotiations that are analogous to the contentiousness-stalemate-constructive dynamic in private-sector negotiations: First, a mutual understanding of a latent opportunity to create public value is formed, followed by a recognition among the players that collective efforts and risks are manageable, and finally the process of collaboration begins. Negotiations in networks will result in consensus only after members have fully explored the issues and interests, and only after significant effort has been made to find creative responses to differences (Innes and Booher, 1999). Such processes are supported by trust-based accommodations and by the dualism of the agency delegate to the network and the network delegate to the agency being the same person. Weiner (1990) suggests that whether collaborating or negotiating, such dual loyalty necessitates a totally new mindset and value stance for managers working within transorganizational systems.

An example of groupware at work occurred as a collaborative task force of governmental and nongovernmental leaders from Iowa created a strategic plan for rural development, under the sponsorship of the National Governors' Association. The Rural Policy Academy network was composed of state program administrators, Agricultural Extension Service executives, agriculture and agribusiness representatives, business-agency heads of peak interest associations, credit and capital executives, and civic leaders. The Rural Policy Academy collaborative, as it was called, approached its task as a "temporary organization," proceeding through process facilitation, brainstorming, problem identification, team building, survey feedback, and so on. Most essential were five task teams or work groups, involving expanded memberships and built around mutually derived goal areas: business development and retention, local government capacity-building, value-added agriculture, health care, and public infrastructure. Over time, each working group found that as it developed systematic procedures and dug into specific issues, individual and/or organizational positions began to recede in favor of new group understandings. Social capital was built as members saw different ways of looking at problems.

Members also learned about different policy arenas and developed new mindsets regarding rural problems. For example, few members of either the business or agriculture work teams knew about the difficulties of access to venture capital or the diminution of an entrepreneurial ethos among young Iowans. The work groups and the entire Rural Policy Academy did become a collaborative, but nevertheless, they could not effectively incorporate all individual and organizational interests brought to the table. Healthy doses of negotiation ensued over dearly held interests and concerns, including the future of small hospitals in nonmetropolitan areas and whether their closing should be facilitated or whether new roles linking them to metropolitan hospitals should be encouraged; and the consolidation of local government facilities, offices, and programs that were established on a countywide basis in an era of slower transportation and different communication. Complex issues like these required considerable negotiation to reach any policy recommendations (Agranoff, 1991). Despite such obstacles, groupware was developed through difficult negotiation.

How Does the Often Neglected or Misunderstood Role of Organizational Power in Network Management Come into Play?

Network power, or the ability to get action by partners or organizations under circumstances where actors are under dual responsibility roles to both organizations and networks, is clouded by the rhetoric of networking. A focus on joint decision forces within networking, such as those previously mentioned, as well as perceptions of equity, masks the potential for coercive behavior in network management. Klijn (1996), for example, characterizes policy networks as interdependent, coequal, patterned relationships. It is possible, however, that different actors occupy different role positions and carry different weights within networks. Some sit in positions with extensive opportunity contexts, filling "structural holes" (Burt, 1992, p. 67), creating unequal opportunity, while others may be less willing or able players. Organizational representatives also differ with regard to the resource dependencies they may bring to the network (Rhodes, 1981), leading to power differences. Clegg and Hardy (1996, p. 679) suggest that "we cannot ignore the facade of 'trust' and the rhetoric of 'collaboration' used to promote vested interest through the manipulation and capitulation by weaker partners." Power concerns should be at the core of any general theory of network management, because we must know whether power moves hinder the kind of synergistic creativity that reciprocal relationships are purported to produce.

Power in networks can be portrayed neutrally, or at least dualistically, as a property that either prevents or facilitates action. Collaboration can involve changes in structures of domination or asymmetries of resources employed in the sustaining of power relations (Gray, 1999). Schapp and van Twist (1997, pp. 66–67) refer to individual veto power in networks, saying that "actors in the network are able to cut themselves off from the steering interventions of other actors." Such veto power can be used in different ways: to exclude certain actors, to ban certain points of view, or to close potential actors outside of the network. On the other hand, there is an enabling component to network power. The use of power does not always include getting the dominant to act or altering their social control. In the "social production" model identified by Stone and his associates (1999, p. 354), it is assumed that social forces (and society's most vexing problems) are characterized by a lack of coherence and that many activities are autonomous with many middle-range accommodations instead of a cohesive system of control. In this type of situation, the main concern is how to bring about enough cooperation among disparate community elements to get things done. This is a "power to" that, under many conditions of ultracomplexity, characterizes situations better than "power over." Moreover, the social production model holds out the hope of constituting new possibilities under conditions of flexible preferences or, better yet, "bringing about a fresh configuration of preferences through opening up new possibilities" (p. 355). The key task in such power configurations is that of capacity building, building critical skills within networks of relationships while enlarging the view of what is possible. It is different from mobilization against the powerful, but it entails enlarging ways of thinking about preferences. The social production model juxtaposed against veto power illustrates just two dimensions of power in networks. As any political scientist can relate, power has many faces. At the minimum, it can inhibit or facilitate collective action, including action within networks.

Are there important operating dimensions of power? Gray (1989) characterizes collaboration as power sharing. The exercise of collaboration involves how power is acquired and challenged in the formation of collaborative efforts. Resource mobilization theorists (Alinsky, 1971; Bachrach and Baratz, 1963; Gamson, 1975) suggest that two sources of power are critical to the problem-setting phase: the power to mobilize and the power to organize. Gray (1999) offers others: the power to strategize; control of information, particularly in the direction-setting phase of collaboration; and the ability to exercise influence or authorize action, which is paramount to implementation. Gray sees this collaboration sequence as a power sharing that implies at least a temporary redistribution of power, enabling stakeholders with differential power levels to engage in domain transformation. She cautions, however, that alternative strategies of engagement can also characterize stakeholder involvement: compliance, when one organization bows to the wishes of the other (or others) because of resource leverage or undermining of legitimacy; contention, or challenging practices held or decisions made by more powerful stakeholders, leading to discursive legitimacy; and contesting, or a means of engagement within the domain of other stakeholders, particularly the more powerful ones. Also, equality of power can be eroded by invoking formal or legal authority, resource control or co-optation of low-power stakeholders. These sequences elaborate the aforementioned duality that power is a property in network management that can facilitate or inhibit collaborative actions.

Dynamics within the Federal–State Rural Development Councils again illustrate these complexities of network power. In their formative years, these multijurisdictional councils as a group did a reasonably adequate job of bringing together the disparate actors and following the five-step sequence of collaborative power identified above. In regard to certain problems related to rural development, particularly those that dealt with intergovernmental regulatory or programmatic barriers to economic and community development, these networks opened up numerous new possibilities. Thus, in regard to the intergovernmental program issues explored by the councils, power was to a considerable degree leveled among partners. Federal, state, association, private sector, and tribal stakeholders were able to explore identified problems in depth, develop workable solutions, and get implementing agencies to yield power and procedure in the interest of solving the problem. In this sense, true social production was possible.

Lurking behind the overt pretenses of network power sharing, however, was the contesting and sometimes contention and/or compliance enforcing of the most powerful stakeholders. In virtually every state, the interest or noninterest of the governor's office proved to be a key force in determining the issues that the councils addressed. In one or two states, the council's agenda proved to be the governor's agenda. In other states, the work of councils could come to a halt should their governors be uninterested or unwilling to support them. Under very limited circumstances could most councils tread on the turf of an administration's rural agenda, if one existed. Rural policy agendas belonged to the governor, so councils were relegated to marginal crossjurisdiction "discussions," "issue papers," and "demonstrations." Moreover, at a network-operating level, most councils have to defer to the power of their two most important stakeholders: the state departments of economic development (agencies also very close to the governors) and USDA/RD, housed in each state and headed by a presidential appointee. These two agencies constitute the sources of discretionary funding for rural development projects. In one state, the power conflict within the council between these two major stakeholders was so intense that the rest of the council tried to mute it by precluding either party from membership in its steering committee. But this was not a deterrent for either, as they wielded their levers behind the scenes. Most important, in this state, the powerful stakeholders limited the council's agenda to issues that did not interfere with their interests (Radin et al., 1996, 1997). In virtually every state that has a council (thirty-five in total), both the "power to" and the "power over" are exhibited.

Power is obviously a more complicated concern in networks than can possibly be depicted here. As an attribute of management, it needs to be raised because so much of the rhetoric of networking emphasizes processes that imply mutuality or where interests are (or are expected to be) checked at the door. One popular book on network management, for example, extols five key features of mutuality: unifying purpose, independent members, voluntary links, multiple leaders, and work at integrated levels (Lipnack and Stamps, 1994). It says much less about the ability of key stakeholders to dominate or how such domination may erode unifying purpose, independent members, and so on. Some empirical research has revealed the reality of power. The work of Milward and Provan (1998) found that network effectiveness was associated with stakeholder exercise of controlling power among community mental-health centers, a monopoly provider that dominated both service delivery and funding provisions for others in the network. Power concerns must be moved to the core of network management research.

Do Public Management Networks Produce Results or Discover Processes and Solutions That Would Not Have Emerged from Work Through a Single Organization?

These questions address the origin of a public management network. That networks are a unique institutional form, consisting of processes different than the spontaneous coordination of markets or the visible management of hierarchy (Powell, 1990), is the premise upon which the study of networks, ours included, is based. Earlier in the chapter, we documented the distinct behaviors of operating in networks, suggesting that there are, indeed, processes that are consistent with work in single organizations. The critical issue in question is whether public management networks produce solutions and results that otherwise would not have occurred through single, hierarchical organizations. Are networks *required* for achieving results in particular problem areas? When the public demands action on certain public issues, are multiple players drawn together to fulfill that demand because it can only be done through a network or because governments will not do it?

One of the most dominant perspectives argues that the pace and quality of social change at this point in history are the primary determinants of the emergence of network forms. This social change thesis is prominent in the writings of futurists (Toffler, 1980), business consultants (Lipnack and Stamps, 1994; Peters, 1992), organization theorists (Clegg, 1990), and in much of the literature on public management networks. Just as the bureaucratic organization was the signature organizational form during the industrial age, the emerging information or knowledge age gives rise to the network, where persons link across internal functions, organizational boundaries, and even geographic boundaries. The world is characterized by extreme complexity and diversity (Dunsire, 1993; Kooiman, 1993), where power is dispersed, not centralized; tasks are becoming dedifferentiated, rather than subdivided and specialized; and society worldwide demands greater freedom and individuation, rather than integration. In such a world, an organizational form based on individuation, dispersed power, and dedifferentiation is necessary; the network structure is that form. Therefore, this is a strong suggestion that a network is the only organizational form designed to be applied to postmodern concerns.

A related perspective is the problem change thesis, which asserts that the types of problems or issues society seeks to address collectively are increasingly wicked; that is, they typically have no definitive formulation and hence no agreed-upon criteria to tell when a solution has been found. Wicked problems are "problems with no solutions, only temporary and imperfect resolutions" (Harmon and Mayer, 1986, p. 9). Tame problems are readily defined and easily decomposable into neat, technical solutions (O'Toole, 1997a), but these have given way in large part to wicked problems. For most of the problems that emerged in the first part of the twentieth century, a bureaucratic organization was ideal—the problems were easily defined, goals were clear, and objectives were measurable. The metaphor of the wicked problem stands in contrast to traditional bureaucratic policy making and implementation. When there is little or no agreement as to the appropriate division of moral, institutional, and legal responsibility for any particular public problem, who can say how the solution to that problem might be achieved (Harmon and Mayer, 1986)? For wicked problems, agreement is forged by jointly steering courses of action and delivering policy outputs that are consistent with the multiplicity of societal interests. Other, more nonconventional modes of organizing, like networks, have emerged to do just that.

There are still questions about whether the emergence of networks is completely natural, as the social change and problem change arguments indicate. The empirical literature offers mixed answers, most of which focus on the types of policy instruments adopted as the key determinant of network emergence. In essence, any examination of public management networks must not disregard the political context. For example, the emergence of intergovernmental networks within the context of municipal wastewater treatment assistance does not appear to be "natural" (O'Toole, 1996) in that their creation was necessary to continue delivering such assistance. In fact, the network emerged from a decision by the federal government (Environmental Protection Agency) to reduce its role as grantor to municipalities and from the ensuing initiative of states to create separate state revolving loan funds as a partial replacement for the lost federal support. This is evidence for the claim that "efforts from political levels to trim the scale of bureaucracy and extent of direct administrative responsibility for accomplishing public purposes . . . accentuate the networking impulse" (O'Toole, 1996, p. 239). The decision to utilize state revolving-loan funds resulted in more complex governing configurations involving new actors with needed resources and technologies. O'Toole concludes that "decisions to shift programs to the states, deregulate, privatize, and employ market-based mechanisms have consequences for interorganizational arrangements and programs in practice" (p. 239). It is unclear whether a networked policy structure is the "best" choice for providing assistance to cities for wastewater treatment, but evidence indicates that it certainly is the best, perhaps the only, for the type of policy instrument being used, which, in this case, is a state-level revolving-loan fund.

Similarly, as the acceptable technology for treating people with severe mental illness shifted in the 1960s from directly provided institutionalization to a reliance on services provided by community health and social service organizations, collaborative service implementation networks of these provider agencies emerged (Provan and Milward, 1991, 1995; Weiss, 1990). Did these public management networks produce results in the mental-health field that otherwise would not have occurred? Once direct provision of government services in hospitals was viewed as an unacceptable policy instrument and, consequently, vertical integration of services through one provider was no longer appropriate, service implementation networks became the only, perhaps the best, organizational form through which mental-health services could be delivered. Therefore, given the type of policy instrument adopted by governments, networks did indeed produce results that otherwise would not have occurred. Harrison and Weiss (1998) use numerous cases to demonstrate how a more inclusive approach to workforce development results in networks of interorganizational relationships that connect the residents of low-income neighborhoods to employers with training positions through mediating institutions such as community colleges, government agencies, and various community-based organizations. Since the most politically acceptable means for employing persons in America is for these persons to find jobs on their own in a competitive market, rather than have the government find jobs for them, extensive networks of employers, trainers, and the unemployed clearly become the best organizational fit for delivering such "services." Like the empirical research cited in these last two paragraphs, which is some of the very best in the field, it is important always to consider the context within which networks emerge and operate. Even in network settings, structure follows strategy.

Finally, over and above the societal-level changes occurring and the shift in the types of acceptable policy instruments used in governing, decisions made in networks may simply be better decisions. Not better in the sense of more efficient—there is nothing particularly efficient about making decisions jointly—in the sense of being more effective, since, ideally, those involved in any given network are not merely steerers, but stakeholders, suppliers, clients, even customers. If the basic problem and challenge of policy and strategy making in many policy settings are for multiple governmental and nongovernmental organizations to jointly steer courses of action and to deliver policy outputs that are consistent with the multiplicity of societal interests, then a policy decision that laboriously, even painfully, meets that test is bound to be viewed as the best decision. When all relevant interests are considered in decision-making, then, at the minimum, the decision will have wider agreement, which still may be the test of the best policy (Lindblom, 1959). Network decision-making can be viewed, in some senses, as being more rational than individual decision-making. Multiple parties mean multiple alternatives to suggest and consider, more information available for all to use, and a decision system that is less bounded by the frailties of individual thinking. Additionally, decisions in networks may not only be the product of a more rational process, but they may also occur as a result of a synergy that can develop when multiple players pursue a common solution. Synergy means that the network of participants will produce better decisions not only because of the larger supply of alternatives and information to consider, but also because the commitment and interaction of the participants stimulate new alternatives that otherwise would not have been considered.

Conclusions and Questions for Future Research

We are able to make some tentative conclusions regarding network management, but the unanswered questions far outnumber the resolved issues. There do appear to be common network management sequences, such as activation, framing, mobilizing, and synthesizing. However, beyond this, we must discover the set of managerial decision rules that network managers currently follow (and should follow) in their quest for performance. What does a network manager do when trust is lacking among the actors? What should she do? What does a network manager do when the goals of the network actors are conflicting? What should he do? What are the best mechanisms to improve decision-making in the network, or to increase productivity, or to address a slacker in the network? Broadly, what are the critical occurrences or situations affecting network operations, and what are the preferred responses to these situations? Extensive observation and in-depth interviewing are required to answer these critical questions.

A number of behavioral process questions remain that could be answered with systematic observation of network processes. For example, the foregoing discussion suggests that information is an important ingredient in interorganizational transactions. Is the information that participants bring to the network the empowering force in collaborative discussion? If so, does this create power imbalances if information is unequal? If the techniques of applied behavioral science are virtually the same but the clustering is different, what is the distinctive clustering in networking? Social capital's role in collaboration is also unfolding. Is social capital necessary to reach collaborative results, or can other features (resources, legal requirements, perception of mutual gain) make up for capital deficiencies? Is social capital (including trust, norms, operations) sufficient to reach mutual outcomes, or are other properties, such as power, negotiation, or resources, paramount? Can collaboration occur when social capital is low or absent from an interagency situation?

Are there new and different dimensions of collective orchestration of joint learning? If joint learning through process is the key, what is the process? To what extent might these elements of collaboration also build groupware? If negotiations are part of the collaborative process, to what extent are network negotiations different from those between single organizations? What negotiation stages follow in networks? In the process, when does joint learning-based mutual decision end and negotiation begin? Does a negotiation imbalance (too much negotiation) reduce the chances of creative synergy? Most importantly, how does negotiation within the network contribute to the development of group abilities to recognize and solve problems?

Power needs to be confronted as a core element in network management, in terms of both control and its social-production forms. The impact of "control over" on synergistic collaboration needs further elaboration. Several questions should drive the research agenda. What techniques can be used to channel negative stakeholder engagement into positive engagement? Do networks need to manage power in the five steps of collaboration—agenda setting, organizing, strategy, direction setting, and action—in different ways than do hierarchies? How does an operating network understand when the sequence of collaboration is breaking down because the power balance is breaking down? How is power channeled from stakeholders' engagement of protecting their interests into social production? How do power brokers in networks build effective social production? What are the effects on creative problem solving of unequal application of power?

Finally, while we know that networks create value by acting as important means of bridging multiple organizations and dealing with complex problems, there is more to be explored. More empirical research is necessary to sort out the distinctiveness and contribution of networks as a decision-making entity (McGuire, forthcoming). Will some problems simply not get solved if not tackled with networks? Or is the use of networks a political or administrative choice? Do governments merely choose to use (or allow the use of) networks to be the primary policy designing and implementing method of organizing because networks are the most effective, the most acceptable (politically or otherwise), or a way to keep or move direct responsibility for a problem out of government? Similarly, is the emergence of networks in public policy and administration due to a shift in the types of policy instruments used by governments? Or, conversely, do networks select policy instruments that are fundamentally different from those selected by bureaucracies? Research that examines how and why networks emerge within the context of particular policy and program areas is necessary to better understand what can be expected from network forms of governance and how to evaluate the solutions that emerge from such forms.

Network management is as complex as the issues it deals with. As government is shifting from operation of hierarchical bureaucracies to governance through networks of public and nonpublic organizations, it is imperative that we begin to understand what is meant by "managing" in networks, how to improve network operation, and when and why to utilize a network. The field still lacks sufficient insight into the completeness, interconnection, implementability, and functioning of networks (Kickert et al., 1997). The solution, of course, is empirical research designed to address these very issues. This chapter is intended to suggest several research directions by discussing the state of knowledge in a few areas. As a core task of governance becomes arranging networks along with managing hierarchies (Milward, 1996), network management is a most essential arena of examination in the fields of management and public administration.

References

Agranoff, R. (1991). *Iowa's rural policy academy: Process and strategic plan.* Report submitted to Aspen Institute/Ford Foundation evaluation study of National Governor's Association Rural Policy Academy. Washington, DC: Aspen Institute.

Agranoff, R. (1996). Managing intergovernmental processes. In James L. Perry (Ed.), *Handbook of public administration* (2nd ed.) (pp. 131–147). San Francisco: Jossey-Bass.

Agranoff, R., & McGuire, M. (1998). Multinetwork management: Collaboration and the hollow state in local economic policy. *Journal of Public Administration Research and Theory, 8*(1), 67–91.

Agranoff, R., & McGuire, M. (1999a). Managing in network settings. *Policy Studies Review, 16*(1), 18–41.

Agranoff, R., & McGuire, M. (1999b). Expanding intergovernmental management's hidden dimensions. *American Review of Public Administration, 29*(4), 352–369.

Alinsky, S. D. (1971). *Rules for radicals.* New York: Vintage Books.

Alter, C., & Hage, J. (1993). *Organizations working together.* Newbury Park, CA: Sage Publications.

Bachrach, P., & Baratz, M. S. (1963). Decisions and non-decisions: An analytical framework. *American Political Science Review*, *56*(4), 641–651.

Bardach, E. (1998). *Managerial craftsmanship: Getting agencies to work together.* Washington, DC: Brookings Institution.

Benson, J. K. (1975). The interorganizational network as political economy. *Administrative Science Quarterly*, *20*, 229–249.

Burt, R. (1992). *Structural holes: The social structure of competition.* Cambridge, MA: Harvard University Press.

Clegg, S. R. (1990). *Modern organizations: Organization studies in the postmodern world.* London: Sage Publications.

Clegg, S. R., & Hardy, C. (1996). Conclusion: Representations. In S. R. Clegg, C. Hardy, and W. R. Nord (Eds.), *Handbook of organization studies* (pp. 676–708). London: Sage Publications.

Coleman, J. S. (1990). *Foundations of social theory.* Cambridge, MA: Harvard University Press.

Dunsire, A. (1993). Modes of governance. In J. Kooiman (Ed.), *Modern governance: New government–society interactions* (pp. 21–34). London: Sage Publications.

Fountain, J. E. (1998). Social capital: Its relationship to innovation in science and technology. *Science and Public Policy*, *25*(2), 103–115.

Galaskiewicz, J., & Zaheer, A. (1999). Networks of competitive advantage. *Research in the Sociology of Organizations*, *16*, 237–261.

Gamson, W. O. A. (1975). *The strategy of social protest.* Homewood, IL: Dorsey Press.

Gray, B. (1989). *Collaborating: Finding common ground for multiparty problems.* San Francisco: Jossey-Bass.

Gray, B. (1999). *Theoretical perspectives on collaboration.* Paper prepared for Collaboration Research Group, Technology University of Sydney, Sydney, Australia.

Hanf, K., & O'Toole, L. J. (1992). Revisiting old friends: Networks, implementation structures and the management of inter-organizational relations. *European Journal of Political Research*, *21*(1/2), 163–180.

Harmon, M. M., & Mayer, R. T. (1986). *Organization theory for public administration.* Glenview, IL: Scott, Foresman and Company.

Harrison, B., & Weiss, M. (1998). *Workforce development networks.* Thousand Oaks, CA: Sage Publications.

Innes, J. E., & Booher, D. E. (1999). Consensus building and complex adaptive systems: A framework for evaluating collaborative planning. *Journal of the American Planning Association*, *65*(4), 412–423.

Kettl, D. F. (1996). Governing at the millennium. In J. L. Perry (Ed.), *Handbook of public administration* (2nd ed.) (pp. 5–18). San Francisco: Jossey-Bass.

Kickert, W. J. M., Klijn, E.-H., & Koppenjan, J. F. M. (1997). Introduction: A management perspective on policy networks. In W. J. M. Kickert, E.-H. Klijn, & J. F. M. Koppenjan (Eds.), *Managing complex networks: Strategies for the public sector* (pp. 1–13). London: Sage Publications.

Kickert, W. J. M., & Koppenjan, J. F. M. (1997). Public management and network management: An overview. In W. J. M. Kickert, E.-H. Klijn, & J. F. M. Koppenjan (Eds.), *Managing complex networks: Strategies for the public sector* (pp. 35–61). London: Sage Publications.

Klijn, E.-H. (1996). Analyzing and managing policy processes in complex networks. *Administration and Society*, *28*(1), 90–119.

Klijn, E.-H., & Teisman, G. R. (1997). Strategies and games in networks. In W. J. M. Kickert, E.-H. Klijn, & J. F. M. Koppenjan (Eds.), *Managing complex networks: Strategies for the public sector* (pp. 98–118). London: Sage Publications.

Kooiman, J. (1993). *Modern governance: New government–society interactions.* London: Sage Publications.

Landau, M. (1991). Multiorganizational systems in public administration. *Journal of Public Administration Research and Theory, 1*(1), 5–18.

Lindblom, C. E. (1959). The science of muddling through. *Public Administration Review, 19*(2), 79–88.

Lipnack, J., & Stamps, J. (1994). *The age of the network.* New York: Wiley.

Mandell, M. P. (1988). Intergovernmental management in interorganizational networks: A revised perspective. *International Journal of Public Administration, 11*(4), 393–416.

Mandell, M. P. (1990). Network management: Strategic behavior in the public sector. In R. W. Gage & M. P. Mandell (Eds.), *Strategies for managing intergovernmental policies and networks* (pp. 29–54). New York: Praeger.

McGuire, M. (forthcoming). Collaborative policy making and administration: The operational demands of local economic development. *Economic Development Quarterly.*

Milward, H. B. (1994). *Mapping the linkage structure of networks.* Paper presented at Conference on Network Analysis on Innovations in Public Programs, LaFollette Institute of Public Affairs, University of Wisconsin.

Milward, H. B. (1996). Symposium on the hollow state: Capacity, control, and performance in interorganizational settings. *Journal of Public Administration Reseach and Theory, 6,* 193–195.

Milward, H. B., & Provan, K. G. (1998). Principles for controlling agents: The political economy of network structure. *Journal of Public Administration Research and Theory, 8*(2), 203–221.

Mossberger, K., & Hale, K. (1999). *Information diffusion in an intergovernmental network: The implementation of school-to-work programs.* Paper delivered at the Annual Meeting of the American Political Science Association, Atlanta, Georgia, September 2–5.

O' Toole, L. J. (1988). Strategies for intergovernmental management: Implementing programs in interorganizational networks. *International Journal of Public Administration, 11*(4), 417–441.

O' Toole, L. J. (1996). Hollowing the infrastructure: Revolving loan programs and network dynamics in the American states. *Journal of Public Administration Research and Theory, 6*(2), 225–242.

O' Toole, L. J. (1997a). Treating networks seriously: Practical and research-based agendas in public administration. *Public Administration Review, 57*(1), 45–52.

O' Toole, L. J. (1997b). Implementing public innovations in network settings. *Administration and Society, 29*(2), 115–134.

Peters, T. (1992). *Liberation management.* New York: Knopf.

Porter, D. O. (1981). Accounting for discretion in social experimentation and program administration. In K. L. Bradbury & A. Downs (Eds.), *Do housing allowances work?* (pp. 110–137). Washington, DC: Brookings Institution.

Powell, W. W. (1990). Neither market nor hierarchy: Network forms of organization. *Research in Organizational Behavior, 12*(3), 295–336.

Provan, K. G., & Milward, H. B. (1991). Institutional-level norms and organizational involvement in a service-implementation network. *Journal of Public Administration Research and Theory, 1*(4), 391–417.

Provan, K. G., & Milward, H. B. (1995). A preliminary theory of interorganizational effectiveness: A comparative study of four community mental health systems. *Administrative Science Quarterly, 40*(1), 1–33.

Putnam, R. (1993). *Making democracy work: Civic traditions in modern Italy.* Princeton, NJ: Princeton University Press.

Radin, B. A., Agranoff, R., Bowman, A. O'M., Buntz, G. C., Ott, S. J., Romzek, B. S., & Wilson, R. H. (1996). *New governance for rural America: Creating intergovernmental partnerships.* Lawrence: University Press of Kansas.

Radin, B. A., Agranoff, R., Bowman, A. O'M., Buntz, G. C., Romzek, B. S., & Wilson, R. H. (1997). *The national rural development partnership after seven years: A glimpse at eight state rural development councils in 1997.* Washington, DC: National Program Office, NRDC.

Rhodes, R. A. W. (1981). *Control and power in central–local relations.* Adershot, UK: Gower.

Schapp, I., & van Twist, M. J. W. (1997). The dynamics of closedness in networks. In W. J. M. Kickert, E.-H. Klijn, & J. F. M. Koppenjan (Eds.), *Managing complex networks: Strategies for the public sector* (pp. 62–78). London: Sage Publications.

Scharpf, F. W. (1978). Interorganizational policy studies: Issues, concepts, and perspectives. In K. Hanf & F. W. Scharpf (Eds.), *Interorganizational policy making* (pp. 345–370). London: Sage Publications.

Senge, P. M. (1990). *The fifth discipline: The art and practice of the learning organization.* New York: Doubleday.

Stoker, G., & Mossberger, K. (1994). Urban regime theory in comparative perspective. *Environment and Planning C: Government and Policy, 12*(2), 195–212.

Stone, C. N. (1989). *Regime politics.* Lawrence: University Press of Kansas.

Stone, C. N. (1999). *The Atlanta experience re-examined: Toward refining the analysis of urban regimes.* Paper presented at the Annual Meeting of the American Political Science Association, Atlanta, Georgia, September 2–5.

Stone, C., Doherty, K., Jones, C., & Ross, T. (1999). Schools and disadvantaged neighborhoods: The community development challenge. In R. F. Ferguson & W. T. Dickens (Eds.), *Urban problems and community development* (pp. 339–380). Washington, DC: Brookings Institution.

Termeer, C. J. A. M., & Koppenjan, J. F. M. (1997). Managing perceptions in networks. In W. J. M. Kickert, E.-H. Klijn, & J. F. M. Koppenjan (Eds.), *Managing complex networks: Strategies for the public sector* (pp. 79–97). London: Sage Publications.

Toffler, A. (1980). *The third wave.* New York: Morrow.

Weiner, M. E. (1990). *Human services management* (2nd ed.). Belmont, CA: Wadsworth.

Weiss, J. A. (1990). Policy instruments: Ideas and inducements in mental health policy. *Journal of Policy Analysis and Management, 9*(2), 178–200.

3

From Subnet to Supranet

A Proposal for a Comparative Network Framework to Examine Network Interactions Across Borders

Matthew S. Mingus

THE MARSH AND RHODES TYPOLOGY (MRT) represents the state of the art in the literature with regard to classifying different types of networks and network structures, yet inadequacies arise when applying this typology to cross-border policy issues and within federal states. This chapter casts the net broadly in describing the existing body of literature on network theory by applying O'Toole's definition of networks, which stresses the interdependence of actors on the modern stage and the diffuseness of their power. The goal is to discuss diverse models of networks, explain how the MRT helps unify this diverse body of literature, describe several shortcomings with this typology in cross-border settings, and recommend a Comparative Network Framework (CNF) that addresses these shortcomings. This goal is worthwhile because rapid globalization[1] of the economy increases the likelihood that any particular network does not exist isolated within the borders of one nation. Indeed, cross-border structures are used every day to help manage these increasingly complex public policy and implementation issues.

This goal is pursued in four sections: Models of Networks, the Marsh and Rhodes Typology (MRT), Cross-Border Networks Highlight Weaknesses of the MRT, and Recommendation for a Comparative Network Framework. The third section fleshes out several shortcomings of the MRT based on my research with the Canada–U.S. Pacific Salmon Treaty (PST), and the concluding section recommends the CNF to explicitly incorporate cross-border contexts involving federalist nations into the literature on networks and network structures. This research suggests that knowledge of the existing *subnets* (subnational, regional, and/or national networks) might eventually help nations design more effective and efficient *supranets* (networks of networks that span international borders) to assist in joint public management.

Models of Networks

O'Toole (1997) states that "networks are structures of interdependence involving multiple organizations or parts thereof, where one unit is not merely the formal subordinate of the others in some larger hierarchical arrangement. . . . Administrators cannot be expected to exercise decisive leverage by virtue of their formal position" (p. 45). O'Toole's definition is a useful one because it is seemingly general enough to incorporate a vast body of research since the mid-1970s on policy networks, policy communities and policy complexes, advocacy coalitions, social networks,[2] policy-issue networks, intergovernmental networks, interorganizational networks, and issue networks. The common threads of these approaches are that they represent a growing field of interorganizational theory as well as the evolution of interest group theories. Miller (1994) highlighted this focus of network research "away from the inner workings of the organization and toward the mosaic of interactions among the sometimes diverse, sometimes narrowly interested parties engaged in the struggle over the allocation of values" (p. 379). This development is in keeping with the more general trend toward systems theory (Katz and Kahn, 1966) and the more flexible, collaborative, and responsive public sector predicted by futurists many decades ago (Bennis and Slater, 1968; Toffler, 1970).

Policy networks, network management, intergovernmental networks, interorganizational networks and network structures, and issue networks are the five leading network models, although they frequently cross paths in the literature. With regard to the policy networks approach, Schneider and Ingram (1997) place policy networks, policy communities, and policy complexes on a continuum, from policy networks, in which there is a "common allegiance to scientific and professional norms as well as a shared perspective and a common body of knowledge"; to policy communities, which are "made up of highly educated and trained specialists in the science and technology" of a particular policy area and are a "closely knit, coherent, stable, and closed form of networks"; to policy complexes, which are "loosely connected networks" that "encompass a large diversity of opinion" and where "all the members agree that utilitarian rationality and science should govern decisions" (pp. 156–157). Policy networks are focused on applying scientific expertise[3] to help develop sector-specific policies (e.g., see Agranoff, 1990; Boase, 1996; Daugbjerg, 1997; Verdier, 1995). Applications on particular management topics are also common, including privatization (Zahariadis and Allen, 1995), intergovernmental management (Gage and Mandell, 1990; Mandell, 1988; Rhodes, 1981), and supranational entities (Nelson, 1996).

Network management, a relative newcomer compared with policy networks, is focused on how political leaders and public administrators can manage existing networks. For example, *Managing Complex Networks* (Kickert, Klijn, and Koppenjan, 1997) is an edited book with chapters that cover the public-management spectrum from game theory and systems theory to implementation processes and the "tools" approach, which focuses on choice of policy instruments. The editors rigorously object to the focus of the new public management on developing a businesslike focus on performance indicators, deregulation, and privatization within government. Instead, they equate public management directly with network management, as they state, "One of the major challenges with which public management as a form of governance is confronted, is to deal with network-like situations, that is, situations of interdependencies. Public management should therefore be seen as network management" (pp. 2–3).

This view of public management as network management comes full circle from the original views of policy networks research, which primarily focused on explaining that government policies frequently failed because experts and self-interested groups had special access to the policy-making arena, with vested interests blocking legitimate proposals for change. Network management is still about policy networks, but the focus shifts toward actively controlling policy networks rather than explaining how they constrain policy development.

Intergovernmental networks have focused on local, regional, state, and national governments as key actors in interdependent relationships. Mandell (1988) describes intergovernmental management networks as exhibiting high degrees of interaction, interdependence, trust, and areas of agreement, ultimately developing beyond mere linking and moving toward being held together to achieve some functional purpose. Working within the parameters of the law and meeting the complex requirements of a wide array of grant programs are also distinguishing characteristics of intergovernmental networks (Gage and Mandell, 1990). The general focus is, therefore, on management and joint program implementation more than on public policy or advocacy.

The approach of interorganizational networks and network structures tends to focus on managerial or implementation issues as well, and originated in organizational theory and development (Hanf and Scharpf, 1978), often with a sociological focus on the resource dependency model (see Klijn, 1997; Mizruchi and Galaskiewicz, 1994). This body of literature was frequently focused on generic administration rather than public administration, as evidenced by numerous key articles in *Administrative Science Quarterly* from the early 1960s to the late 1970s. Examples of this approach now abound in the field of public administration, especially community-development programs such as workforce development, economic development, and community-based substance-abuse prevention (Chisholm, 1998; Harrison and Weiss, 1998; Mandell, 1999a; Mingus, 1994). An identifying characteristic of this approach is that networks are frequently created by design to achieve specific intended purposes, whereas the policy networks literature assumes that a network is a naturally occurring phenomenon that can be explained by thorough research.

In contrast to these four approaches, issue networks assume rapidly changing, dynamic networks that ebb and flow in a quantumlike manner.[4] Heclo (1978) tells us that "an issue network is a shared-knowledge group having to do with some aspect (or, as defined by the network, some problem) of public policy" (p. 103). He presents issue networks as a supplement to the iron triangle theory by arguing that "instead of power commensurate with responsibility, issue networks seek influence commensurate with their understanding of the various, complex social choices being made" (p. 103). In other words, in a rapidly changing information society, well-informed activists come from many corners, and their knowledge is valued because of a strong perceived need on the part of government to be "right" when making decisions.

Key differences of this approach include the idea that nonprofessionals may have extensive influence and that the focus is on broad policy concerns rather than a narrow policy subfield. An issue network might be concerned about protecting consumers from the mythical "all-powerful, multinational corporation," whereas a related policy network might be focused on deregulating the natural gas industry to create a more efficient economy. Miller (1994) highlighted the contrast when he described the need for the policy network model to replace the traditional progressivist model in public administration:

> By using the term [policy] network, I refer to social relations that are recurring, but are less formal and bounded than social relations institutionalized in organizational roles. Nonetheless, network relations are sufficiently regular that sense-making, trust-building, or value-sharing may occur. (p. 379)

The contrast is that while Heclo assumes sense making by basing his definition on shared knowledge, he does not assume that either trust building or value sharing occurs in issue networks. Therefore, Heclo implicitly discounts the possibility that personal interaction of issue-network participants might help them communicate better, learn from one another, and alter their values over time, thereby moving intractable policy issues toward closure. The issue networks model might not fit within Mandell's (1999b, pp. 7, 13) focus on "networks and network structures" because organizations may still be working separately to get their own needs met and because the focus is on power without the "other face" of building trust.

This maze of terms and models represents a critical problem for developing a field of comparative network theory, which focuses on how subnets interact across borders to form supranets. Identical terms are regularly used to describe different concepts, and the same concepts are described in different ways, because of the interdisciplinary nature of public administration. Table 3.1 draws broadly from the literature to make comparisons among these five network models in terms of six meaningful categories:

Table 3.1
GENERAL COMPARISONS OF FIVE NETWORK MODELS

	Policy or Administration as Main Focus	Breadth of Focus (Narrow, Moderate, Broad)	Natural or Deliberate Design	Stability of Network (High, Medium, Low)	Members Mostly Professional or Amateur	Agreement on Rational/ Scientific Methodology
Policy Networks	Policy	Narrow	Natural	High	Professional	Yes
Network Management	Both	Moderate	Both	Medium	Professional	Yes
Intergovernmental Networks	Administration	Narrow	Both	High	Professional	Mostly
Interorganizational Networks and Network Structures	Both	Full Range	Both	Medium or High	Both	Maybe
Issue Networks	Policy	Broad	Natural	Low	Both	Maybe

1. *Policy or Administration as Main Focus:* Do networks generally focus on policy issues or on management and implementation issues?

2. *Breadth of Focus (Narrow, Moderate, Broad):* Are networks generally highly focused (e.g., oil policy), moderately focused (e.g., energy policy), or broadly focused (e.g., natural resources and the environment)?

3. *Natural or Deliberate Design:* Are networks mostly a naturally occurring form of social organization, or are they usually created and designed to accomplish specific tasks?

4. *Stability of Network (High, Medium, Low):* How resistant to change are networks?

5. *Members Mostly Professional or Amateur:* Are technocrats of various types at the core of networks, or do lay people and the general public play an assertive role?

6. *Agreement on Rational/Scientific Methodology:* Do network participants agree on the rational/scientific approach, or does significant conflict exist regarding what "information" and "thought processes" are relevant for making decisions?

The comparisons in table 3.1 reveal a strong focus of network theory on policy issues, a slight lean toward narrow policy subfields, and a clear dominance of professionals, such as public administrators, technicians, scientists, and so on. While the models vary considerably, there is almost universal commitment to the rational/scientific method for those models that are professionally based and a weaker commitment in more community-based networks. In addition, the newer models—especially intergovernmental networks and network management—are frequently focused on implementation and administrative issues rather than on public policy. Mandell's view of networks and network structures would come the closest to subsuming all the other categories, but narrowing the field to one model runs the risk of losing sight of important distinguishing characteristics. In fact, the intergovernmental networks model might easily be included with interorganizational networks but has been kept separate here because of the overall focus on cross-border interactions among federalist states.

The Marsh and Rhodes Typology (MRT)

Typologies take this idea of comparing networks a step further by attempting to unify this theoretical field into a clear classification schema for discussing and comparing specific networks. This research examined existing typologies and used the strongest one from this author's perspective as the starting point for asking, "From the perspective of cross-national governance, what is missing?" This seemed like a reasonable approach, because typologies are essentially comparative tools and so existing research should have some cumulative knowledge to offer as a starting point for this cross-border focus.

Typologies in general have not flourished within American public administration, perhaps because this pragmatic field has a love–hate relationship with academia (e.g., see King, 1998). In contrast, typologies often guide European research or research in more theoretical fields, such as sociology and linguistics. Substantial efforts to develop typologies for network theory have been made in Europe, including the Rhodes Typology (1981), the Wilks and Wright Typology[5] (1987), and the Marsh and Rhodes Typology, or MRT (Marsh and Rhodes, 1992).

Rhodes originally studied "the government" as one organization (a unitary state) rather than studying a system of more-or-less autonomous governments (a federalist state). While Rhodes consistently used the phrase "policy networks" in studying subgovernments, probably because he emphasized relationships among political institutions, the American research on subgovernments (sometimes "policy networks," other times "intergovernmental networks") has a stronger focus on individuals as key figures in networks. Also, Rhodes focused on the sectoral level, whereas American research on policy networks was often on the subsectoral or subsubsectoral levels. Perhaps these differences are endemic to the American system, as both specialization and individualism are characteristics of this system (Stillman, 1998, pp. 59–60).

A decade after the Rhodes Typology was published, Rob Rhodes went back to the drawing board with collaborator David Marsh in an effort to learn from the criticisms of his original typology and to incorporate their criticisms of the Wilks and Wright approach.[6] The Marsh and Rhodes Typology was then developed to create a common understanding of many of the terms that had developed in this body of literature. It has made strides in this area, including influencing Dutch researchers to adopt policy networks as the generic term within the network-management model, although the MRT is based heavily in the unitary state and does not consider cross-border networks. Its complementary purpose was to outline the distinguishing characteristics of policy networks.

This typology uses *policy networks* as the overall generic term for the field,[7] varying on a continuum from policy communities, where the relationships are quite close, to issue networks, where relationships are distant or loose (Rhodes, 1997, pp. 43–45). Nevertheless, this typology is not within the confines of the policy networks model discussed earlier, because its creators sought to pull that model, the issue-networks model, and others together into a coherent framework for talking about networks of public/private interactions. To do this, eight variables within four categories are used to distinguish any particular policy network, as represented in table 3.2. The four categories are membership, integration, resources, and power. The typology describes two ideal types of policy networks: *policy communities*, which are focused, coherent, and stable; and *issue networks*, which are large, loose, and more ephemeral. Any particular policy network, within this typological schema, can be represented by a set of points on eight continuums related to membership, integration, resources, and power.

The MRT is state of the art because it was developed and refined over more than a decade through a competition of ideas in the academic literature, and because it has been more successful than its two predecessors in its explicit attempt to encompass the whole spectrum of network models. Indeed, Marsh

Table 3.2

TYPES OF POLICY NETWORKS (MARSH AND RHODES TYPOLOGY)

Dimension	Policy Community	Issue Network
Membership		
Size	Limited number, some consciously excluded	Large and open
Interests	Economic and/or professional	Whole range of affected interests
Integration		
Frequency of interaction	Frequent and high quality among all members	Contacts fluctuate in frequency and intensity
Continuity	Stable membership and values	Access fluctuates significantly
Consensus	Members share values and accept legitimacy of the outcome	Some agreement exists, conflicts are present
Resources		
Distribution within network	All participants have resources to exchange	Most participants are consultative, limited number have resources
Distribution within member organizations	Hierarchical, leaders can deliver their members	Participants have variable abilities to regulate actions of their members
Power	Balanced enough for positive sum game	Unequal power leading to zero sum game

Source: Adapted from Marsh and Rhodes, 1992, p. 251.

(1998, p. 7) decided to use the MRT as the starting point for his edited volume *Comparing Policy Networks, Public Policy and Management*. Because it uses three key terms already in common usage, this typology represented a significant advancement in reducing the proliferation of new terms such as "policy issue networks" (Skok, 1995) and "interorganizational policy networks" (Wamsley and Zald, 1983). In addition, the MRT represented a turn toward a typology that allows one to compare fairly similar or dramatically different networks.

Cross-Border Networks Highlight Weaknesses of the MRT

While the MRT is strong and represents an advancement over its predecessors, weaknesses are apparent that should be avoided in developing an inclusive typology for cross-border settings. The remainder of this chapter suggests some of these weaknesses that are in need of correction if one typology is to encompass the whole range of network concepts. For convenience, these weaknesses are grouped into three general areas: implementation, intergovernmental structure, and internationalization.

Implementation

The MRT seems to be missing the common focus of network management, intergovernmental networks, and interorganizational networks on administrative issues or implementation. Neither ideal type in this model captures the hands-on, working-level or service-delivery network. In addition, it is difficult to imagine how something between the two ideal types in this model could focus on these issues. While this inattention to administration is in keeping with the strong focus of network models on policy issues that is identified earlier, it also leaves out a notable focus of three of the models.

When networks are working with other networks, an exclusive focus on policy can generate negative dynamics. Specifically, in comparing the networks of Alaska, British Columbia, Washington, and Oregon with regard to the U.S.–Canada Pacific Salmon Treaty (PST), concerns arise when some of the networks are concerned about policy issues while others are concerned about policy and implementation. In essence, day-to-day management issues created divisive situations that stalled discussions regarding longer-term policy concerns.

Management versus policy, therefore, is a meaningful variable absent from the MRT. It may be possible to differentiate between the two by thinking of the likelihood of coordinated action being initiated by the network in the short term, because short-term actions may create both positive and negative feedback loops that impact the ability to achieve longer-term policy coordination. While this analysis is based on networks working with other networks across an international border, it stands to reason that the same dynamic would be at play in many networks where day-to-day administration or policy implementation is a concern.

Intergovernmental Structure

The whole central–subcentral or intergovernmental aspect that was the basis for Rhodes's original research (e.g., 1981, 1991) is conspicuously absent from the MRT. This intergovernmental aspect, specifically central–subcentral relations, may be assumed by Marsh and Rhodes rather than being incorporated into their typology as a distinguishing element of various networks. The difficulty of assuming a particular distribution of powers within a nation becomes quite apparent when one seeks to apply their research to compare networks across borders or to examine the interaction of networks across borders, especially when one or more of the nations involved is a nonunitary state.

For example, research on the PST reveals that federalism, specifically the level of government that is in control for a particular policy issue, is an important—if not overriding—factor. In the three relevant states, the state governments assert primary control with regard to salmon, while in Canada, the federal government has primary jurisdiction. It has taken decades of interaction on this issue and thirteen years with a binational treaty in force for the Canadian minister of fisheries to start negotiating directly with state governors. This interaction is clearly outside of the treaty structure and yet was necessary to reach agreement in the supranet because of differences between the subnets. This dynamic seems too significant, and too specific, to group into the MRT category for "distribution of resources within the network" or for the overall "distribution of power." If both Canada and the United States were unitary states, this concern might take on the appearance of integrating local needs into national policy-making, and thus might avoid cross-border interaction between different levels of government. It should be noted, however, that U.S.–Canadian governmental interaction is extremely informal, frequently occurring between subnational units of government or between federal departments rather than federal diplomats or politicians (Swanson, 1978; Watts, 1993).

The significance of this concern is that any comparisons of networks must be explicit about the division of powers when networks are to be compared across international borders or if the goal is to determine the potential compatibility of cross-border networks and network structures. This is important, because leaving out this factor makes an implicit assumption that subnational governments cooperate with one another and with their national government, while subnational governments can be a force for either cooperation or competition (Boeckelman, 1996). Much of this subnational competition in the case of the PST has occurred in U.S. federal court (*Confederated Tribes and Bands of the Yakima Indian Nation v. Baldrige; United States v. Washington*). Furthermore, subnational–national competition is the very essence of the relationship between Canada and British Columbia on this issue, with provincial politicians distancing themselves from the recent binding agreement and both state departments giving credit for the agreement to everyone except the provincial government (Albright and Axworthy, 1999).

John M. Kline (1993, pp. 202, 205) of Georgetown University explained the dynamic of interdependence that drives this research quite well:

> Global political and economic interdependence stimulates the negotiation of new international accords, but also requires the creation of societal adjustment and support mechanisms that are often best developed and implemented by subnational entities. In other words, national adaptation to international change can depend heavily on the responsiveness of subnational governments. . . . Local, state, and regional growth prospects and socio-economic adjustment needs became inextricably tied to international economic forces.

Internationalization

As stated, the MRT has predominantly British foundations rather than international foundations. This is reflected in the above comments on intergovernmental structure but has additional implications. Networks are frequently used to understand and even explain how policy decisions are reached within different sectors of a given society and are infrequently used to make comparisons involving more than one nation. A body of research is starting to make these international comparisons (Brinkerhoff, 1999; Daugbjerg, 1998; Marsh, 1998; Mingus, 1999), yet the MRT is not well suited to such comparisons.

Evidence of this weakness is found in Brinkerhoff's (1999) three case studies in the developing world, wherein he proposes regime type, level of trust, legal framework and regulations, and the nature of the policy to be implemented as potentially important variables. These variables are largely missing in the MRT. It may make sense to avoid level of trust, because the Marsh and Rhodes categories for resources and power more fully address this dynamic, and to avoid nature of the policy, because it might be a recipe for a different network theory for each sector, subsector, and so on. However, regime type and legal framework are hard to dismiss as the network heuristic is increasingly pushed into international usage. Similarly, my research on the PST suggests that the locus of power within government (political, diplomatic, or administrative) is significant, yet this might easily be overlooked using the MRT.

My research also differs from previous research comparing networks in that it does not stop at comparing networks from different nations; it also focuses on interactions among networks from three states and one province on a cross-border issue—conservation and sharing of Pacific salmon as a potentially renewable cross-border resource—involving an international entity, the Pacific Salmon Commission. In order to focus on this goal, it was necessary to introduce the concepts of subnet and supranet. For network theory to be inclusive on the international front, it must find a way to grapple with these network interactions in addition to a way to compare networks that have formed within different types of regimes or governmental structures. Clearly these are interrelated, yet incorporating cross-border network interactions into the MRT may prove exceedingly difficult.

To recap, the MRT depicted in table 3.2 is strong until one seeks to apply it to implementation issues (day-to-day or street-level management), international comparisons across regime types or legal structures, and issues involving cross-border policy-making and management. These are areas where there is opportunity for new theory to incorporate the valuable ideas of Marsh and Rhodes, and then move beyond the idea that comparing networks must occur within any one nation rather than across nations or for multinational entities.

Recommendation for a Comparative Network Framework

The MRT guides some key issues for a comparative network discussion, such as the common strength of user groups in the four state and provincial subnets involved in the PST supranet and the overall power imbalance that tilts toward Alaska as the subnets relate with one another, in part because the return migration for most Pacific salmon is through Alaskan waters first. Comparison of these subnets places them all at the policy community end of the MRT continuum—primarily resembling tight public–private relationships—but the balance of power for the PST supranet approaches the issue network side of the continuum. Significant differences exist among the subnets, ranking the B.C. network closest to the middle of the continuum on many of the eight dimensions. However, this typology does not help us assess or predict cross-national network compatibility. A framework is needed specifically for the cross-border aspects of these comparisons.

This can be likened to the mixed scanning approach to decision-making, where Amatai Etzioni sought to reconcile Charles Lindblom's branch and root methods of policy analysis by explaining that both exist simultaneously. Etzioni (1967, 1986) argued that fundamental changes at the macro level may exist, supported by what appears to be an entirely incremental process at the micro level. His model was dualistic by "combining (a) high-order, fundamental policy-making processes which set basic directions and (b) incremental ones which prepare for fundamental decisions and work them out after they have been reached" (Etzioni, 1967, p. 385). My argument is that at a national level, the main weakness of the Marsh and Rhodes Typology is its avoidance of administration or implementation issues, and that at the cross-national level, a complementary tool is needed to compare networks and guide discussions of network interactions. The Comparative Network Framework (CNF) presented in table 3.3 is a proposed tool to guide this cross-national discussion. It fills the gaps discussed in the preceding section, not by replacing or amending the MRT, but by adding a conceptual layer above the MRT.

The long-term intent is to shift into a predictive mode by seeking to answer the question, "How can we know that subnets are compatible before designing a supranet?" The CNF is proposed as a model for determining subnetwork compatibility at the broadest level by stressing four issues related to this broad-level compatibility. Within the formal power structure, the two issues are the locus of power within government (administrative, diplomatic, or political) and the level of government with primary control (national or subnational). With regard to network symmetry, the two issues are the structural focus of the network (implementation issues, policy issues, or a holistic approach) and the participant interests (broad range of interests or fairly similar to one another). In the search for predictive power, a specific hypothesis worth testing would be that the more similarity that exists in these four categories, the lower the likelihood of incompatibility as the subnets form into a supranet. Additionally, differences in any one of the categories might guide useful discussions to help design mechanisms that can assist a supranet in compensating for potential incompatibilities.

Explanation of Incompatibilities Within the PST Supranet

While comparative network theory is unlikely to explain away all the problems related to the PST, because much of the issue is related to biology, climatology, electoral politics, and the hundred-plus-year history of agreements regarding Pacific salmon, the CNF provides a strong explanation for the fundamental incompatibilities of these subnets.

Table 3.3
COMPARATIVE NETWORK FRAMEWORK

		Formal Power Structure	
		Level with Primary Control	
		National Control	*Subnational Control*
Locus of Power within Government	Political Power	BC	—
	Diplomatic Power	—	—
	Agency Power	Canada	OR, WA, AK, United States

		Network Symmetry	
		Participant Interests	
		Broad Range	*Fairly Similar*
Structural Focus of Network	Holistic Approach	BC, Canada	WA
	Policy Issues	—	OR, AK, United States
	Implementation Issues	—	—

One key problem already touched upon is that the three states have primary control in the United States, while the federal government has primary control in Canada. Complicating this further, power within the state governments is concentrated within the fishery-management agencies, while power within the B.C. government has been at the political level because Premier Glen Clark has been very active. Another compatibility concern is that the interests of network participants in the states are primarily the interests of the fishers, while the range of interests is broader in Canada, specifically with environmental groups being active within the B.C. network. Finally, British Columbia and Washington are concerned about both implementation and policy, because the Fraser River Panel of the Pacific Salmon Commission actually manages the fishery along both sides of the border area. Alaska and Oregon, on the other hand, are mostly concerned with policy, because the Northern and Southern Panels do not have fishery management responsibilities. The potential for policy disputes to create day-to-day management problems during the salmon fishing seasons is thus greater for two of the subnets than for the remaining subnets.

The dynamics of these four incompatibilities—misaligned federal jurisdictions, misaligned internal locus of power, differing range of active interest groups, and policy versus implementation focus—capture the nature of the most serious problems with the PST, and they appear to be potential problems with regard to the interaction of networks between any two federalist nations. The four factors in the CNF are essentially these four compatibility issues, and three of the four concepts apply to unitary systems or confederations as well, because only the "level of government with primary control" is a federal-specific concept. In addition, whether power within government is predominantly political, diplomatic, or bureaucratic gets to the heart of regime type, so long as military power is considered a nondemocratic form of political power (Heady, 1984; Konig, 1998).

Explanatory Power of the CNF

Significantly, two of these problem areas could have been identified before the PST was signed—the differing levels of government with primary control and the fact that two of the states would not be invested in the supranet with regard to implementation issues. A different model *might* have emerged with the following three elements:

1. The PST could have legitimized direct Canada–Oregon, Canada–Washington, and Canada–Alaska negotiation processes to help reach two-party agreements, perhaps as a prelude to overall agreement. Fisheries Minister David Anderson has started this approach recently and is doing it in an extraconstitutional manner rather than with clear legitimacy. This approach also fits with recent advice that two-party games and side payments must be considered to rescue the treaty from the edges of insignificance (Munro, McDorman, and McKelvey 1998). Likewise, Alaska–Washington, Alaska–Oregon, and Oregon–Washington components, and the role of southern U.S. tribal governments, might also have been incorporated in the PST design to increase clarity and legitimacy instead of whitewashing the true complexity of the negotiations.

2. Clearer means for incorporating the interests of British Columbia within the system of federal management that has plagued the Canada–B.C. relationship for the past decade might have been incorporated in the PST or outlined in a Canada-only side agreement. The locus of power within the government in British Columbia has shifted to the political level under Premier Clark precisely because of a growing frustration at the stifled representation. The Strangway-Ruckleshaus report (1998) and a recent Suzuki Foundation report (Glavin, 1998) highlight this rift, which was also apparent from my personal interviews with key negotiators.

3. Separate panels for managing the Fraser River fishery and developing sharing arrangements for this fishery might have been incorporated in the PST design. Such a system might better protect the salmon resource from the negotiation-directed fish wars that have occurred (Egan, 1997; Wood, 1995). The mission of the International Pacific Salmon Fisheries Commission to manage the Fraser River fishery on a limited scale was

folded into the role of the Pacific Salmon Commission's Fraser River
Panel for convenience purposes and perhaps with little forethought to
this policy versus implementation dynamic.

While this analysis has the advantages of hindsight, and it may not be possible to retrofit the PST, the first two of these issues have received attention in
recent policy recommendations, and the CNF provides some theoretical justification for seriously considering such innovative approaches to help these two
federal nations cooperate more effectively.

Conclusions

Thinking in terms of networks runs the risk of devaluing the status of governments. Governments are responsible for making decisions in the public interest—broadly defined—and networks may narrow the definition of public interest considerably if such networks become the primary sources of input for
administrators. Recent criticisms of the PST structure and operations suggest that
this is the case with regard to Pacific salmon and that fishing industry voices,
especially commercial fishers, drive both the agreements and disagreements
within the existing process, often to the detriment of the salmon, the environment, and even the local fishing communities (Bergman and Haw, 1998; Glavin,
1998). This view is also supported by an analysis of my personal interviews conducted with PST negotiators from both sides of the border. Miller (1996)
summed this up nicely when she said, "However, perhaps the best description of
management within each jurisdiction still is that it represents an effort to prevent
the worst excesses of overharvesting while appeasing a vociferous collection of
competing user groups" (p. 117).

On the other hand, rather than devaluing government, developing clear
descriptions of network dynamics may be a useful application of the network
approach as a heuristic device to identify specific potential problems in democratic administration. If all relevant interests are not included in the networks of
public administrators, then democratic administration may be derailed by the
power of selected interests. How public administrators working on a particular
issue define "relevant" may be an important clue.

For example, in spite of persistent conflicts, the subnets on both sides of the
border tend to value the role of scientists in providing information to make
resource utilization decisions; the application of analytical techniques to identify
problems and prepare useful plans; the use of the political process for reaching
decisions in specific situations (often choosing both means and ends); and the
rights of groups, particularly those with vested economic interests, to be involved
in the decision-making process. The bulk of these characteristics fit within the
descriptive power of the MRT and thus justify adding the CNF as a conceptual
layer above the MRT rather than seeking to extensively revise the typology. This
research also suggests that Marsh and Rhodes need to visit the issue of networks
that are focused on administrative or implementation issues in an effort to either
revise the MRT or explain how they see these issues in relation to their typology.

Finally, the Comparative Network Framework deserves further research, as evidence related to the PST suggests that this framework may have predictive power that could be useful to those who design supranets. It is true, however, that the evidence at this stage is based on exploratory, interpretive research and the predictions embrace the power of hindsight. These methodological reasons suggest that further discussion and research are the prudent course, especially research involving additional attempts at cross-border governance.

Notes

1. There was a thirteenfold increase (in real terms) in global trade of goods and services from 1950 to 1990 (Fry, 1993, pp. 124, 126), and communications and shipping costs are now "between one-third and one-twentieth of their 1950 levels," thus spurring a rapid increase in cross-border economic and governmental activity (Boeckelman, 1996, p. 2).

2. While most social networks literature has a minimal focus on public policy and administration, the work of Knoke (1993, 1994) and his colleagues is a refreshing exception.

3. The Advocacy Coalition Framework of Sabatier and Jenkins-Smith (1993, p. 110) is broader than the policy networks model primarily because it seeks to "fuse cognitive and political factors in order to better explain change." This approach postulates that resistant-to-change core values hamper coalitions from adapting to fundamental changes in the policy environment, and therefore dominant coalitions are occasionally replaced by new coalitions whose values are more in tune with the current policy environment. As such, the focus is on values rather than the scientific method, thus offering a true competing model for policy change.

4. One policy network definition highlights this contrast: "We define policy networks as *(more or less) stable patterns of social relations between interdependent actors, which take shape around policy problems and/or programs*" (Kickert, Klijn, and Koppenjan, 1997, p. 6, emphasis in original).

5. Wilks and Wright also examined government–industry relations in Japan and the United States.

6. The Rhodes Typology came under attack because its five network types (policy/territorial community, professional networks, intergovernmental networks, producer networks, and issue networks) did not appear to form a continuum, because it focused exclusively on structural issues and therefore left out interpersonal relations, and because it focused at the sectoral level while much policy research seeks to explain subsectoral policy decisions. Wilks and Wright borrowed the American focus on subsectors to argue that it was not useful to focus on government–industry relations, because the dynamics of such relationships vary extensively; for example, even within the chemicals sector, there exist wide variations for subsectors, such as basic chemicals, pharmaceuticals, agrochemical, paints, personal hygiene, and so forth (Wilks and Wright, 1987). A policy network, in their terminology, would focus on a specific subsector, while the entire sector, chemicals in the above example, would relate to a policy community. "Policy universe," a term Wilks and Wright introduced, would refer to the population of potential actors that share a concern about industrial policy. This typology received a number of criticisms, mostly aimed at its use of terms already in popular currency for dramatically different meanings, the creation of new terms such as policy universe, and their long list of factors to explain the variations among network types. For example, policy communities were generally considered

to be tightly integrated networks, yet the Wilks and Wright Typology, in Rhodes's view (1997, p. 42), uses the phrase to represent loosely integrated issue networks.

7. The term *policy networks*, therefore, distinguishes networks in public administration from other types of networks, such as production networks, local-area networks, telecommunications networks, or personal networks.

References

Agranoff, R. (1990). Responding to human crises: Intergovernmental policy networks. In R. W. Gage & M. P. Mandell (Eds.), *Strategies for managing intergovernmental policies and networks* (pp. 57–80). New York: Praeger.

Albright, M. K., & Axworthy, L. (1999). *Joint statement on the pacific salmon agreement.* Press Release. Washington DC: U.S. Department of State.

Bennis, W. G., & Slater, P. E. (1968). *The temporary society.* New York: Harper & Row.

Bergman, P. K., & Haw, F. (1998). *Failure of the Pacific Salmon Treaty: Causes, effects, and solutions* (unpublished manuscript). Olympia, WA.

Boase, J. P. (1996). Institutions, institutionalized networks and policy choices: Health policy in the U.S. and Canada. *Governance: An International Journal of Policy and Administration, 9*(3), 287–310.

Boeckelman, K. (1996). Federal systems in the global economy: Research issues. *Publius: The Journal of Federalism, 26*(1), 1–10.

Brinkerhoff, D. W. (1999). State–civil society networks for policy implementation in developing countries. *Policy Studies Review, 16*(1), 123–147.

Chisholm, R. F. (1998, May). *Developing interorganizational networks: Lessons from three applications.* Paper presented at the 59th National Conference of the American Society of Public Administration, Seattle, WA.

Confederated Tribes and Bands of the Yakima Indian Nation v. Baldrige. 898 F. Supp. 1477 (W.D. Wash. 1995), aff'd, 91 F.3d 1366 (9th Cir. 1996) (The "Confederated Tribes Injunction").

Daugbjerg, C. (1997). Policy networks and agricultural policy reforms: Explaining deregulation in Sweden and re-regulation in the European community. *Governance: An International Journal of Policy and Administration, 10*(2), 123–142.

Daugbjerg, C. (1998). Linking policy networks and environmental policies: Nitrate policymaking in Denmark and Sweden, 1970–1995. *Public Administration, 76*(2), 275–294.

Egan, T. (1997). Salmon war in northwest moves to larger scale. *New York Times,* September 12.

Etzioni, A. (1967). Mixed scanning: A "third" approach to decision making. *Public Administration Review, 27*(5), 385–392.

Etzioni, A. (1986). Mixed scanning revisited. *Public Administration Review, 46*(1), 8–14.

Fry, E. H. (1993). The U.S. states and foreign economic policy: Federalism in the "new world order." In B. Hocking (Ed.), *Foreign relations and federal states* (pp. 122–139). London: Leicester University Press.

Gage, R. W., & Mandell, M. P. (Eds.). (1990). *Strategies for managing intergovernmental policies and networks.* New York: Praeger.

Glavin, T. (1998). *Last call: The will to save Pacific salmon.* Vancouver, BC: David Suzuki Foundation.

Hanf, K., & Scharpf, F. W. (Eds.). (1978). *Interorganizational policy making.* London: Sage Publications.

Harrison, B., & Weiss, M. (1998). *Workforce development networks: Community-based organizations and regional alliances.* Thousand Oaks, CA: Sage Publications.

Heady, F. (1984). *Public administration: A comparative perspective* (3rd ed.). New York: Marcel Dekker.

Heclo, H. (1978). Issue networks and the executive establishment. In A. King (Ed.), *The new American political system* (pp. 87–124). Washington, DC: American Enterprise Institute for Public Policy Research.

Katz, D., & Kahn, R. L. (1966). *The social psychology of organizations.* New York: Wiley.

Kickert, W. J. M., Klijn, E.-H., & Koppenjan, J. F. M. (Eds.). (1997). *Managing complex networks: Strategies for the public sector.* London: Sage Publications.

King, C. S. (1998). Reflective scholarship: Healing the scholarship/practice wounds. *Administrative Theory & Praxis, 20*(2), 159–171.

Klijn, E.-H. (1997). Policy networks: An overview. In Kickert, W. J. M., Klijn, E.-H., & Koppenjan, J. F. M. (Eds.). *Managing complex networks: Strategies for the public sectors* (pp. 14–34). London: Sage Publications.

Kline, J. M. (1993). United States' federalism and foreign policy. In Brown, D. M., & Fry, E. H. (Eds.), *States and provinces in the international economy* (pp. 201–231). Berkeley, CA: Institute of Government Studies Press.

Knoke, D. (1993). Networks as political glue: Explaining public policy making. In Wilson, W. J. (Ed.), *Sociology and the public agenda* (pp. 164–184). Newbury Park, CA: Sage Publications.

Knoke, D. (1994). Networks of elite structure and decision making. In Wasserman, S., & Galaskiewicz, J. (Eds.), *Advances in social network analysis* (pp. 274–294). Thousand Oaks, CA: Sage Publications.

Konig, K. (1998). Three worlds of public administration modernization. *International Journal of Organizational Theory and Behavior, 1*(4), 481–520.

Mandell, M. P. (1988). Intergovernmental management in interorganizational networks: A revised perspective. *International Journal of Public Administration 11*(4), 396–416.

Mandell, M. P. (1999a). Community collaborations: Working through network structures. *Policy Studies Review, 16*(1), 42–64.

Mandell, M. P. (1999b). The impact of collaborative efforts: Changing the face of public policy through networks and network structures. *Policy Studies Review, 16*(1), 4–17.

Marsh, D. (Ed.). (1998). *Comparing policy networks, public policy and management.* Buckingham, UK: Open University Press.

Marsh, D., & Rhodes, R. A. W. (Eds.). (1992). *Policy networks in British government.* Oxford: Clarendon Press.

Miller, H. T. (1994). Post-progressive public administration: Lessons from policy networks. *Public Administration Review, 54*(4), 378–385.

Miller, K. A. (1996). Salmon stock variability and the political economy of the Pacific Salmon Treaty. *Contemporary Economic Policy, 14*(3), 112–129.

Mingus, M. S. (Ed.). (1994). *Part of the solution: Useful information from the front lines of community partnership development.* Providence, RI: Behavioral Health Resources Press.

Mingus, M. S. (1999). *Comparative network theory: An interpretive study of the Canada–United States Pacific Salmon Treaty* (unpublished manuscript). Graduate School of Public Affairs, University of Colorado at Denver.

Mizruchi, M. S., & Galaskiewicz, J. (1994). Networks of interorganizational relations. In Wasserman, S., & Galaskiewicz, J. (Eds.), *Advances in social network analysis* (pp. 230–253). Thousand Oaks, CA: Sage Publications.

Munro, G., McDorman, T., & McKelvey, R. (1998). *Canadian–American public policy: Transboundary fishery resources and the Canada–United States Pacific Salmon Treaty.* Orono: Canadian–American Center, University of Maine.

Nelson, P. J. (1996). Internationalizing economic and environmental policy: Transnational NGO networks and the World Bank's expanding influence. *Millennium: Journal of International Studies, 25*(3), 605–633.

O'Toole, L. J., Jr. (1997). Treating networks seriously: Practical and research-based agendas in public administration. *Public Administration Review, 57*(1), 45–52.

Rhodes, R. A. W. (1981). *Control and power in central–local government relationships.* Farnborough, UK: Gower.

Rhodes, R. A. W. (1991). Policy networks and sub–central government. In Thompson, G., Frances, J., Levacic, R., & Mitchell, J. (Eds.), *Markets, hierarchies and networks* (pp. 203–214). London: Sage Publications.

Rhodes, R. A. W. (1997). *Understanding governance: Policy networks, governance, reflexivity and accountability.* Buckingham, UK: Open University Press.

Sabatier, P. A., & Jenkins-Smith, H. C. (1993). *Policy change and learning. An advocacy coalition approach.* Boulder, CO: Westview Press.

Schneider, A. L., & Ingram, H. (1997). *Policy design for democracy.* Lawrence: University Press of Kansas.

Skok, J. E. (1995). Policy-issue networks and the public-policy cycle: A structural–functional framework for public administration. *Public Administration Review, 55*(4), 325–332.

Stillman, R., II. (1998). *Preface to public administration: A search for themes and direction* (rev. ed.). Burke, VA: Chatelaine Press.

Strangway, D. W., & Ruckleshaus, W. D. (1998, January 12). Pacific salmon report to the prime minister of Canada and the president of the United States <http://www.ncr.dfo.ca/communic/treaty/pac_sal/report.html>.

Swanson, R. F. (1978). *Intergovernmental perspectives on the Canada–U.S. relationship.* New York: New York University Press.

Toffler, A. (1970). *Future shock.* New York: Random House.

United States v. Washington. 384 F. Supp. 312 (W.D. Wash. 1974), aff'd, 500 F.2d 676 (9th Cir. 1975), cert. denied, 423 U.S. 1086 (1976) (The "Boldt Decision").

Verdier, D. (1995). The politics of public aid to private industry. *Comparative Political Studies, 28*(1), 3–42.

Wamsley, G. L., & Zald, M. N. (1983). The environment of public managers: Managing turbulence. In Eddy, W. B. (Ed.), *Handbook of organization management* (pp. 501–529). New York: Marcel Dekker.

Watts, R. L. (1993). Representation in North American federations: A comparative perspective. In Olson, D. M., & Franks, C. E. S. (Eds.), *Representation and policy formation in federal systems* (pp. 291–321). Berkeley, CA: Institute of Governmental Studies Press.

Wilks, S., & Wright, M. (Eds.). (1987). *Comparative government–industry relations: Western Europe, the United States, and Japan.* New York: Oxford University Press.

Wood, C. (1995). The west coast war: Canada's fisheries minister takes aim at Alaska's fleet. *Maclean's* (July 17), 12–13.

Zahariadis, N., & Allen, C. S. (1995). Ideas, networks, and policy streams: Privatization in Britain and Germany. *Policy Studies Review, 14*(1/2), 71–98.

4

Assessing and Modeling Determinants of Capacity for Action in Networked Public Programs

Glenn W. Rainey, Jr. & Terry Busson

T HE EMPHASIS IN RECENT YEARS on reinvention, decentralization, and devolution in federal programs in the United States has given rise to a new
wave of cooperative programs involving multiple jurisdictions, agencies,
firms, and nonprofit organizations (or NGOs), accompanied by political rhetoric
about the superior performance potential of decentralized and localized administration. Students of public administration, attempting to find a systematic basis
for explaining the dynamics of networked programs and evaluating their effectiveness, have responded in part with a renewed interest in network theory (e.g.,
Milward, 1996). The modeling of organizational networks continues, however,
to be a complex undertaking with a variety of unresolved conceptual and operational issues, including a paucity of comparative modeling that specifies variable
attributes of networked organizations and the related contingencies that affect
their performance.

Improved understanding of networked or cooperative programs has importance both for effective administration and for strategic national policy. Moreover, the policy and administrative implications are interdependent. "Effectiveness" is directly related to both policy goals and administrative means, and the

developmental interdependence of the two has been well demonstrated. The issue of network effectiveness is therefore inseparable from the question of who wants networked arrangements, why, and to accomplish what purposes.

The emphasis on federal devolution has been accompanied by initiatives in delegation, federal pass-throughs, privatization, and reduction or termination of public programs. Some significant part of this activity reflects the sloughing off to the nonprofit sector of services perviously performed by governments, associated with a variety of symbolic expressions about the natural goodness and desirability of local government and limited government, frustration with the presumed ineffectiveness of government services (of which more continue to be desired), antipathy to "bureaucracy" (O'Toole, 1997), and, during the Reagan administration, the call for private charity to replace government responsibilities. The shift in administrative methodology might reasonably be taken to imply that the alternative arrangements that are contemplated offer a known potential for improved effectiveness. If network theory is any clue, this is not so.

Network modeling can be useful because it can focus attention on the properties (e.g., integration, external control, stability, resource munificence—Provan and Milward, 1995) that tend to be associated with the effectiveness of cooperative multiorganizational endeavors—such as service and product outcomes or self-preservation. Much of the literature on network dynamics has not carried forward, however, to link network properties to performance or effectiveness, and network theory carries a variety of conceptual paradoxes, anomalies, and ambiguities that reflect the more general problem of analyzing multicollectivity behavior.

In its extensive but rather controversial academic history, network modeling has been applied to problems in sociology (e.g., Wellman and Berkowitz, 1988, p. 3), analysis of business organizations and cooperative relations between business firms and stakeholders (e.g., Carroll, 1989; Freeman, 1984; Iacobucci, 1996), and as a natural concomitant to a presumed movement toward cooperative alliances and interdependencies among firms in the context of globalization and high technology (e.g., Nadler, 1992, p. 5). Network concepts have also been linked to concepts from economics, such as game theory, transaction cost analysis, and public choice theory (O'Toole, 1997).

There is not much systematic conceptual integration among the disciplines, however, and at least some sociologists have been straightforward in noting a "long-standing gap between theoretical promise and empirical performance" in structural analysis (Wellman and Berkowitz, 1988, p. 7). In the business literature as well, network modeling may be regarded as an area of inquiry of narrow applicability, relevant primarily to small populations of organizations characterized by high interdependence among small firms, particularly in high-technology niches of the market (e.g., Perrow, 1992). While networked public programs are presumably being touted as a means of flexibly and are creatively addressing complex problems, their impact on performance is admitted to be, at best, unpredictable and hard to measure (O'Toole, 1997).

The concept of "effectiveness" in complex programs becomes no simpler

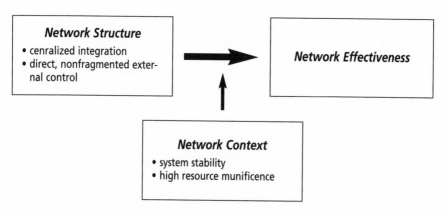

FIGURE **4.1** The Provan and Milward preliminary model of network effectiveness.

from being associated with the network concept, and as Provan and Milward note in their effort to remedy the problem, much of the network literature concentrates on the properties and dynamics of networks without specifying linkages to outcomes (Provan and Milward, 1995). Research agendas have been advanced to refine approaches to network analysis (e.g., O'Toole, 1997), including the straightforward need to explore "dimensions of network structure that may help to explain and mediate program and service delivery results" (O'Toole, 1997, p. 50) as well as linkages to environmental contexts.

This chapter will employ a comparison of three different multijurisdictional programs to build a preliminary contingency model of network effectiveness, advance a more comparative perspective on network dynamics in public administration, and draw implications for strategic policy and the policy-making process.

Conceptual Issues in Network Analysis

A point of departure for this effort has been provided by the particularly energetic and thoughtful comparative study of mental-health services networks in four cities undertaken by Provan and Milward (1995), subsequently reinterpreted in terms of organizational economics in an effort to improve theoretical modeling (Milward and Provan, 1998). They propose that "networks will be effective under structural conditions of centralized integration and direct, nonfragmented external control, but that effectiveness will be highest when the system is also stable and environmental resources are relatively munificent" (1995, p. 23). They conclude that, among other things, a network's effectiveness (measured by subjective assessments from administrators and clients) is particularly facilitated when there is a strong, centrally controlling agency at its core.

In their analysis, Provan and Milward proposed the preliminary model of network effectiveness shown in figure 4.1. The model is striking in its extreme simplicity and conceptual ambiguity, and it clearly implies broad dimensions of variance among networks, including variation across different types of networks. "Effectiveness" is not differentiated at all, despite the fact that Provan and Milward had found it to be a multidimensional construct—in mental-health services meaning one thing to case managers and something else to clients and families. It is quite reasonable to expect that the meaning of the term will also vary according to program goals. Measurement of outcomes has been a long-standing problem in public programs that do not produce tangible or observable outputs, and one of the classic consequences is that managers in those programs tend to fall back on process measures (such as numbers of clients served) as opposed to outcome measures (clients effectively served) (Rainey, 1997, see especially pp. 135–136).

"Structure" in the model is defined in terms of the administrative control variables of "integration" and "external control." It is not clear how other important organizational attributes such as technology or organizational culture fit the model. Moreover, the relationship between structure and "context" is conceptually ambiguous in that "external control" somehow appears as a feature of structure, but not of context. It is also implausible, in that context is represented only as an intervening variable between structure and effectiveness, thus ignoring the effects that context may have directly upon structure.

"Context," in turn, is defined only in terms of stability and resource munificence. Absent are the physical, cultural, and political policy attributes that might play a major role in conditioning network operation and performance, and which will interact developmentally with structure. All public programs must, for example, translate idealized goals into practice and may recast the goals to a greater or lesser degree in the process. May the idealized goals be construed to be an element of context, and the interpreted goals part of structure?

To say that groups of collectivities cooperate more effectively when they are coordinated around a central authority or force, and/or directed toward common goals by an external force, enjoy stability in membership and relations, and have plenty of resources, should not surprise us, and even smacks of closet hierarchicalism. Subsequent questions must be answered. For example:

- How do different types of program goals relate to different types of network effectiveness, and to the interactive dynamics among network properties?

- What are the different ways in which resource munificence or centralized integration can be developed, and how do they trade off against each other or complement each other?

- What are the design options for networks, and what implications do design options have for the interaction between goals and network properties?

An elaborated model of network dynamics and effectiveness will require enhanced understanding of both structural dynamics and their interaction with environmental forces. "Network structure" must be expanded beyond internal centralization and mechanisms of external control, "network context" must be expanded beyond issues of resources and stability, and an initial effort must be made to differentiate the concept of "network effectiveness." Moreover, the expanded conceptualization must incorporate the interdependence between environment and structure, moving beyond generic or industrial perspectives, which use dimensions such as capacity, turbulence, or complexity that are simply inadequate for understanding the dynamics of public program networks. Such concepts tend to neglect the substantive content of human and social behavior, such as the specific content of policy goals, cultural values, environmental conditions, and legal constraints.

Therefore, the specification of environmental linkages must begin with a scan of environmental conditions for networks. One example of a preliminary list of conditions is provided by Rainey (1997, p. 79), who identifies seven general conditions: technological, legal, political, economic, demographic, ecological, and cultural. These general conditions do not interface cleanly with the simpler structure-context-effectiveness model proposed by Provan and Milward. Structure includes not only organizational infrastructure, but control, oversight, and administrative support systems as well, and will overlap with political and legal conditions. It may also include the prevailing technology of service or production. Context may be construed to include cultural conditions, technological opportunities, environmental constraints and munificence, and goal expectations. Effectiveness remains an undifferentiated dependent variable. Thus any attempt to intrepret the relationship between the structure-context-effectiveness model and environmental conditions forces consideration of a much more inclusive array of variables. What follows below illustrates this point.

Structure

Structure includes system infrastructure, encompassing the design of the network itself, as well as oversight, control, and support systems. Design will have to include a developmental perspective: Intended network designs may vary within a policy area—for example, policy may impose relatively central control for a while and then change to emphasis on autonomy and self-coordination. Design also includes the implementational aspects of goal content, including the number of different goals, and their clarity, specificity, and observability. Finally, design must include the prevailing production or service technology, which extends to both engineering and administrative arrangements. The methods by which the structure is integrated may include authoritative oversight or control, such as by a central agency, work processes that compel cooperation, shared commitment by participants, or some combination of such factors.

Context

Context includes the following:

• Environmental constraint and munificence, encompassing physical opportunities and constraints, environmental infrastructure and resource munificence, and established or emergent policy channels. Ecology and demography may also reasonably be incorporated under environmental factors. In a fully specified causal model, they would be exogenous variables influencing such other key elements as program goals and economic conditions. Because the simpler objective here is to identify key components for a model, ecology and demography are incorporated indirectly, on the assumption that their effects will be primarily manifested in such other factors and economic conditions and program goals.

- Cultural values and ethos, including collaborative versus individualistic culture and habits, and an emphasis on quality of life.

- Technological options and opportunities, including potential new physical technology, administrative technology, and related expectations.

- Imposed goals, including symbolic or idealized expectations, and susceptibility to psychological or political partitioning; for example, separating interest in quality of life from antipathy to government action.

Effectiveness and Outcomes

Effectiveness is in the eye of the beholder, but its assessment must begin with the definition and measurement of program outcomes. The attempt to link public policy and its implementation to outcomes poses a paradox: To make the linkage, goals must be clearly defined. Yet it is virtually an established principle of public administration that social goals are often ambiguous and politically charged, resulting in highly accommodational approaches to implementation (Matland, 1995). The broader and more socially encompassing the goal, the more ambiguous it is likely to be, and the more likely it is that administration must address the question of whose goals are to govern. And there is an important corollary: A goal that is stated in unambiguous terms but grossly underfunded or undersupported is still ambiguous from the standpoint of the administrator.

Administration of vaguely defined goals requires administrators to operationalize them, and in the process, administrators may usually be expected to modify the goals to fit pragmatic constraints while offering gestures of support for the policy ideals that were originally announced. If standards of performance are to be applied realistically, they must incorporate adjustments for the pragmatic conditions that the administrators must address. As noted earlier, it is virtually axiomatic that as goals become more abstract and intangible, administrators will tend to fall back on process indicators (such as the number of clients served) rather than substantive outcomes (effectiveness of service) in evaluation. Yet the two are not completely independent. Process outcomes such as the volume, speed, and cost of completed tasks, the application of resources to prominent problems, or improvements in administrative arrangements and procedures may be direct indicators of important social goals such as client access and uniform delivery of services across society. Assessment of program effectiveness will therefore presumably involve not only the amount and quality of substantive services directly delivered, but also the extent of formal and practical public access to services.

The case-history assessment of three programs is intended to compare and further specify the content of these five key attributes: infrastructure, environmental constraints and munificence, goals, cultural values, and technological options and opportunities. The objectives are to specify in greater detail the content of these attributes for networked public programs, expand the conception of the attributes themselves when appropriate, and provide a more detailed conception of network effectiveness.

Program Profiles

Solid Waste Networks

Solid waste management (SWM) is primarily a function of local jurisdictions in the United States. Pressures toward innovation and improved control of waste flow and environmental impact in SWM by local governments have historically emanated from several environmental sources. Leaders in the solid waste administrative community have long been concerned that traditional methods of disposal, and particularly landfill capacity and viability, cannot indefinitely absorb unlimited growth and need to be both more efficient and replaced as much as possible by other means. This recognition, together with more general interest in quality of physical environment, led to an increasing federal role in actively pushing for changes, first through the Solid Waste Disposal Act of 1965, and then through guidelines and pressure emanating from a 1990 report, *Agenda for Action*, issued by the Environmental Protection Agency (Center for Regionalization of Solid Waste Management, 1997, section 3, pp. 3–4). During the early 1990s, federal action to promote more effective containment in landfills created additional pressures for change, with increased costs in landfill management.

As a result, a progressive philosophy developed within the solid waste policy and administrative community that envisioned reduced and more efficient use of landfills, diversion of solid waste into recovery programs such as recycling and incineration, enhanced public education and reduction in solid waste, and generally improved environmental quality. Accompanying the development of external pressure and the new philosophy were technological advances in transportation, disposal, and diversion of solid waste, probably due in part to the general advance in transportation and related technologies, and in part to direct expression of need from the solid waste community.

One important strategy for meeting the new pressures for diversion and containment was regionalized management. Supporting and encouraging regionalization, the Solid Waste Association of North America (SWANA) developed technical materials and in the process developed eleven short case histories of regional alliances and authorities, most of which appeared during the 1980s (Center for Regionalization of Solid Waste Management, 1992, 1997).[1] These case studies cover a range of variations in program scope and design in seven states across the continent and will be assumed to provide a fairly comprehensive overview of environmental conditions, organizational options, and variations in program content.

Structurally, the majority of the eleven SW networks reviewed by SWANA serve areas of one to three counties, typically moderately to heavily urbanized, but not in major metropolitan centers. (Delaware might well be construed to fit within this group; Los Angeles County is an obvious exception.) Where workforce sizes were reported, they tended to be less than a hundred employees at the time the case studies were reported (but some, at least, have since grown dramatically). Agreements have taken the form of informal and consultative cooperation, joint powers agreements, special purpose districts, contractual agreements, or regional authorities or districts (Center for Regionalization of Solid Waste Management, 1997, section 3, p. 16). They are commonly implemented under a multijurisdictional board that oversees an administrator. Board members may be voluntary, paid professionals, or *ex officio* political officials; representation of jurisdictions on boards may incorporate varied mixtures of city, county, and special district officials; the structure may incorporate an executive directorate in a single administrative structure or may require coordination of several agencies.

Detailed reexamination of these cases is beyond the scope of this chapter. Their implications for modeling public program networks may be summarized, however, since the emphasis is more on the identification of important variables than on a precise measurement of their empirical distribution. The case studies were augmented by selective interviewing of managers of some of these networks during the fall of 1999.

A number of attributes appear common to SW networks as a class. Obviously, a geographically delimited area of service seems to be a prerequisite to SW network development. Within this area, there must be sufficient volume of waste flow to justify a local administrative entity, as well as sufficient economic resources to support start-up costs and sufficient political receptivity or leadership to generate the critical mass for innovation. Another general feature of SW networks is that their goals are relatively specific, tangible, and practical, and are therefore also relatively measurable—in terms of absolute and relative reliance on landfills, environmental damage and related citations and penalties, diversion activity and its costs and benefits, and public-education activity. Most of these networks also have the ability to generate independent funding, through tipping and other user fees, as well as through sales of such things as energy, recyclables, and solid waste by-products. Mechanical technology also appears to be a relatively stable and uniform influence—established methods for collection, transfer, disposal, incineration, recycling, and containment appear to be accessible to any of the networks; utilization varies with other factors, such as the ambition of the undertaking, political commitment, and available resources.

In other key dimensions, the eleven vary, often widely. Among the variable attributes that appear to have encouraged the formation of networks, and that channel formation of the multiple goals against which effectiveness will be assessed, are these:

- Direct pressure of limited landfill capacity.
- Willingness of local officials to invest up-front funds and grant other revenue-generating authority.
- Development of administrative authorities as opposed to cooperative service agreements.
- Development of administrative infrastructure, with a general manager or executive director.
- Control of supporting facilities and services, such as landfills and incineration facilities, either directly or through subcontracting.
- Compulsory state legislation and/or receptiveness at the state level to enabling legislation to create authorities where such legislation was required.
- A history of cooperation among local jurisdictions and/or a culture of receptivity to environmental-quality initiatives or efficient management of local services.
- Administrative progressivism, reflected in planning initiatives, concern for long-term economic development, and so on.
- Public and political receptivity to fee-supported, cooperative governmental initiatives.

Administrative reports and interviews with solid waste administrators suggest that the outputs of SW networks vary. Most or all consolidate and improve economies in landfill use. The more ambitious and successful combine improvements in the availability and utilization of landfills with extensive and growing diversion programs, while generating reserve revenues in the process. Solid waste administrators indicate that solid waste authorities in general provide considerable leverage for public jurisdictions against private service providers. Such multijurisdictional or networked arrangements appear, however, to have very limited practical applicability across the country. Administrators pointed out that many smaller jurisdictions will not have the resources to develop them. Indeed, stronger federal containment regulations have increased costs, even as consolidation among private providers has further decreased the relative financial and political leverage of small public jurisdictions. Moreover, market forces have produced a surge in new landfill space, thereby reducing, for the moment, the impetus toward other solutions. Even where such arrangements are feasible, the more ambitious services, such as extensive diversion programs and public education, tend to develop only under particularly favorable conditions involving the size of the jurisdiction, culture, economics, and political support.

The influence of some variables is so intertwined with others that their effect on network viability remains ambiguous, at least for the time being. For example, common sense would suggest that politically fragmented service areas would tend to impede network formation and effectiveness. Yet the Lancaster County Solid Waste Authority serves all sixty municipalities in the county. In that particular case, the authority emerged as a county initiative, in response to a county solid waste plan, which was in turn a response to several compulsory state statutes.

The Job Training Partnership Act Program (JTPA)

The development of the Job Training Partnership Act Program (JTPA) was a reaction to the Comprehensive Employment and Training Act (CETA) program, which was predominantly a public-service employment program. The goal of CETA was training that would result in long-term, private-sector employment, and for the most part this just didn't happen (U.S. Department of Labor, 1997, p. A-3). The Job Training Partnership Act (Public Law 97-300) was enacted on October 13, 1982. The reaction to the CETA program was embodied in antipathy to temporary jobs created within public agencies and in a new effort to emphasize permanent jobs in the private sector. Cosponsored by two unlikely allies, Dan Quayle and Ted Kennedy, JTPA expressed high hopes for preparing men and women to enter into the workforce and giving them the tools to expand their opportunities. The federal government provided most of the money; the states provided additional shares to augment the allowable administrative costs.

The Job Training Partnership Act Program was designed to be a private-sector training program administered on a substate regional level by private industry councils (PICs). These PICs were to be made up of at least one-half private business representatives, with a businessperson as chair. Each PIC was responsible for developing a local job-training plan, selecting grant recipients and administrative entities to run the program, and overseeing its implementation. The PICs oversee multicounty service-delivery areas (SDAs) and are responsible for all eligible residents in their SDA. States, for the most part, were to replace the federal government in monitoring performance of the local programs. In reality, however, the federal government maintained a strong hand in setting performance standards and driving both the type of training offered and standards of eligibility through administrative oversight actions and a series of amendments in 1992 (U.S. Department of Labor, 1997, pp. 1, 3, 4).

State and local planning and oversight were given to state job-training coordination councils (SJTCCs). An SJTCC had to be made up of at least one-third business representatives, and the chair could not be a government employee. A set of performance standards established by the federal government, in effect, drove the actions of the PICs and the reporting requirements established by the SJTCCs. Federally mandated operational performance measures included specific outcomes, such as job-placement rates, job retention, and average wage at job placement. These were intended to improve outcomes over and above the rates that would have occurred without the program. States also had options to add oversight requirements at this and other points in the process.

Since the states were the initial recipients of the federal grants, the federal government could and did require them to make some decisions. They were charged with ensuring that the reporting and performance standards were met. In order to do this, most states imposed a cost-accounting system to ensure that the money was expended within federal guidelines. Each state also established its own uniform reporting system, although since many states did not have standard management information systems (MIS), much of the reporting and monitoring met only minimum federal standards and did not result in a fully planned evaluation system that could support comparative analysis of program participation and outcomes. Rather, performance was monitored through these systems in part on the basis of follow-up surveys of trainees, and the survey results were plugged into formulas used to determine future funding for the SDAs. The SDAs therefore paid close attention to the results of the surveys and to their impact under the standards. One particularly clear and heavily weighted standard was that 70 percent of the training graduates would be employed for thirteen weeks after completing the program. Therefore, nationwide, the results on this standard hovered somewhat above the required figure. The program participants, however, tended to be unemployed high-school graduates, who did not fit the profile of those most in need.

The JTPA system clearly incorporated a paradox. PICs are to drive the system to meet the needs of the local service area, but the federal outcome standards drive the training toward the general statistical standards, in part because each year's funding is based on how successful the SDA was in the previous year in meeting such outcome standards as job-placement rates, job retention, and average wage rate. In addition, the states were given the task of reporting on performance, setting additional performance standards as necessary, as well as the establishment of monitoring systems to ensure and evaluate results.

The PICs varied in the scope and quality of their planning and in their use of the various training and education programs, resulting in very different long-term employment and wage rates. Numerous states were faced with a lack of good data or comparative MIS systems, or had administrative structures that were weak or lacked the capacity to act quickly. As a result of these and other criticisms, the federal government set some new standards dealing with planning, evaluation, and the need to serve the hard-core unemployed and those on welfare. The results of these changes, which were designed to improve service delivery and performance, varied widely depending on the environmental, cultural, and technical conditions found in the various state systems.

The program was mandated by federal action in all of the states, but there were wide variations in local economies, education systems, training resources, eligible workers, and the commitment of the states and PICs to provide clear goals and objectives for local programs. Run as a "market-driven" program, JTPA uses allocational formulas established by the federal and state governments to distribute funding. In addition to performance standards, these formulas incorporate factors to compensate for local variations in clientele characteristics and market opportunities, but these are the only program measures that take local variations in opportunity structure into account.

Within SDAs, the administrative arrangements were left up to the PICs. A variety of different arrangements was worked out, depending on what was available to the PIC and how it chose to organize its training efforts. The organization seemed to revolve around what the needs of the population were, what the job market was like, and what training organizations were available to provide services. As has so often been the case in American policy-making, idealized goals had to be operationalized with inadequate resources. The JTPA program has always been underfunded, with only about 10 percent of the eligible population being served in any one year.

Within the administrative "network" of the SDA, the new PICs could exercise relatively direct administrative control of SDA staff, who might be contractually housed in a variety of host agencies. Programmatically, however, the PICs and the SDA staff then had to graft together service arrangements with existing administrative entities previously involved in job training and/or placement. These would typically include such state-operated entities as regional employment-services offices and vocational training schools and providers. Officially, the state cabinet department might have authority to exercise considerable influence over these preexisting entities and push them into close compliance. But the regional entities also might have considerable *de facto* political clout and autonomy. Moreover, the JTPA program would often represent only one component of the activities of these entities, and perhaps not a very significant component at that. In addition, the SDA staff would often be established as a component of a host agency, such as a council of governments, and would itself work in the context of multiple activities and programs that might be completely unrelated to JTPA. In this administrative context, the states were able to exercise influence on behalf of integration and cooperation in the JTPA networks, but their influence was more negotiated than authoritative, and the regional entities had considerable leeway to determine their levels of commitment. While local PICs were required to set their goals for education, training, and retraining, the federal and state governments also set goals that each SDA had to meet in order to get its funding and any incentive money for the next year. In addition to pressures to serve hard-to-serve clients, these goals included standards for job-placement percentage, job retention thirteen weeks after completion of training, and wages at placement. States adopted other goals to meet objectives set by governors or state legislatures. (Interview with JTPA official.)

In the JTPA program, administrative practices and program content interact in complex patterns with local economic conditions, culture, and the preexisting administrative and technological capabilities. For example, the attitudes and leadership in the PICs have tended to reflect the culture of the geographic region served and in turn affected administrative professionalism and the choice of options offered to eligibles. These internal variables reflect the differences from SDA to SDA and state to state.

Both culture and local economic conditions influence the type of education and training offered to clients. While some SDAs have strongly supported technical and community college training and even higher education for some, others have stopped with a GED and then pushed for some low-level dead-end job. Still others used on-the-job training as a primary source of job creation. A few SDAs supported training for jobs that would tend to take their clients out of state in search of good-paying high-tech jobs, while others trained individuals for jobs that were low-skilled and even on the way out. Still others provided training for small or in-home businesses that would meet the needs of rural families with limited ability to move where more jobs might be.

Administrative/organizational options are limited by the knowledge and expertise of the voluntary PIC boards and the choices they make in selecting administrative organizations. The limits of state control and data-analysis requirements are often driven by political considerations and accountability standards.

The JTPA resulted in a national program that, with widespread variations in the content and quality of service, provided some kind of systematic training in all parts of the country, to a modest fraction of the population in need, and placed approximately two-thirds of its graduates in employment that lasted at least a few months. A dissatisfied Congress intervened in job-training policy again in August 1998, passing the Workforce Investment Act (WIA) (Public Law 105-220). This act is presumably replacing JTPA with a revised administrative system that, among other things, is supposed to further reduce federal and state involvement and rely even more heavily on control by local boards or committees.

The School-to-Work Program

The School-to-Work Opportunities Act (Public Law 103-239), signed into law in May 1994, authorized development grants to support state efforts in designing school-to-work transition strategies. In its idealized form, the act does the following:

- Provides states and local communities with seed money to build school-to-work systems to prepare young people for high-skill, high-wage jobs or education.
- Requires that every school-to-work system have three essential elements: work-based learning, school-based learning, and connective activities.
- Specifies that school-to-work systems integrate school-based and work-based learning, academic and vocational education, and postsecondary education.
- Encourages partnerships among key stakeholders, including educators, employers, and labor and community-based organizations.
- Considers existing programs such as tech prep, youth apprenticeship, cooperative education, and career academies as building blocks for the program.
- Administers implementation funds in "waves" to allow states and local districts to develop sound plans and learn from efforts elsewhere.
- Provides technical assistance and support to enable school-to-work systems in each state to continue successfully after the federal investment ends. (School-to-Work transitions, 1996, p. 3.)

Planning dollars were available in 1994, with money available to the first group of eight states: Kentucky, Maine, Massachusetts, Michigan, New Jersey, New York, Oregon, and Wisconsin. The program embodied several key goals, among them promoting and demonstrating good academic and occupational competencies; broad-based career education, guidance, and counseling programs, including self- and career awareness for students through fifth grade and the development of career goals by eighth grade; and the development of specific business links through such means as internships for teachers, bringing business into the classroom, trips to businesses for students, and advisory committees for business ties. Other components included workplace exposure, such as job shadowing, school-based enterprises, "tech prep," internships for teachers and students, and a programmatic focus on careers for all students. The final component was actual work experience through after-school and summer jobs in one of the participating businesses or industries (School-to-Work transitions, 1996, p. 5).

The program was to be different from JTPA in that it was to have a minimum of direction from the federal government and only limited oversight from the state government. Two broad goals were envisioned at the federal level in addition to the ideas expressed in the components above: to shake the school culture away from precollege to a work-transition program, not a vocational education program; and that the state would pick up the program and run it when the developmental money ran out after five years (interview with School-to-Work official).

The programs were to be run at the local level, but the exact nature of the local organizations was to be determined by the local networks. In most states, the state government worked with various groups, such as school administrators, school boards, vocational education units, and business and labor organizations, to develop some sort of regional or county entity to administer the program. In Kentucky, a School-to-Work office in the Workforce Development Cabinet decided to establish labor market areas (LMAs) composed of multicounty areas with widespread representation. Local individuals were recruited to establish these councils, and they established their goals and selected an administrative unit to choose individuals to organize the programs in each school district. In Oregon, the Workforce Quality Council is responsible for state policy and individual school districts for the local control of the programs. In Wisconsin, the Executive Cabinet for a Quality Work Force set state guidelines in cooperation with the Department of Public Instruction and its Office of School-to-Work Transition. Local school boards were to approve plans for each of their schools under broad state guidelines (interview with School-to-Work official). In numerous situations, state and local educational systems already provided career preparation and work-experience programs, to which School-to-Work activities would have to somehow be added and administratively adjusted.

While the states used different approaches in various important respects, they all tended to rely for program oversight on councils of business, labor, education, and in some cases parents and students. The councils were charged with formulating plans to develop programmatic components, setting up administrative and performance standards for the program, and monitoring spending.

During the early stages of the program, federal agencies attempted to exercise administrative oversight and quality control over states and the local administrative arms through a number of traditional measures, but the administrative authority for oversight was limited and ambiguous, and the federal methods and goals tended to be inconsistent and variable. One method of oversight was program audits, but audit policies varied among federal departments involved with the program. The Department of Education apparently took a broad and relatively flexible view of the rules and regulations, while the Department of Labor seemed to take a more narrow and restrictive view, based on its experience with JTPA. Another early oversight tactic was the use of special program money that was made available to states for specific uses, such as the development of total quality management (TQM) and customer-satisfaction systems.

It is unclear how many School-to-Work programs are committed to continue the programs beyond the end of the federal funding. Some states, such as Florida, Wisconsin, Oregon, and Tennessee, will probably continue and even expand their programs, but these states had some model in place prior to the federal program. Others, like Kentucky, will fold the program into an existing agency, probably with no new money. Unlike JTPA, which was to some large extent grafted onto the state workforce development or labor departments and the regional employment-services offices, and solid waste networks, which developed as extensions of counties, cities, or regional governments, School-to-Work in most cases became devolution at its most extreme—organizational arrangements were to emerge from local initiative.

It is particularly difficult to define and assess any operational outcomes of the School-to-Work program. Systematic data on participant outcomes appear to be largely nonexistent. Evaluation tends to be anecdotal and exhortatory. Interviews with officials involved in the program suggest that the results have typically been a series of disparate work-experience and career-planning activities, of widely varying scope and quality. There is simply no evidence or reason to assume that the program has had siginificant effects on the educational attainment or career preparation of more than a small minority of American schoolchildren.

Summarizing Variations Within and Between Networked Programs

The program profiles highlight major variations among networks within each program and between programs, which are represented in table 4.1. The variations are summarized in approximate but not absolute order of the table.

Solid Waste Networks

Formed by some local governments in response to external pressures, solid waste authorities lack intensive external oversight and must typically be created as new agencies, but tend to form cohesively around the relatively clear and workable service technologies that are available to them, with the particular advantage that they can establish their own sources of revenue. The needs they address are relatively tangible, visible, and measurable. The scope of their activities can vary

Table 4.1

**COMPARISON OF SOLID WASTE NETWORKS, JTPA, AND STW
ON SELECTED ATTRIBUTES RELATED TO PERFORMANCE**

Attribute	Solid Waste	JTPA	STW
Structure			
Integrative oversight	low	moderate	low
Integrative process	high	moderate	low
Integrative commitment	variable	variable	variable
Availability of preexisting agencies	low	high	high
Context			
Goal observability	high	moderate	low
Access to funding	high	moderate	low
Access to needed program technology	high	moderate	low
Cultural support	variable	variable	variable
Economic opportunity	variable	variable	variable
Outcomes			
Services delivered to public	variable	moderate	low
Consistency in legal access to services, across networks	high	high	high
Consistency in legal access to services, across society	low	high	high
Consistency in service delivery, across networks	moderate	moderate	low
Consistency in service delivery, across society	low	moderate	low

quite widely, however, in part because of the diversity of local cultural norms about quality of life, collective social responsibility, and political cooperation, and in part because local economies differ both in the kinds of solid waste problems to be solved and in slack resources that may be accessed. Legal access to supply the kinds of services they can provide seems to be quite uniform within the authorities, but most local governments in the United States either have not generated such cooperative ventures or cannot afford to, one factor being variability in state enabling legislation. Actual service delivery varies among networks, from cooperative disposal arrangements to disposal accompanied by diversion, marketing, and public-education programs. Again, however, such authorities are available in only a minority of communities across American society.

The JTPA Program

Grafted by federal mandate onto a series of existing state and local training agencies and programs across the nation, the JTPA program was pulled together by mandated performance standards and traditionally established processes and technology for conducting job training but pulled apart by the traditional independence of many local agencies, the limited enforcement powers of oversight agencies, and its own emphasis on delegation of program authority to the PICs. Commitment to cooperative endeavor, cultural values of personal and community development, and economic opportunities for job development and placement varied across the states and across the PICs within states. The goals of the program, as administratively operationalized, included specified outcomes for participants and quantitative objectives that could be fairly easily measured (client placements and initial salary) as well as social or qualitative objectives that could not (long-term career development and economic development). The program depended on externally provided funding from the federal government and the states, and the funding always fell short of the rhetorical ideals of the program. Thus the unemployed would have legal access to the program across the entire nation, and across every PIC, but the services delivered tended to be oriented to relatively short-term training and placement for large numbers of relatively employable clients, rather than the neediest ideally targeted, and access to actual service would have to be rationed both across PICs and across the country because of limited resources.

The School-To-Work Program

Also federally mandated, but lacking the administrative oversight arrangements and performance standards of the JTPA program, the School-to-Work program would generally search out host agencies from among a variety of existing ones, and under some circumstances create them. The multiple methods and locuses of career education, the variations in their application across the ages of children, and the presence of preexisting career-education programs in some locations but not others create more challenges to integrated administration than natural channels and pressures for integration. Once again, wide variations may be observed across states and across LMAs within states in cultural support for career development among children as well as in economic opportunities for cooperative programs with businesses and for improved career opportunities for graduates. The goals of the program are inherently vague and intangible, and push measurement toward short-term administrative process (participation by children in programs) as opposed to long-term outcomes (improved careers). The absence of permanent federal funding has created a short time horizon for administrative personnel and implies that the program will survive only where local or state resources can be generated to keep it going. It may be difficult to even know whether the program has survived, since it may do so by merging into other, preexisting career-education activities. Thus, though from a statutory standpoint the program exists everywhere in the nation, in fact the services delivered vary

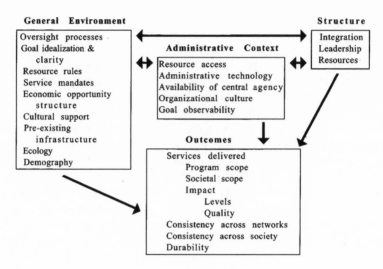

FIGURE 4.2 Elaborated model of network effectiveness.

widely across LMAs and across states, but for the most part are restricted to various kinds of experiential education offered on a fragmented basis.

An Expanded Model

A simple structure-context-effectiveness model cannot encompass the complex interactions revealed by the case studies. An attempt to capture a broader range of variables and more carefully specify causal and interactive relationships is shown in figure 4.2. The expanded model is not intended to be a fully specified multivariate causal model of network effectiveness, but to summarize categories of key cause-and-effect variables. Certain structural features of the model should be noted in particular: Environment, administrative context, and structure are portrayed as interactive; in general, environmental variables may be expected to interact recursively with features of administrative context and network structure to influence internal administration and service outcomes. This contrasts with the Provan and Milward model, which treated context as an intervening variable between structure and outcomes. To the extent that simple, sequential, causal relationships do exist among these groups of variables, our experience suggests that features of context will largely be antecedent to both structure and outcomes, and that the emergence and operation of networks must be treated as an evolutionary and developmental process, requiring explanatory analysis oriented toward organic rather than mechanistic modeling.

Implications for Policy and Administration

The accumulating experience with networked programs supports some conclusions that have implications for further research. First, networked, decentralized approaches to administration do not obviate basic requirements of organizational effectiveness, such as adequate resources, realistic goals, and integrative structures and processes. The mechanisms of integration may take the form of a dominant central agency, as Provan and Milward suggest, but our observations show that they may take other forms as well, including technologies that require cooperation for mutual success, externally imposed standards and processes backed by resource sanctions, or (at least hypothetically) widely shared cultural norms and social goals for which a networked approach serves as a facilitator.

Networked arrangements do, however, bring with them their own special requirement as an administrative methodology and present administrators with important choices among trade-offs. They may be able to choose between integrative arrangements that rely on a central agency within a network, or impose external sanctions and standards, or rely instead on commitment generated internally within the network. Networked programs that provide direct client service or involve cooperation among other entities with revenue-generating powers may or may not be able to establish dedicated or independent revenue streams, depending upon enabling statutes and program design. If students of public policy are serious about understanding networked and devolved arrangements, further understanding must be developed of the trade-offs between different approaches to networked administration and their costs and benefits.

The research agenda will need as well to include attention to capacity for action in a broader comparative context that encompasses the interaction between structure and environment and contrasts networks to other organizational arrangements. If networked, relatively decentralized programs are to be substituted for so-called "traditional" hierarchical arrangements, and if the rationale is that they will be somehow more effective in carrying out central policy goals, the implication is that they will have stronger capacity for effective action than the bureaucracies they are to replace. It is not clear, however, why anyone should take this for granted. If networks may vary in such attributes as integration, resource munificence, and stability, then a clear implication is that there are networks that are unstable, impoverished, and anarchic. As Rosenbloom (1998) has noted, reinvention and decentralization initiatives within the federal bureaucracy tend to assume high levels of constructive commitment and responsibility among the employees to whom autonomy will be delegated. Decentralized, unregulated, cooperative or networked programs in the federal system make similar assumptions about the commitment of individual and institutional participants.

The experiences of solid waste networks, JTPA training networks, and School-to-Work LMAs suggest that such arrangements are likely to fall short of serving certain potentially important national policy objectives. All three do, indeed, appear to have created opportunities for invention at the program-delivery level. At the same time, they place great reliance on the capability, resources, and commitment of disparate, multiple agencies and actors, with widely varying results, including varying levels of effectiveness. Programs generated in locations where there are resources, commitment, and perhaps previously developed experience and infrastructure may be expected to perform relatively well. Programs in locations lacking these advantages are likely to be broadly ineffective. Ironically, the JPTA program, which retained important elements of federal oversight (and which policy-makers have already sought to redesign and further decentralize), has been the most consistent of the three in providing a basic, more or less comparable service to American society as a whole. Solid waste management networks can provide excellent results under appropriate conditions, but, at least as a practical matter, the conditions seem to be infrequent and widely scattered. The most decentralized program, with the most ambiguous objectives, School-to-Work, will need great luck to produce any long-lasting, socially widespread, demonstrable results.

Careless and overextended use of such arrangements will undermine the ability of industrial societies to identify and meet broad national goals with measurable outcomes, to provide services equitably to all eligible citizens, and to identify adequate resources to meet stated goals. They will inevitably incorporate elements of social Darwinism, as genuinely unregulated markets do. Rather than lift the society to new levels of attainment through a brave new era of collective action, policy-makers may devolve a modern industrial society as they devolve its government.

To address these implications in future analysis and policy, it will be necessary to understand not only the dynamics of networked programs themselves, but the role such programs play in the larger policy process. The question is practical and blunt: Why would policy-makers adopt administrative arrangements that carry a clear risk of weak and uneven implementation? As already noted, it makes no sense to assume that they have a profound but secret understanding of these arrangements that managers and social scientists have missed in decades of searching.

Some quite different explanations are plausible. One is that networked arrangements are a reactive strategy borne of several types of desperation—other approaches have left a trail of dissatisfaction, whether realistic or not, so why not try an entrepreneurial adventure in decentralization and see if it helps? Another plausible explanation, however, is that decentralized, networked administration, which certainly appears to be associated with a movement toward reduced central governmental authority in the United States, is simply consistent with a philosophy of cheap, weak government that appeals to many large, influential economic interests.

This question of who wants networked arrangements and why has direct implications for our understanding of how and why such arrangements emerge and what can or cannot be done about their effectiveness. Policy-makers who choose them out of reactivity or desperation might be willing to learn from experience and modify their approaches. To the extent that policy-makers are acting out of subservience to economically and culturally dominant interests in the society, it is those interests that must learn and change.

Note

1. The eleven are the *Bi-County Integrated Waste Management Authority* (Cities of Live Oak, Marysville, Wheatland and Yuba City, California); *County Districts of Los Angeles County* (California); *Delaware Solid Waste Authority*; *Great River Regional Solid Waste Authority (GRRWA)* (Fort Madison, Iowa); *Lancaster County Solid Waste Management Authority* (Pennsylvania); *Monterey Regional Waste Management District* (Monterey County, California); *Northern Tier Solid Waste Authority (NTSWA)* (Bradford, Sullivan, and Tioga Counties, Pennsylvania); *Regional Solid Waste Systems, Inc.* (Portland, Maine); *Solid Waste Authority of Central Ohio* (Franklin County, Ohio); *Solid Waste Authority of Palm Beach County* (Florida); *South Central Iowa, Solid Waste Management Association* (Tracy, Iowa).

References

Carroll, A. B. (1989). *Business and society: Ethics and stakeholder management.* Cincinnati: South-Western Publishing.

Center for Regionalization of Solid Waste Management. (1992, October). *Regionalizing municipal solid waste management: Facing a political challenge with a political response: A series of case studies.* Silver Spring, MD: Solid Waste Association of North America.

Center for Regionalization of Solid Waste Management. (1997). *SWANA Center for Regionalization of Municipal Solid Waste Management: Regional guidance document and center information.* Silver Spring, MD: Solid Waste Association of North America, dated January 1995.

Freeman, R. E. (1984). *Strategic management: A stakeholder approach.* Boston: Pittman Publishing.

Iacobucci, D. (Ed.). (1996). *Networks in marketing.* Thousand Oaks, CA: Sage Publications.

Job Training Partnership Act, Public Law 97-300 (October 13, 1982).

Matland, R. E. (1995). Synthesizing the implementation literature: The ambiguity-conflict model of policy implementation. *Journal of Public Administration Research and Theory, 5*(2), 145–174.

Milward, H. B. (Ed.). (1996). Symposium on the hollow state: Capacity, control, and performance in interorganizational settings. *Journal of Public Administration Research and Theory, 6*(2), 193–314.

Milward, H. B., & Provan, K. G. (1998). Principles for controlling agents: The political economy of network structure. *Journal of Public Administration Research and Theory, 8*(2), 203–221.

Nadler, D. A. (1992). Introduction: Organizational architecture: A metaphor for change. In D. A. Nadler, M. S. Gerstein, R. A. Shaw, & Associates (Eds.), *Organizational architecture: Designs for changing organizations* (pp. 1–8). San Francisco: Jossey-Bass.

O'Toole, L. J., Jr. (1997). Treating networks seriously: Practical and research-based agendas in public administration. *Public Administration Review, 57*(1), January–February, 45–52.

Perrow, C. (1992). Small-firm networks. In N. Nohria & Robert G. Eccles (Eds.), *Networks and organizations: Structure, form, and action* (pp. 445–470). Boston: Harvard Business School Press.

Provan, K. G., & Milward, H. B. (1995). A preliminary theory of interorganizational network effectiveness: A comparative study of four community mental health systems. *Administrative Science Quarterly, 40*(1), 1–33.

Rainey, H. G. (1997). *Understanding and managing public organizations.* San Francisco: Jossey-Bass.

Rosenbloom, D. H. (1998). *Public administration: Understanding management, politics, and law in the public sector.* New York: McGraw-Hill.

School-to-Work Opportunities Act, Public Law 103-239 (1994, May 4).

School-to-Work transitions. (1996, spring). *ERIC Review, 4*(2).

U.S. Department of Labor. (1997). Employment and Training Administration, Implementation of the 1992 Job Training Partnership Act (JTPA) Amendments. Washington, DC.

Wellman, B., & Berkowitz, S. D. (1988). Introduction: Studying social structures. In B. Wellman & S. D. Berkowitz (Eds.), *Social structures: A network approach* (pp.1–14). Cambridge: Cambridge University Press.

Workforce Investment Act of 1998, Public Law 105-220 (1998, August 7).

Other Works Consulted

Bloom, H. S., et al. (1992). *The national JTPA study: Title IIA impacts on earnings and employment at 18 months.* Abt Associates.

Brown, P. (Ed.). (1995). *Promoting a dialogue on school-to-work transition.* Washington, DC: Center for Policy Research, National Governors' Association.

Erlichson, B. A., & Van Horn, C. E. (1999, June). *School-to-work governance: A national review.* Consortium for Policy Research in Education.

Hill, C. W. L., & Jones, T. M. (1992). Stakeholder-agency theory. *Journal of Management Studies, 29*(2), 131–154.

Kazis, R., & Barton, P. E. (1993). *Improving the transition from school-to-work in the United States.* Boston: Jobs for the Future.

Larson, A. (1992). Network dyads in entrepreneurial settings: A study of the governance of exchange relationships. *Administrative Science Quarterly, 37*(1), 76–104.

Medrich, E. (1998, November). *School-to-work progress measures.* MPR Associates.

Rosenbaum, J. E., Kariya, T., Settersten, R., & Maier, T. (1990). Market and network theories of the transition from high school to work: Their application to industrialized societies. In W. R. Scott and J. Blake (Eds.), *Annual Review of Sociology, 16*, 263–299. Palo Alto, CA: Annual Reviews.

U.S. Department of Education. (1994). *School-to-work: What does the research say about it?* Washington, DC: Office of Research, Department of Education.

U.S. Department of Education, and U.S. Department of Labor. (1998). *Implementation of the School-to-Work Opportunities Act of 1994.* Joint Report to Congress.

U.S. General Accounting Office. (1989). *Job Training Partnership Act: Services and outcomes for participants with differing needs.* Washington, DC: GAO.

U.S. General Accounting Office. (1993). *Transition from school to work.* Washington, DC: GAO.

Wasserman, S., & Galaskiewicz, J. (Eds.). (1994). *Advances in social network analysis: Research in the social and behavioral sciences.* Thousand Oaks, CA: Sage Publications.

5

Multiorganizational, Multisector, and Multi-community Organizations

Setting the Research Agenda

Beverly A. Cigler

NEW WAYS OF ORGANIZING ARE EMERGING for mobilizing human, financial, and other resources necessary for facilitating multiorganizational action across sectors (public, private, nonprofit) and communities (multicommunity collaboratives) that share common problems. These alliances require new types of interactions, purposes, operations, and agreements—all increasing organizational complexity. Problem-solving organizations, for example, are more complex than those solely sharing information.

Collaboration involves an intensity of linkages (increased resource commitments, a sharing of tasks and decision rules, and common goals). Truly collaborative organizations foster a feeling of "shared destiny." Increased importance is given to nurturing an ability to network people, money, and facilities. Multicommunity collaboration can also include greater formality of organization, often evolving from handshakes to more formal legal, written contracts.

This chapter examines aspects of the organizing and managing dimensions of multicommunity collaboration. Previously published research, which received limited distribution through government reports and conference proceedings (Cigler, 1992a, 1992b; Cigler et al., 1994) and one journal article (Cigler, 1999), reported that collaborations can vary along a continuum involving simple information sharing, cooperative, coordinative, and truly collaborative interaction in which actors recognize a "shared destiny." Significantly, the research found that the new emergent organizations studied had themselves evolved along such a continuum of partnerships over many years. Also uncovered were several "preconditions" that explain the emergence of partnership organizations with the small communities in each region studied.

No measure of organizational "success" was built into the research design (Milward and Provan, 1998; Provan and Milward, 1995) because of the impossibility of making such a judgment before embarking on the research, which occurred in the early 1990s and was "baseline" for studying multicommunity collaboration. It was possible, however, to reflect on the impacts of specific projects and/or the process of collaboration itself engaged in by the organizations studied. The research, then, is more closely aligned to the work of Alter and Hage (1993) and Alexander (1995), who look at types of coordination in interorganizational networks, rather than work that attempts to measure outcomes. The research summarized here focuses on the emergence of new multiorganizational entities but differs in emphasis from the work of Provan and Milward (1995, 1998), for example, who have been more concerned with networks built on contractual ties than those evolving from historical patterns of collaboration. Uzzi (1997) found that both types of networks can coexist, and Jones, Hesterly, and Borgatti (1997) looked at both the formal roles of contracts and the informal features of networks such as reputation and trust, concluding that social coordination and control are more important to network governance. The research discussed in this chapter examines alliances that are not built initially on formal authority or legal foundations. Issues related to power relationships among the participating or creating organizations and the building of trust relationships are studied and found to be very important.

This chapter summarizes the research methodology; explains the *continuum of partnerships* examined by the research; summarizes a set of "preconditions" that help explain the *emergence* of multiorganizational, multisector, and multicommunity organizations; and focuses on the development of *research questions* that flow from the case study selection process and the findings on the continuum of partnerships and the preconditions for multiorganizational emergence.

Research Design

The research occurred in several phases. First, criteria were developed for selecting the specific three case study sites. The selection criteria were as follows:

- Alliances that were rural or nonmetropolitan in character. This would permit examination of complex organizations but not necessarily as complex as those in more urban settings. The eventual fieldwork and baseline information gathering associated with the project would, it was thought, benefit from this selection criterion.

- Geographic dispersion of research sites. Among three sites, at least one was sought from Canada so that the research would have a more comparative focus.

- Alliances that led to organizations in existence for approximately five years. This would indicate organizational stability and long-term interest in major change. It would also permit the exploration of more than the initial stages of organizational development, as the aim was to study both organizational emergence and maintenance.

- Voluntary alliances—that is, grass-roots or self-help organizations. The intent was to avoid selecting organizations that were mandated by government, especially the national, state, or provincial levels.

- Alliances with broad-based interests in systemic change, based on multifaceted approaches to community economic development. This criterion permitted examination of complex alliances on holistic issues, rather than those that focused on isolated topics.

- Alliances that included five or more communities. This would also permit the exploration of more than the initial stages of organizational development.

- Alliances that involved many sectors within each member community. For example, intermunicipal organizations that involved government bodies but exclude other sectors (private, nonprofit) were not suitable candidates for further research, nor were multicommunity groups that did not include any government involvement.

- Alliances that were representative of communities in terms of race, gender, and socioeconomic status.

The next research phase involved a national telephone survey of knowledgeable elites across the fifty states and Canada who were familiar with complex (multiorganizational, multisector, and multicommunity) organizations in the area of community economic development. The calls, guided by a short questionnaire that depicted the team agreement of selection criteria, were to elicit a set of initial organizations to consider for in-depth field research.

Representatives from a dozen organizations that appeared to meet the criteria were then interviewed by phone, constituting the third phase of the research. The research team, composed of a sociologist, an economist, a planner, and a political scientist, had to then reconsider some of the original selection criteria. For example, none of the twelve organizations, based on interviews with their founders or with the knowledgeable elites who participated in the snowballing to identify organizations for study, were truly "self-help" in the sense of not receiving any type of external capacity-building assistance. That is, all of the organizations uncovered by the telephone survey received some type of financial or technical assistance as they emerged. Other sites did not meet the five-years-in-existence criterion; instead, the present organizations evolved from long-standing earlier efforts over many years, still affording the opportunity to study organization emergence. In the assessment of the research team, none of the organizational alliances were truly representative of communities in terms of race, gender, and socioeconomic status. Finally, some sites were much more grass-roots or self-developmental in nature than other organizations considered for additional research.

Based on the telephone interviews with founders and board members of potential organizations for study, three areas were selected for intensive field-work. The research team judged these to be the best "fit" to the selection criteria. The study areas include two regions in the United States, in Michigan and Nebraska, and a third in Alberta, Canada. The Michigan organization represents four nonmetropolitan communities, including a county, and the Nebraska organization includes ten rural communities dispersed over a large area. The lone Canadian site includes fourteen rural communities attempting to collaborate over a wide geographic area.

The initial research, as well as a restudy two years later, examined the emergence of the new organizations as well as the factors that facilitate their "maintenance." The findings summarized here stem from the study of the emergence of the organizations.

A Continuum of Partnerships

The initial national search for candidate organizations for study, and a second round of interviews with major candidates, revealed that partnerships themselves vary widely. Specifically, the array of partnerships examined varied along a continuum involving networking, cooperative, coordinative, and collaborative action (Cigler, 1992a, 1992b, developed from Habana-Hafner, Reed, and Associates, 1989, and Mulford and Rogers, 1982). The various partnership types on the continuum differ in complexity of purposes (for example, information sharing versus complicated, joint problem-solving), intensity of linkages (based on common goals, decision rules, shared tasks, and resource commitments), and the formality of agreements reached (informality versus formality of rules guiding operating structures, policies, and procedures).

The case studies focused on formalized collaboration that resulted in the creation of new organizations to work on systemic or holistic problems within a region. However, much was learned about the various types of partnerships, especially since the three emergent organizations themselves had evolved along the points on the continuum.

The three organizations drew primarily on nonstate public-sector actors, namely, an array of private and nonprofit groups. The organizations emerged slowly with rich histories. Emergence evolved from a set of conditions that are defined as "preconditions" for organizational emergence. Significantly, the three emergent organizations originally began with loose linkages and networking and only much later were formalized.

Organizations working together with very loose linkages are networking partnerships (Gilroy and Swan, 1984), usually existing for information exchange. Members join or disconnect with ease, without threatening the partnership's existence. Informality governs procedural and structural patterns; member units can maintain their organizational autonomy. Resource sharing primarily involves the exchange of ideas, news, and reports.

A second type, cooperative partnerships, can also be relatively simple in terms of organizational purpose, with relatively low levels of intensity in linkages and agreements that can range from informal to somewhat formal. Organizations can cooperate on one or more activities but do not generally have marginal costs to participants, are staffed by middle- or lower-level personnel, and entail the use of relatively few resources (Andranovich, 1991).

Organizations that work together with more closely linked connections are seen as a coordinating partnership (Rogers and Whetten, 1982). The purpose involves tasks that require a commitment of resources beyond information sharing and generally entails specific shared, common goals established by the member units. Membership is more stable, with attention given to who joins and the consequences of member units leaving. More formality surrounds process and structural patterns of the coordination. Significantly, each member unit agrees to some loss of autonomy, with possible effects on its internal organization. As such, higher-level officials tend to participate because the stakes of participation are relatively high. Resource commitments, for example, involve some amount of each member's assets, such as time, funds, personnel, or facilities. In general, this type of partnership is more visible than the networking and cooperative types, since its tasks or activities require a higher degree of tangible processes and structures.

The fourth type of partnership, collaborative, involves strong linkages among members. The purpose is specific, often complex, and usually long-term. Membership is very stable. The addition or reduction of members is an issue that could produce significant and often detrimental changes in the partnership, including its failure. Formal process and structural patterns of collaboration are usually expressed in writing, generally as legal documents. When a collaborative partnership emerges, each member unit has delegated considerable autonomy to the collaboration. Resource commitment is similarly significant. Collaborative efforts are highly visible to others in the community or region. These organizations can be very complex, involving multiorganizational, multisector, and multicommunity partnerships. Less complex types of partnerships usually develop before a highly collaborative entity emerges.

The three case studies used for this discussion each followed the continuum pattern in their development. Government created none of the organizations, so their authority base differs from the traditional organization empowered to deal with community economic development. Instead, the mostly nonstate actors from the private and nonprofit sectors achieve a semblance of "legitimacy" from their relatively strong fund of knowledge, access to information, and the relative ease at which they can continuously renegotiate their organizational goals and strategies.

In each case of an emergent organization, the public sector was the "weak link" in terms of driving organizational creation, vision, mission, goals, resources, and other factors. Yet in each case, the key actors made efforts to include governmental representatives because ultimate decisions, such as the recruitment, retention, or development of homegrown businesses, required governmental authority to offer subsidies, to tax, to zone, and so forth. Some of the organizations created "shadow" devices for doing what needed to be done for economic development, but without the usual constraints in which government operates. For example, a new authority was promoted by one of the emergent organizations to allow more flexibility for financing than the existing county government economic-development agency. The authority was created, and the board members of the emergent organization explained that accountability was ensured simply because the board was so large and so representative of traditionally competing groups that it naturally served as a check on excesses. Finally, all of the organizations had an imbalance in terms of nonstate actors, with private groups more predominant than nonprofit organizations, thus neglecting the "community" part of community economic development.

Examination of points on the continuum of partnerships suggests a number of other considerations regarding partnership development. The more complex the partnership, the more likely it is to involve an issue that requires an integrated set of actions for resolution. Thus, interdependence extends beyond coordination and cooperation to the need for a collaborative policy community, highlighting the need to be concerned with issues of responsibility, accountability, and responsiveness. Issues of divided authority suggest increased concern with the stability of the goal structure and the need for development of various skills, such as process skills, analytical skills, people skills, or mediation skills. That is, as partnerships grow from simple information sharing and perhaps coordination to more coordinating and collaborative relationships, the need for skills also shifts—from planning, organizing, and leading to mediating, guiding, and influencing.

Similarly, initial concerns are with shared visions and defining purpose and goals. As interactions increase in complexity and formality, there is a need to clarify the self-interest of the participating organizations in the new organization being formed, often resulting in conflict. Also, greater attention is directed to establishing priorities and expectations of participants, achieving mutual trust, and confronting both the potentials and the pitfalls of the endeavor.

Future Research Needs Flowing from
the Partnership Continuum

- Do complex and/or successful partnerships evolve along a continuum from simple to complex? This could be assessed by examining such variables as organizational purposes (for example, information sharing versus complicated, joint problem solving), intensity of linkages (vision, mission, and goal development; resource commitments; shared tasks; and decision rules), and the formality of agreements reached to guide operating structures, policies, and procedures.

- Is it useful to study organizations over time utilizing a typology developed from the interactions posited for points on the continuum of partnerships? This may help to understand how individuals and organizations move from competitive to collaborative relations. The case study research suggests that trust relationships be built among individuals from small successes on less contentious issues (joint festivals, for example). The built trust then helps forge a willingness to work on projects that require more commitment. Different processes and leadership skills appear to be central at different points in the developmental continuum.

- What is the basis for legitimacy for organizations that do not possess the traditional reins of government authority? Is it a relative monopoly on information? Or is it the ability to bypass traditional restraints on government and thus to achieve flexibility in a fast-paced and continually changing environment?

- When government is the "weak sector" within a collaboration, what are the effects on accountability, traditionally defined as linkages and responsiveness to citizens? Since part of vision creation involves the notion of inclusiveness, how do these organizations build broad support, and how do they recruit participants and yet balance representation with the need to take quick and flexible action?

- If the new emergent organizations are examples of the building of social capital, how representative are they of the entire community, and how responsive are they to the needs of the entire community?

- Why are organizations that traditionally compete willing to commit resources and to trust the emergent organizations?

- What changes occur in the culture and operations of the existing organizations as they gain experience with collaborative partnerships?

- What is government's role in these new types of organizations that are not governed through top-down processes? Is it as a catalyst or facilitator (which was not the case in the three case studies)? Is it a source of legitimacy for the organization without the traditional notions of accountability? Is participation by government a way to avoid accountability while gaining more flexibility?

- The new emergent organizations are touted as seamless approaches for dealing with problems that spill over boundaries, but their formation (and functioning) poses many boundary questions in need of research. These include issues of authority boundaries, or the "who is in charge of what?" question. Similarly, the question about "who does what?" related to the boundaries for completing the tasks necessary for achieving legitimacy and empowerment is relevant. Thorny questions regarding issues of self-interest related to "what's in it for my existing organization?" have to be addressed. Other researchable questions involve how collaboration can be solidified in a new unit by establishing a clear identity that does not tamper with existing identities of participating organizations.

Partnerships as Organizational Change

Truly collaborative ventures are system-changing (McDonnell, 1988). They require a recasting of the fundamental structure or purpose of the participating units, their culture, incentive/sanction systems, and their core processes (Downs, 1967). Existing research relies heavily on resource dependence theory (e.g., Pfeffer and Salancik, 1978; Thompson, 1967) and transaction cost analysis (e.g., Powell, 1990; Williamson, 1975) to explain the reasons for collaborative ventures. The assumption is that knowledge of resource dependency leads organizational actors toward collaborative partnerships. Jones, Hesterly, and Borgatti (1997) attempted to develop a general theory of how network governance emerges. They argue that exchange attributes of network members lead to the development of a social structure, and through the social structure, control mechanisms develop to allow for the efficient governance of the network. The researchers relied on both transactions cost economics and Granovetter's (1985) structural embeddedness of networks. The work, however, relates to private firms and nonprofit agencies engaged in creating products or services based on implicit and open-ended contracts. As such, the types of environmental contingencies and coordinated exchanges may not be representative of the types of societal problems indicated by research on community economic development or other complex, holistic issues that involve public values.

Nine Preconditions for Organizational Emergence

The three case studies uncovered a set of nine "preconditions" that help explain the emergence of multicommunity collaborative organizations. Whether a particular precondition is "necessary and/or sufficient" for complex collaborations to occur was not established by the research; that is, the three exploratory case studies did not posit a causal theory. Instead, the preconditions highlight aspects of emergent multiorganizational, multisector, and multicommunity collaboration in need of scrutiny before further theory development can occur. Practical strategies for facilitating partnership formation are also derived from the preconditions findings. This section reports on the preconditions and their implications for additional research.

The first two preconditions, a disaster occurrence and fiscal or perceived fiscal stress, are interrelated. They all preceded the other so-called preconditions in the case study areas, suggesting their importance to the development of collaborative ventures. A *disaster occurrence* or *multiple disasters* (such as the Midwest farm crisis, with economic and population losses; a chemical disaster, flooding, and loss of key businesses; rural depopulation) serve as triggering events that lead to exchange relationships among participating communities, which then form new collaborative organizations. Similarly, *fiscal stress* or *perceived stress* often result from the disaster occurrences and create crises for the basic industries in the area. The triggering event of a disaster or otherwise dire circumstance suggests that resource dependence alone may not be enough to drive collaboration. Instead, circumstances may trigger thinking about resource dependence, but other contextual and organizational process factors (preconditions) extend the resource dependency and transaction cost explanations.

Another set of related preconditions uncovered by the case studies relates to capacity building by external agents. Without the "push" of public opinion calling for collaborative behavior, leaders may need the "pull" of incentives such as technical or financial assistance in order to hone the skills necessary to mobilize for action and to harness resources needed for collective action. *Outside capacity building* (by state government, foundations, and professional associations) was necessary in the case study areas for strengthening and broadening leadership. The capacity-building activities of the U.S. state and national governments and the provincial policies in Canada assumed that solutions to local-development problems had to emanate locally from a strong self-help perspective. However, support for local partnership efforts was very important to the emergent organizations. Among the three case study areas, levels and types of resource commitment by outside capacity builders varied greatly, and in two of the cases, the emergent organizations would not have been created without financial inducements from national and state or provincial governments. Disasters and real or perceived fiscal stress were triggering events for organizational formation, but the "pull" of incentives from external agents was instrumental in the formation of the organizations studied. The most diversified and arguably the most successful of the three case study areas also had the longest history of external funding and other capacity building (for example, strong cooperative-extension service and foundation funding).

In addition to financial incentives for inducing collaborative activities, another capacity-building type of precondition found in the research was the presence of *collaborative skills-building* expertise in the study areas. In all cases, the development of such skills was also a factor of supportive capacity building by those external to the areas studied. This was especially the case for the emergent organizations' board members in the least well-staffed areas. Board members took part in government-sponsored visioning and strategic-planning exercises in two of the case study areas. The third organization, also the one to have the most external financial assistance, had an executive director and other paid staff who also possessed an array of collaborative skills.

The set of capacity-building type of preconditions offers practical suggestions to governments and foundations that provide inducements for collaborative ventures. An example is the granting of more points for a funding proposal based on an initiative being a collaboration among communities. Similarly, funding to teach collaborative skills and/or to implement regional-visioning and strategic-planning processes, as is done by several states, may be a useful catalyst to partnership formations.

The findings regarding capacity building also extend resource-dependency theories in several ways. First, it must be remembered that the research team's national survey to find collaborative organizations for additional study could not uncover even one organization that had emerged without some type of capacity-building assistance external to the organization. Completely self-help or grass-roots organizations did not exist. Second, the linkages found in the research between the collaborative organizations and the outside capacity builders suggest the relevance of Granovetter's (1985) thesis on the "strength of weak ties." The multiorganizational leaders had relatively weak ties with a wide variety of entities unlike the organizations themselves, and those weak linkages were beneficial in the emergence of the new organizations.

Another important precondition, found in all three case study areas, was the *existence of a policy entrepreneur* or group of entrepreneurs. Organizational formation was tied to an identifiable policy entrepreneur (King and Roberts, 1991). Their energies and talents charted the ability of the organizations to harness the capability needed to organize. These "sparkplugs" (DeWitt, Batie, and Norris, 1988) offered unfailing energy and commitment to organizational emergence and development. Significantly, the entrepreneurs came from a variety of sectors and occupations (a local newspaper executive and a small businessperson; the former economic-development coordinator for a county and a prominent local banker; a high-school teacher with an interest in economic development). A common attribute of the entrepreneurs was an asset-based perspective on the region, rather than a focus on problems. The array of political, analytical, and people skills possessed by the movers in creating the organizations enabled them to mobilize key support for their visions.

The existence of an entrepreneur to promote collaboration appears to be tied to yet another precondition, the *building of a political constituency for cooperation*. Broad-based political constituencies did not exist to promote partnership development in any of the three case study areas. Natural political constituencies for the promotion of collaborative ventures are rare. However, proximity to and interaction with local institutions of higher education had a positive effect on the development of the emergent organizations that completed the most successful specific projects. This is an environmental factor neglected in the existing literature. Agranoff and McGuire (1999), however, have noted the importance of activation skills in tapping knowledge and resources to obtain the money, information, and expertise necessary for managing in a network setting.

The lack of broad-based supportive constituencies emerging to promote cooperative activity helps explain why elected political leadership (who possess authority and some financial resources to facilitate formal collaborative action within and across communities) was not motivated by the "push" of public opinion to engage in collective action to deal with common problems in the study areas. Local governments were not the initiators of the partnership organizations. The lack of a natural supportive political constituency also helps explain why the initiators of the multicommunity partnerships had difficulty in generating local officials' support.

The partnership-type organizations in all three case study areas also did not emerge with broad-based representation from all sectors and income, racial, and other groups, as was the case with all of the initial organizations considered for the field research. The emergent collaborative organizations were dominated by a few individuals with vested interests—that is, business-community leaders acting as entrepreneurs in the creation of the organizations. The lone organization that had the most broad-based board representation had national funding that required such representation on its board.

   Early and continued support by elected local officials is yet another precondition uncovered by the research. Because of financial capacity-building assistance, two of the organizations were required to have board representation by local government, although the government officials were not the leaders or key entrepreneurs in the organizational formations. In the third case, elected leadership was relatively insignificant. Representation was self-selected, and feedback to the local government was unsystematic. The failure of elected officials to be proactive in the formation of all three organizations is a contrast to the notion of government as a catalyst or facilitator. On the other hand, the low level of activity by elected officials posed problems for all of the organizations when they were in need of authoritative support for activities.

   A final set of preconditions relates to characteristics of leadership for multiorganizational, multisector, and multicommunity organizations. Specifically, in each case study, organizational leaders attempted to demonstrate early advantages of thinking regionally about common problems and tying such to financial return. This precondition was labeled the *promotion of visible advantages of cooperation for participating communities*. Actors from the various sectors within the participating communities in each region saw early positive results from collaboration. Examples included the widespread use of a slogan and bumper sticker to promote regional thinking, the seeking of extensive state and national news coverage of the collaborations, and the development of regional phone books. All of the early activities spurred later collective action of a more significant nature and were part of the "continuum of partnerships."

   Related to the promotion of visible advantages of cooperation is another precondition, an *early focus on visible, effective strategies*. Doing such stimulated interest in the organization and helped build interested and supportive constituencies. Similarly, quick sure-bet successes also generated more trust among participating units. The three cases differed in their early successes, thus helping to determine future organizational strength. This precondition relates directly to the continuum of partnerships in that relatively uncontentious issues involving low levels of intensity of interaction can more easily lead to success early in a partnership, compared to dealing with issues initially perceived as "win–lose." In the case study areas, communities and organizations coordinating a series of festivals to celebrate the region, for example, had a greater chance of early success than the decisions involved in deciding where a new plant should locate and how income from it might be shared across the region. Building first on celebrations and then working together on amenity-type projects laid the groundwork for dealing with more conflictual community economic-development issues. An early focus on some "wins" seemed to link two major skill categories in ways that promote success. Interpersonal skills, such as team building and effective communication, were honed at the same time that problem-solving and decision-making skills were improved.

Research Needs Flowing from the Preconditions

- Are disasters (natural or human-made) and fiscal or perceived fiscal stress preconditions for the types of cooperative thinking associated with resource dependency and transaction cost theories as explanations of organizational emergence? That is, is the spirit of cooperation honed by experience with dire circumstances? This is an especially important question for the emergence of truly grass-roots or self-help organizations.

- What are the effects of capacity-building mechanisms such as government or foundation funding and/or technical assistance (for visioning and strategic planning) as inducements to spur partnership development and collaborative thinking? How does such capacity building relate to resource-dependency thinking and action? How important is the role of government financial- or technical-capacity building to the emergence of partnerships?

- Does leadership behavior in developing a multiorganizational, multisector, multicommunity organization differ from leadership in the traditional top-down organization? The work of Mandell (1990) and Agranoff and McGuire (1998, 1999) seems especially important in terms of examining framing, mobilizing, and activation leadership behaviors.

- What is the role of government in these new organizations?

- What are the mechanisms for accountability in these new organizations when government is a "weak" partner?

- Are some of these new emergent organizations another form of "hidden" government, similar to special districts and authorities, which operate with greater flexibility than fully visible governments? Are new types of policy instruments being used by these organizations?

- How flexible are these new emergent organizations, based on seemingly seamless networks across organizations, sectors, and communities, in adapting to rapid change?

- How flexible are these new emergent organizations in devising procedural mechanisms for dealing with complex issues?

- What adaptations are made by the new emergent organizations, and to what degree of success, to achieve a type of accountability similar to government's traditional absolute responsibility?

- Who monitors, or should monitor, the outcomes of the emergent organizations' activities?

- Are the new emergent organizations representative and responsive when operating on holistic community problems, such as community economic development?

- Are the new organizations a form of social capital building, or are they a perpetuation of elite dominance in community decision-making?

Conclusions

Participation in complex partnerships necessitates changes within and among participating organizations. Truly collaborative ventures can restructure political boundaries, as in the case of government mergers. Partnerships of any type require some recasting of the fundamental structure or purpose of the participating local units, as well as their operation.

The existence of entrepreneurs to help forge new organizations is not enough. Champions for the organizations must be nurtured. To study partnerships is to examine organizational change. For small communities, this generally also means a focus on the key roles played by external change agents, such as technical-assistance providers. Successful communities of the future will chart their own course, based on their particular characteristics—but they appear to need help to do so, based on the research summarized here.

The precondition findings help focus on important areas of study when examining points along the partnership continuum. A combination of preconditions goes far toward explaining the emergence and potential for the organizations studied. Innovative types of capacity building that hone collaborative skills play important roles in preparing communities and their organizations for the changes associated with complex partnerships. Local decision-makers and leaders, as well as the general public, will likely need information about the possibilities, opportunities, benefits, and costs of partnerships. Without more understanding of the strategic benefits of partnerships to meet regional governance needs, emergence is less likely.

The continuum of partnerships and the preconditions offer much practical advice. If collaborative ventures emerge from disaster occurrences and real or perceived fiscal stress, entrepreneurs can present information in ways to citizens and leaders that demonstrate an impending "disaster" if existing conditions don't change. If so-called "self-help" collaboratives rarely emerge without extensive capacity building by external agents, state governments and foundations might offer useful help. This need not necessarily be financial aid. Collaborative skills building through visioning processes and strategic planning facilitate partnership formations, as do the development and dissemination of information about the advantages and payoffs of partnerships. Individuals from all sectors will likely need help in developing boundary-management skills to deal with the relationships that must be built in a partnership. Special attention may need to be given to bringing elected governmental officials into partnerships early in their formation and to protecting against volunteer burnout as initial policy entrepreneurs feel the pressures of time constraints.

Partnerships vary widely in complexity, so their management and organizational needs and skills also vary. The continuum of partnerships may be a very useful device for understanding the too-often-neglected managerial aspects of partnership formation. Partnership development is very time-consuming, and any lessons learned from research can help prevent volunteer burnout, a finding from the "maintenance" phase of the case study research.

Acknowledgment

This chapter was supported, in part, by research supported by a grant from the U.S. Department of Agriculture, National Research Initiative (NRICCP Project Number 93-337401-9088).

References

Agranoff, R., & McGuire, M. (1998). Multinetwork management: Collaboration and the hollow state in local economic policy. *Journal of Public Administration Research and Theory, 8,* 67–91.

Agranoff, R., & McGuire, M. (1999). Managing in network settings. *Policy Studies Review, 16*(1), 18–41.

Alexander, E. R. (1995). *How organizations act together: Interorganizational coordination in theory and practice.* Amsterdam: Gordon & Breach Publishers.

Alter, C., & Hage, J. (1993). *Organizations working together.* Sage Library of Social Research 191. Newbury Park, CA: Sage Publications.

Andranovich, G. (1991, April). *Interlocal cooperation: An overview of organization and policy management in rural and smaller jurisdictions.* Pullman: Program for Local Government Education, Washington State University.

Cigler, B. A. (1992a). From networking to collaboration: Intercommunity relations. *Proceedings of the National Public Management Research Conference,* Syracuse University.

Cigler, B. A. (1992b). Pre-conditions for multicommunity collaborations. In P. F. Korsching, T. O. Borich, & J. Stewart (Eds.), *Multicommunity collaboration: An evolving rural revitalization strategy* (pp. 53–74). Conference Proceedings. Ames: North Central Regional Center for Rural Development, University of Iowa.

Cigler, B. A. (1999). Pre-conditions for the emergence of multicommunity collaborative organizations. *Policy Studies Review, 16*(1), 86–102.

Cigler, B. A., Jansen, A. C., Ryan, V. D., & Stabler, J. C. (1994). *Toward an understanding of multicommunity collaboration.* Staff Report No. 9403. Agriculture and Rural Economy Division, U.S. Department of Agriculture.

DeWitt, J., Batie, S. S., & Norris, K. (1988). *Brighter future for rural America? Strategies for communities and states.* Washington, DC: National Governors' Association.

Downs, A. (1967). *Inside bureaucracy.* Boston: Little, Brown.

Gilroy, N., & Swan, J. (Eds.). (1984). *Building networks.* Dubuque, IA: Kendall/Hunt Publishing.

Granovetter, M. (1985). Economic action and social structure: The problem of embeddedness. *American Journal of Sociology, 91,* 481–510.

Habana-Hafner, S., Reed, H. B., & Associates. (1989). *Partnerships for community development: Resources for practitioners and trainers.* Amherst: Center for Organizational and Community Development, University of Massachusetts.

Jones, C., Hesterly, W., & Borgatti, S. P. (1997). A general theory of network governance: Exchange conditions and social mechanisms. *Academy of Management Review, 22,* 911–945.

King, P. J., & Roberts, N. C. (1991). Policy entrepreneurs: Their activity structure and function in the policy process. *Journal of Public Administration Research and Theory, 1*(2): 147–175.

Korsching, P. F., Borich, T. O., & Steward, J. (Eds.). (1992). *Multicommunity collabora-tion: An evolving rural revitalization strategy.* Conference Proceedings. Ames: North Central Regional Center for Rural Development, University of Iowa.

Mandell, M. P. (1990). Network management: Strategic behavior in the public sector. In R. W. Gage & M. P. Mandell (Eds.), *Strategies for managing intergovernmental poli-cies and networks* (pp. 29–54). New York: Praeger.

McDonnell, L. (1988). *Policy design as instrument design.* Paper presented at the 1988 Annual Meeting of the American Political Science Association, Washington, DC.

Milward, H. B., & Provan, K. G. (1998). Principles for controlling agents: The political economy of network structure. *Journal of Public Administration Research and Theory, 8,* 203–221.

Mulford, C. L., & Rogers, D. L. (1982). Definitions and models. In D. L. Rogers & D. A. Whetten (Eds.), *Interoganizational coordination* (pp. 9–31). Ames: Iowa State University Press.

Pfeffer, J., & Salancik, G. (1978). *The external control of organizations: A resource-dependence perspective.* New York: Harper & Row.

Powell, W. (1990). Neither market nor hierarchy: Network forms of organization. In *Re-search in Organizational Behavior,* vol. 12 (pp. 295–336). Greenwich, CT: JAI Press.

Provan, K. G., & Milward, H. B. (1995). A preliminary theory of network effectiveness: A comparative study of four community mental health systems. *Administrative Science Quarterly, 40,* 1–33.

Rogers, D. L., & Whetten, D. A. (Eds.). (1982). *Interorganizational coordination.* Ames: Iowa State University Press.

Thompson, J. (1967). *Organizations in action.* New York: McGraw-Hill.

Uzzi, B. (1997). Social structure and competition in interfirm networks: The paradox of embeddedness. *Administrative Science Quarterly, 42,* 35–67.

Williamson, O. (1975). *Markets and hierarchies: Analysis and antitrust implications.* New York: Free Press.

PART TWO

Behavioral Implications of Networks

6

Environmental Networks
Relying on Process or Outcome for Motivation

Lisa S. Nelson

A N INTERORGANIZATIONAL NETWORK IS A GROUP of people working together, each of whom represents an organization seeking to advance its
goals through collaboration with other organizations (Kickert and Koppenjan, 1997). Interorganizational networks address a variety of policy and administrative issues. Environmental and natural resources networks are often
organized to resolve regulatory conflicts or to plan land use in a region, among
other purposes (Knight and Landres, 1998; MacKenzie, 1996). In response to
changing notions of what is necessary to protect the environment, most of
today's environmental networks are being established to guide particular places
toward more sustainable practices. The goal of sustainability supports viable
communities and economic activities, as well as the environment. Membership
in environmental networks now typically includes "nonenvironmental" members, such as representatives from affected industries or general-purpose governments. Environmental networks have evolved from coalitions of environmental
groups seeking to defeat opponents in the political arena, to collaborations in
which people who might formerly have been on opposite sides of the issue now
try to work together.

Because collaboration among former antagonists is still a novelty, there is
often a temptation in a new network to count the achievement of a workable and
cooperative process as a sufficient accomplishment. However, this is rarely suf-

ficient to sustain the motivation of all network participants. This chapter explores four elements of motivation in environmental networks: differences between organizational and participant preferences, accountability and changing goals, coercion and trust, and the risks and benefits of expanding participation. These elements emerged as important themes in earlier work (Nelson, 2000). Environmental and natural resources network-management examples illustrate the situations described.

Differences Between Organizational and Participant Preferences

Why do organizations participate in collaborative arrangements? The sources of motivation are sometimes external, sometimes internal, and sometimes mutual. External motivations often come to public agencies through legislation. Internal motivations may arise when an organization determines that its mission would be served by initiating collaboration with other organizations. Mutual motivation arises when a number of organizations perceive the possible benefits of collaboration at roughly the same time, and leadership is not clearly the province of one participant (Luke, 1998). Progress toward sustainability may be the intention in each situation, as legislators, senior administrators, and field-level administrators have at different times taken the lead in recognizing the need to transcend jurisdictional boundaries. Legislation often calls for collaborative planning or problem solving and assigns one organization the role of the "lead" or network manager (Kickert et al., 1997). The agency absorbs the task of initiating and maintaining the network. For example, the Bureau of Land Management is required to involve the public and coordinate with local communities, states, Indian tribes, and other federal agencies in its land-use decisions because of the Federal Land Policy and Management Act, the National Environmental Policy Act, and other resource-specific laws. Promoting collaborative management has now become a strategic goal of the agency (Bureau of Land Management, 1999).

An example of internally driven motivation for collaboration is the case of a water-supply agency that initiated collaboration following a change in its mission. The new mission required promoting programs that others would implement. A participatory collaborative process with the agency's stakeholders successfully served the mission. Such processes can help agencies "make their plans more practical, obtain essential political support, and establish a mechanism for on-going plan-review and adjustment" (deHaven-Smith and Wodraska, 1996, p. 371).

In the above cases, external and internal motivations to form a network view collaboration as a policy instrument to carry out a predefined goal. In contrast, networks based on mutual motivation are initiated to address common problems or opportunities. Mutually motivated collaboration may also occur as an effort to move beyond the rule-making and program-implementation conflicts that previously polarized affected interests, a situation common to many forest programs (Ellefson et al., 1997, p. 428). An alternative model of mutually motivated collaboration is provided in regional strategic planning, where communities that share circumstances decide to lay aside economic competition among themselves so as to be stronger competitors with other regions (Dodge and Montgomery, 1995). Luke (1998) makes a good case that many public problems are beyond the capacity of a single organization to solve. The necessary leadership style in these contexts is quite different from the strong, authoritative styles we have come to expect in single organizations. Leadership may even rotate among participants as the situation develops.

Motivations for organizations to collaborate with others may thus come from policy, mission, and mutual interest. Networks provide a chance for the member organizations to achieve policy goals that they could not reach independently. One of the major challenges facing environmental stewardship is that some of the most grass-roots collaborative efforts on behalf of economic development often exclude, deliberately or inadvertently, considerations of environmental sustainability. Networks of all kinds face interesting questions regarding how to structure public involvement.

The organizational purposes that drive upper management to authorize participation in interorganizational networks are, in effect, the organization's motivations. The individuals who represent organizations in a network have motivations that parallel those of organizations, but they differ in important respects. If an organization has made a commitment to participate, staff members will be assigned to represent it as part of their regular duties and may or may not buy into the project. This is a microversion of the organization that receives a mandate to develop collaboration. When an individual independently or through persuasion comes to see that some organizational tasks require cooperation beyond organizational boundaries, that individual is more likely to be motivated. Independent initiative or buy-in by individuals is a microversion of mutual motivation, because the individual perceives the interdependence of the situation and the value of participation. For example, in natural-resources field offices, individual managers often have the autonomy to join and cultivate local and region-specific collaborations in addition to those that are required. Participation may yield common approaches to problems with visitors or address issues of overlapping jurisdictions.

A professional commitment to improving environmental quality can be another important source of motivation for individual participants. Rabe (1996) found a high willingness among environmental professionals to support alternative strategies for achieving integration of pollution-control strategies across media (air, water, and land). Ideas to innovate across media have found willing listeners in key political institutions and among young professionals in the agencies. Nelson and Weschler (1996) propose a new dimension of administrative ethics, in which an enlightened citizen-administrator makes commitments to community sustainability and democratic processes. Such a person would seek out those collaborative stewardship projects that would benefit the community. In other issue areas as well, policy entrepreneurs or brokers are the keys to persuading organizations to invest their time and resources, and to solve particular problems and achieve common goals (Cigler et al., 1994; Kickert and Koppenjan, 1997; Mandell, 1990).

Top-down mandates to collaborate locally are likely to be less motivating for an agency representative than an independent decision made in response to a specific situation. Natural-resource managers may resist such directives on two grounds. First, collaboration may sound like another in a long line of directives coming from headquarters without additional financial support. Second, local managers may feel that collaboration is not justified for all decisions, and that routine technical decisions should remain in the domain of the professional (Keown, 1998). However, outside stakeholders may contest the boundaries of this domain. Such a contest may in fact serve as the impetus for a top-down mandate.

The quality of interaction can be an encouraging or discouraging motivational factor for network participants. Fox and Miller's warrants for discourse (sincerity, situation-regarding intentionality, willing attention, and substantive contribution) are pertinent to the goal of sustaining motivation among individuals (1995). Voluntary collaborative action may attract participants who simply want to stay informed or to be seen at such meetings but are not fully committed to the group's goals. Such behavior may be seen as undesirable, but often it takes time for participating individuals (and their organizations) to assess whether the collaborative effort is worthwhile. Rubin (1997, p. 134) points out:

> Individuals who represent their organizations around the coalition table are busy
> staff members in their own organizations, with tasks to perform and bosses to
> whom they must report. Coalition work often takes a back seat to the press of day-
> to-day responsibilities. And even when individuals agree at a coalition meeting to
> take a position or perform a task, they often lack the authority or power to fulfill
> their coalition promises.

In practice, violators of these warrants are often tolerated if their participation is important enough to the network or if expanded participation is a goal of the group.

Leadership influences the motivation of participants. Kickert and Koppenjan (1997) place the results and success of network management in the hands of the people who participate in them. They must demonstrate leadership, particularly in devising new options, and they must be successful in representing the collaborative effort to their home organizations, so that these home organizations will keep to the agreed procedures (p. 58). They point out that such success hinges on the commitment power possessed by the individuals in their organizations. The person chosen to represent the organization may be a measure of the organization's commitment.

Professional commitment, leadership, and the quality of network processes are likely to have more impact on individual motivation than on organizational motivation. Natural-resource agencies in particular have nearly fifteen years of experience bringing in new professional expertise to strengthen the environmental-protection dimensions of their missions. As these more motivated individuals rise in their organizations, it is likely that they will be able to make stronger proactive contributions, emerging as leaders, even in the externally "mandated" networks. The internal and mutual motivations for network collaboration from their organizations will also be strengthened as a result.

Accountability and Changing Goals

Public organizations and their representatives face dilemmas in negotiating the dual roles of network participation. On the one hand, they are accountable to the public and to their legislative mandates. On the other, network participation and collaboration require trust and accountability to the other members of the network. What if the goals of the network change as a result of the discussions that ensue within the network? New goals may reflect collaborative insight, but they may also be problematic for the attentive public outside the network. Concern for this dilemma can inhibit the development of the collaborative processes necessary to ensure long-term motivation. Network participants must keep the public informed and educated about substantive findings and plans in the network. Otherwise, the network will be put on hold while the members work to repair unmet expectations in their home agencies and the interested public. Frequent interruptions and waiting can erode network motivation.

Improved process and network institutionalization are treated at times in the network literature as equal to or even more important than the achievement of the goals that bring networks together. Klijn and Teisman (1997) turn the conventional measure of goal achievement on its head. They suggest that the joint interest of the participants lies in developing an enriched target set, rather than holding fast to the *a priori* goals of one or more participants. Additional criteria for success, in their view, would include the number of linkages participants are able to construct and the development of effective arrangements for organizing mutual interaction (pp. 113–117). Kickert et al. (1997) extend this argument, saying that goal attainment is a fallacious criterion since network interactions are strategic, not operational. They point out that if effectiveness and efficiency are the goals of the network, then the network has become an instrument of whichever organization has gained control of the steering (p. 172). They suggest that such an outcome will block interaction and damage relations.

Dodge and Montgomery (1995) also focus on process and participation measures as the evidence for successful regional strategic planning. Communities that wish to work together as a regional network and apply strategic-planning principles engage in a variety of activities, including monitoring change and responding to opportunities and threats, building strengths and overcoming shortcomings, periodically redefining and publicizing vision and competitive niches, actively pursuing financing, extensively involving stakeholders and building staff skills, and developing partnerships with other regions (pp. 22–23).

In some environmental networks, establishing the targets by which to measure progress is a daunting task. Especially where ecosystems are badly damaged and rehabilitation and restoration are the goals, groups find it difficult to agree on quantitative measures. In the case of the Remedial Action Plans made to clean degraded areas of concern around the Great Lakes, Hartig et al. have recommended both short- and long-term targets so that incremental improvements can be recognized (1997). For example, a short-term target could be doubling the number of acres currently in conservation tillage over a five-year period; a long-term target could be to halve the sediment load that the Maumee River drops in Lake Erie by the year 2025.

Sometimes, as in the regional strategic-planning example, developing a strong process is the goal, so there is no conflict over the issue of network accountability. Enriching the set of goals may be a great achievement. However, to the extent that the network was given a mission from an external source, or to the extent that representatives were authorized to participate based on the expectation of achieving a preset goal, the "goal displacement" that may result from genuine deliberation will have to be explained to external constituencies.

Finally, when and how soon should measurable progress goals be named? In most environmental stewardship networks, outcome goals are important. Luke (1998) discusses two different approaches to defining success: fidelity to the action plan agreed to at the outset, or progress toward the agreed-upon outcome. He believes the latter is the more effective measure, because it leads to the sorts of long-term, continuous learning that can better maintain momentum. Collaborative implementation should be flexible enough to respond to feedback, stimulate policy learning, and enhance the relationships among key stakeholders (see discussion in Luke, 1998, pp. 124–126).

To counter a lack of commitment, free riding, or the sudden withdrawal of support at a crucial moment, Kickert et al. (1997) suggest that network managers must induce those involved to make a commitment, perhaps informally, perhaps through a contract or covenant, or perhaps even by engaging legal advisers (p. 176). De Bruijn and Ringeling (1997) also stress individual commitment to process norms, arguing that this will translate itself into commitment to the substantive outcomes of the collaboration. However, commanding commitment is a risky business if the collaboration is voluntary.

Uncertainty, trust, commitment, and the evenness of sharing the workload and credit among coalition members are interrelated issues. Unevenness of effort can lead to resentment; resources for staff support may fluctuate or fade; disagreements over decisions may occur that cannot be set aside; personality conflicts may arise. De Bruijn and Ringeling (1997) suggest that public organizations in networks face a dilemma. If they are pressured to demonstrate achievements in the short term, they may sacrifice the construction of long-term relationships by pushing other member organizations too hard (p. 165).

This is where the role of leaders, as indicated in the previous section, plays a critical role. In some settings, it may be possible for leaders to establish and enforce expectations that everyone contribute and that the group as a whole be credited for accomplishments. In others, there may be so much at stake that members require formal contracting or covenanting to regulate themselves. Less formally, social pressure can enforce group norms. Reference to outside expectations for the network can help it move forward when minor internal issues threaten to use up too much energy. Luke has found that positive interpersonal connections are crucial for carrying out commitments (1998, p. 125). Pressuring coalition members to conform to group expectations assumes a stability that may not be present, especially in the early stages of the collaboration. If participation is relatively voluntary, if addressing the issue is new for many members, or if new members join over a long period of time, such enforcement efforts may be counterproductive. In such cases, leaders must rely on more frequent reference to the purpose of the collaboration to keep members on track. Being held accountable for goals and the need to build networks are not always complementary responsibilities. The conflict can reduce motivation. Leaders can work to change perceptions, particularly among outside funders and government entities that are looking for results.

Institutionalization of collaboration may have mixed results on motivation. Some of the key participants may have their motivation grow because they see the formalization of network roles and procedures as a sign of progress and achievement. Formalization may also improve public access. Others may have enjoyed the flexibility and informality of the start-up atmosphere and will need some encouragement to adapt.

Finally, the goal of broad community-based participation requires patience. Network participants who are committed to environmental goals will likely have a strong moral commitment to establishing and improving on stewardship ethics and practices. They hold themselves accountable to improvements in environmental quality. Regional and local networks, to the extent that they are inclusive of members whose top priorities differ, or who are participating as watchdogs for interests that fear environmentally oriented activities, will have to moderate their speed and style in order to maintain inclusiveness. Network participants and leaders who recognize the importance of bringing a diverse group together to steer a region toward environmental sustainability must allow and encourage members to communicate often with the groups they represent about the activities of the network.

Coercion and Trust

Trust among participants is widely viewed as a critical ingredient in a successful collaborative process. Building trust faces several obstacles. Rubin, focusing on interest-group coalitions, points out that participating organizations must be sure that the coalition shares their fundamental goals. Coalitions are time-consuming, often cannot control disagreements among members, and often exhibit problems associated with inequality among members in terms of work effort and taking credit for results (Rubin, 1997). These are risks for networks as well. Kickert and Koppenjan warn that "network interaction takes place between representatives whose representativeness and commitment power is [*sic*] not always guaranteed" (1997, p. 58). This uncertainty creates stress for the more highly motivated participants in the collaboration.

Organizations' satisfaction with collaborative participation is strongly influenced by the occurrence or avoidance of unpleasant surprises, such as unexpected demands for financing either the planning process or the implementation of the plan. Stakeholders in a region can avoid this by making an agreement at the beginning that clarifies mutual responsibilities (Dodge and Montgomery, 1995, p. 19). In a similar vein, a network's ability to self-regulate and contain costs can go far in avoiding the problems that organizations and their representatives may experience (Kickert and Koppenjan, 1997). Commitment and performance by organizations in a network are intertwined with the relationship of the organization's representative to both the organization and the other network representatives.

One of the central issues regarding motivation in collaborative efforts is the degree of coercion that may be present. May et al. (1996) evaluate the trade-offs between coercive and cooperative intergovernmental management regimes from the perspective of implementing national or state environmental-policy goals. Coercive regimes may gain procedural compliance and achieve some minimum regulatory objectives. However, they may prevent local innovations, limit substantive compliance, and risk backlash from the regulated community. Cooperative regimes foster local ownership of programs and enhance the prospects for implementation and effective environmental management. The choice of a cooperative regime over a coercive regime risks that implementation will be uneven, if the community is uninterested in the goals of the policy. For example, federal and state oversight agencies may wait indefinitely for a local community to develop the required plan. Indeed, the potential for regulation is credited with bringing many industries to the table. However, overt coercion invites discord and is not conducive to establishing a sustained pattern of motivated collaboration. Without coercion, the softer tools of shared objectives and normative commitment need to be revisited periodically and recharged if necessary. Research on public-lands planning shows that in situations where trust is low and interests are highly divergent, participants may blame failure on a lack of procedural rules. Meeting structure and decision-making rules may be necessary for trust and progress (Moote et al., 1997, pp. 887–889).

Nelson and Weschler (1998) suggest that formalized settings for increased deliberation, such as those found in the implementation networks of the Great Lakes Remedial Action Plans, can help build long-term collaborations. A variety of techniques, including shared geographic information systems (GIS), can be used to support such frameworks. Dodge and Montgomery recommend several actions to institutionalize regional strategic planning. These include providing financial and training support for participants, and conducting assessment of both the implementation of the chosen strategies and the "state of the region." They also encourage reducing economic, fiscal, and racial disparities among the communities of the region (1995, p. 164). In this model of collaboration, ongoing behind-the-scenes effort supports intense episodes of collaborative planning.

May et al. have found that in local disaster planning, national and state agencies that seek cooperation from local governments have three choices: They can do nothing, waiting for a disaster to catalyze constituency demands for action;

they can foster constituency demands by providing information on hazards and preventive, sustainable practices; or they can establish participatory-planning processes "to create a consensus on the need for government action" (1996, p. 202). Coercion is not viewed as a practical tool for locally based environmental planning. These authors argue that successful collaboration on the relatively low-conflict goal of reducing risk through hazards planning can lay the groundwork and build trust for satisfying broader concerns of environmental management and sustainability. In a similar vein, many federal environmental and resource agencies are pursuing local collaborations to enhance cooperation with their missions (see Environmental Protection Agency, 1999; National Park Service, 1999; Natural Resources Conservation Service, 1999). Dozens of nonprofit groups have taken leadership roles in local collaborative efforts.

Committing to participation in a network involves a variety of costs for both the individual participants and the organizations that they represent. May et al. (1996) classify the obstacles to local commitment to hazards planning as psychological, political, and practical. In their example, which they cast as "the commitment conundrum," local government officials, like other individuals, have a tendency to resist investment in avoiding low-probability risks such as damage from hundred-year floods. Political and constituency support for environmental planning is also likely to be reactive rather than proactive, further constraining the local officials' endorsement of planning or increased regulation. This is consistent with Cigler's work discussing crisis as one of the preconditions for collaboration (Cigler et al., 1994). Other obstacles might include the lack of expertise and resources necessary to conduct the planning and mitigation, which are frequent problems in smaller communities (May et al., 1996, pp. 198–202). To overcome the obstacles and the costs of collaboration, potential participants must be educated in advance on the goal of sustainability and the problems other communities have faced as a result of not considering the long-term consequences of ignoring environmental quality.

Risks and Benefits of Expanding Participation

Many of the issues that environmental networks grapple with are dependent upon changes in community and public attitudes and practices. Public participation has been found to be critically important for the successful stewardship of natural resources (Cortner and Moote, 1994). It is crucial to achieving deliberative practice in community governance, which is a key element in discussions about a sustainable future. It is here that the previous dilemma of the accountability of the participants to both the network and their "home" organizations is compounded by each organization's degree of accountability to the public. If a local government's goals emerge as dominant in a natural-resources network setting, does the national public suffer at the expense of the local public? Or, if national policy dominates collaborative field-level planning for natural-resources extraction, do local communities carry an unfair burden? Expanding participation may help resolve this dilemma.

May et al. (1996) have a list of preconditions for cooperative policies that includes a shared set of policy objectives, a normative commitment to the policy goals by local officials (or lacking that, strong incentives provided by higher levels), facilitative noninterventionist leadership by the higher level, problem tractability, cross-policy consistency, and most important, active involvement of a range of community groups. The last can be nurtured to overcome local government resistance if it exists (pp. 223–227).

Perhaps a level playing field is impossible to establish in environmental and natural-resources networks. Fox and Miller (1995) point out that governments will govern, and unequal power will be applied: "It is still possible to claim, though, that the more the discursive ideal is approached, the more authentic the encounters will be, the less will government be 'they' and the more will it be 'we'" (p. 128). Unfortunately, the role of public participation in complex network settings continues to be viewed instrumentally, as something that serves other purposes rather than as a norm in itself. In other cases, it is ignored or treated as an amplification of the problem of having to explain the same issues over and over again as new participants join the discussion. Environmental stewardship seems especially susceptible to this problem, because those who are intent on improving environmental quality are often concerned about missing time-dependent opportunities to limit further degradation or preserve threatened natural features. Essentially, environmental stewardship is a long-term project, and administrators who share this vision will need to build opportunities for more extensive deliberation, and be willing to let unexpected preferences emerge and develop, if they are to model commitment to democratic governance. Genuine deliberation may lead to results that require explanation to the network members' home bases.

Motivation is clearly affected by expectations about network achievements and the quality of the processes used to attain them. This is good news for collaborations that set improved forms of environmental stewardship as their goal, because the motivation should be strong for both the organizations and representatives that choose to participate. The motivation for extending these processes to develop community self-governance is more likely to be based on some practical connection to the stewardship goal than to democratic principles. Expanding the scope of decision-making can risk the accomplishment of predetermined goals. For now, enthusiasm for expanding participation occurs mainly in situations where the success of implementation depends on community support.

Leaving specific decisions to experts and affected interests may or may not incrementally erode a community's ability to govern itself. Nor is there any guarantee that broadened participation will lead to the best decision. However, in the long run, which is the time frame of environmental stewardship, it will be the pattern of decision-making established by the community as a whole that will dominate the quality of environmental stewardship. Educating environmental networks and their external constituencies to expect improvements in community self-governance as well as environmental stewardship should be a high priority.

This broadened set of expectations may motivate additional support from onlookers and strengthen and validate the motivation of network participants and their organizations.

Implications

What are the practical lessons for environmental networks that emerge from the preceding discussion? First, networks need to decide upon the mix of improvements in process and substance by which they will measure their achievements. Should collaborative effort be evaluated based on the processes developed or on the achievement of substantive goals? Participating organizations and their representatives may differ on this issue. It is likely that organizations will be more concerned with the outcomes, so that they can justify the direct and indirect expenses of participation to key stakeholders. Quality-of-process issues may be more important to the individual representatives, although it is likely that achievements will be important as well. To borrow another criterion from Fox and Miller (1995), a successful collaboration will engage in high-quality interactions that over time consistently produce good ideas on "what to do next." In other words, norms for process (community self-governance) and outcome (environmental stewardship) will be satisfied. Professionals who are themselves involved in networks must periodically compare the process and substantive goals of the network with those of their own organization vis-à-vis the network. Professionals who assign others to represent the organization to a network must periodically meet with the representatives to get a sense of how these goals and the progress toward them compare.

Second, network leaders and the professionals who participate in them must be extremely attentive to the communication processes between network members and the organizations or constituents whom they represent. This is important for the internal planning and decision processes of the network, but it is also important in establishing the legitimacy of the network and its activities. Professionals need to be alert for divergent interests that may emerge to block participation and support, and communicate the potential problem to both the network and the home organization.

Third, the degree of coercion or potential for coercion shapes the tone and long-term viability of the network. Network participants must be cognizant of how the potential for coercive action by some participants can distort communication. Participants who have such power should carefully weigh its use. Participants without such power, namely, those who might be ultimately subject to a regulatory action by the former, might seek guarantees of restraint. Among equals, trust is an important factor in sustaining motivation. Trust partly hinges on resolving uncertainty regarding whether representatives can make commitments on behalf of their organizations. Network participants should first clarify for themselves the boundaries of their ability to make organizational commitments to be sure of not making false promises. Trust also involves determining how to fairly share the workload and credit for the network's achievements. Network leaders should be very attentive to these issues, without allowing the atmosphere to become coercive.

Fourth, motivating environmental-network participants to simultaneously improve environmental quality and the community and region's governance processes through an expanded participation process is daunting. However, it is critical in establishing the culture change necessary to move toward sustainability. Whenever possible, networked professionals should find ways to broaden the community of concern for the issues they are addressing. This could take the form of encouraging members to provide volunteer opportunities. It could also involve linking environmental quality to other community issues such as youth, jobs, and the cost of services. Arranging for educational events to promote issue awareness is often a good starting place for networks, because the events can be formatted to present different sides of the issue. In this way, network participants do not feel that they have sold out their original values for the sake of consensus, and they can better maintain accountability to the organizations they represent. Over time, repeated events increase both public awareness and demand for real, rather than superficial or stopgap, improvements.

Conclusions

Organization and network leaders have an important role to play in building the long-term patterns of communication among organizations and their representatives that are so critical in the construction of more sustainable environmental practices. They must attend to the dynamics of the network and to the relationship between the network and the organizations represented there, and they must assess what is necessary to maintain the motivation of the individual participants in this context. Reaching agreement on desirable goals is no small accomplishment. Networks that are formed out of mutual interest and need seem to face less problems in this regard than networks that are formed from some external and possibly coercive stimulus. Organization and network leaders may need to initially be careful about whom they recruit in order to establish an initial level of trust and a general direction. Farsighted leaders will continually work to expand the network and its impact in the region, because they will realize that the environmental issues they are addressing involve many small decisions made throughout society. Accomplishments will initially focus on public education and building trust but will eventually lead to changes in practice—often by network participants, but also among those outside the network—that will make measurable improvements in environmental quality.

References

Bureau of Land Management. (1999). *BLM strategic goal: Promote collaborative management* <http://www.blm.gov/nhp/BLMinfo/stratplan/1997/5collaborative.html>. Site visited October 18, 1999.

Cigler, B. A., Jansen, A. C., Ryan, V. D., & Stabler, J. C. (1994). *Toward an understanding of multicommunity collaboration.* Staff Report No. 9403. Agriculture and Rural Economy Division, U.S. Department of Agriculture.

Cortner, H. J., & Moote, M. A. (1994). Trends and issues in land and water resources management. *Environmental Management, 18*(2), 167–173.

De Bruijn, J. A., & Ringeling, A. B. (1997). Normative notes: Perspectives on networks. In W. J. M. Kickert, E.-H. Klijn, & J. F. M. Koppenjan (Eds.), *Managing complex networks: Strategies for the public sector* (pp. 152–165). London: Sage Publications.

deHaven-Smith, L., & Wodraska, J. R. (1996). Consensus-building for integrated resource planning. *Public Administration Review, 56*(4), 367–371.

Dodge, W. R., & Montgomery, K. (1995). *Shaping a region's future: A guide to strategic decision-making for regions.* Washington, DC: National League of Cities.

Ellefson, P. V., Cheng, A. S., & Moulton, R. J. (1997). State forest practice regulatory programs: An approach to implementing ecosystem management on private forest lands in the United States. *Environmental Management, 21*(3), 421–432.

Environmental Protection Agency. (1999). *SLATE networks: State, local, and tribal environmental networks* <http://www.epa.gov/epapages/slate>. Site visited October 18, 1999.

Fox, C., & Miller, H. (1995). *Postmodern public administration: Toward discourse.* Thousand Oaks, CA: Sage Publications.

Hartig, J. H., Zarull, M. A., Reynoldson, T. B., Mikol, G., Harris, V. A., Randall, R. G., & Cairns, V. W. (1997). Quantifying targets for rehabilitating degraded areas of the Great Lakes. *Environmental Management, 21*(5), 713–723.

Keown, L. D. (1998). What's all the hype about collaboration? *Natural Resources and Environmental Administration, 19*(3), 8–10.

Kickert, W. J. M., Klijn, E.-H., & Koppenjan, J. F. M. (Eds.). (1997). *Managing complex networks: Strategies for the public sector.* London: Sage Publications.

Kickert, W. J. M., & Koppenjan, J. F. M. (1997). Public management and network management: An overview. In W. J. M. Kickert, E.-H. Klijn, & J. F. M. Koppenjan (Eds.), *Managing complex networks: Strategies for the public sector* (pp. 35–61). London: Sage Publications.

Klijn, E.-H., & Teisman, G. R. (1997). Strategies and games in networks. In W. J. M. Kickert, E.-H. Klijn, & J. F. M. Koppenjan (Eds.), *Managing complex networks: Strategies for the public sector* (pp. 98–118). London: Sage Publications.

Knight, R. L., & Landres, P. B. (Eds.). (1998). *Stewardship across boundaries.* Washington, DC: Island Press.

Luke, J. S. (1998). *Catalytic leadership: Strategies for an interconnected world.* San Francisco: Jossey-Bass.

MacKenzie, S. H. (1996). *Integrated resource planning and management.* Washington, DC: Island Press.

Mandell, M. P. (1990). Network management: Strategic behavior in the public sector. In R. Gage & M. P. Mandell (Eds.), *Strategies for managing intergovernmental policy networks* (pp. 29–54). New York: Praeger.

May, P. J., Burby, R. J., Ericksen, N. J., Handmer, J. W., Dixon, J. E., Michaels, S., & Smith, D. I. (1996). *Environmental management and governance: Intergovernmental approaches to hazards and sustainability.* London: Routledge.

Moote, M. A., McClaran, M. P., & Chickering, D. K. (1997). Theory in practice: Applying participatory democracy theory to public land planning. *Environmental Management, 21*, 887–889.

National Park Service. (1999). *Working with partners* <http://www.nps.gov/partners. html>. Site visited October 18, 1999.

Natural Resources Conservation Service. (1999). *Whom we work with* <http://www.nrcs. usda.gov/WhomWrk.html>. Site visited October 18, 1999.

Nelson, L. S. (2000). Motivation and evaluation in environmental management networks. *International Journal of Organization Theory and Behavior*, 3(3/4), 413–433.

Nelson, L. S., & Weschler, L. F. (1996). Community sustainability as a dimension of administrative ethics. *Administrative Theory and Praxis*, *18*(1), 13–26.

Nelson, L. S., & Weschler, L. F. (1998). Institutional readiness for integrated watershed management: The case of the Maumee River. *Social Science Journal*, *35*(4), 565–576.

Rabe, B. J. (1996). An empirical examination of innovations in integrated environmental management: The case of the Great Lakes basin. *Public Administration Review*, *56*(4), 372–381.

Rubin, B. R. (1997). *A citizen's guide to politics in America: How the system works and how to work the system.* Armonk, NY: M. E. Sharpe.

7

Bringing about Change in a Public School System

An Interorganizational Network Approach

Rupert F. Chisholm

ROOTS OF THE CHANGE PROCESS described in this chapter go back to early 1993. At that time, a retired minister convened representatives of the "social-concerns" committees of several churches to identify and explore ways of dealing with social issues. I was a somewhat reluctant and skeptical participant in the first meeting. Since that time, the Inter-Church Network for Social Concerns (INSC) has gradually developed into an interorganizational system that identifies (i.e., surfaces) broad issues facing the community and helps catalyze action to deal with them. This chapter covers INSC work in confronting race relations in the public school system and triggering action to bring about constructive change, looking at the conceptual foundation, a brief history and context of network development, community workshops to explore the issue and set change goals, action to bring about change, institutionalizing the change in the community, and outcomes.

Conceptual Foundation

Three basic concepts provide the basis for the change and development work conducted in this situation. First, Trist's (1983, 1985) interorganizational network ideas served as a broad model of the type of system developed and managed. Second, action research (e.g., Chisholm and Elden, 1993; Lewin, 1946; Susman and Evered, 1978) guided the basic process used to bring about change. Finally, open-systems theory posits that deep-seated change of a system requires extensive engagement of the environment in which that system operates. That is, fundamental change is more likely to occur via an outside-in strategy than from inside out (Katz and Kahn, 1978).

Interorganizational Network

The network construct has emerged as a key form of organization in the late twentieth century (Chisholm, 1998). And the development and use of networks are likely to increase for the foreseeable future. Several observers predict that networks will become the key type of organization in the next twenty-five years or so (e.g., Alter and Hage, 1993; Hage and Powers, 1992).

The project used the socioecological perspective of interorganizational networks (Finsrud, 1995; Trist, 1983, 1985) to conceptualize and guide the development process. From this perspective, the basic orientation of an individual member organization is to the higher-level purpose that binds the set of organizations together. Organizations belong to networks to enable them to deal with metaproblems that single members cannot handle alone. Such an orientation affects the basic perspective and all aspects of the functioning system.

Loose coupling of members to the network constitutes another feature of these systems. Members represent independent organizations that are physically dispersed and only meet occasionally as required to carry out the higher-level system purpose. Belonging to a network is voluntary, with minimal formal organizational structures and processes to bind member organizations into the system. Cohesiveness results from pursuing a shared purpose and from social and psychological processes. Networks also rest on a horizontal rather than a hierarchical organizing principle: One organization or member does not have a superior–subordinate relationship with another.

In addition, network organizations are controlled by members, not by a centralized source of power. Members develop the purpose, mission, and goals for initiating and managing projects and work activities. The organization is self-regulating (members direct and control activities) and rests upon a shared understanding of the basic issue or metaproblem. In short, the organization *is* the way members devise to relate to each other in carrying out the work necessary to actuate a shared vision of a larger issue domain. A shared vision provides the context for orienting activities to the larger environment. Continuously maintaining this orientation at the domain level is critical to develop and maintain networks.

Action Research

An action research (AR) approach provided the second conceptual base for developing the network. Essentially, AR attempts to generate understanding of a network or organization as an integral part of the development process. Following the AR approach, development work in this case used repeated cycles of diagnosing, planning, implementing, collecting, and analyzing data on outcomes, discussing outcomes with system members, reaching conclusions, and defining new sets of action steps (Chisholm and Elden, 1993).

Development results from active engagement with members of the system and external stakeholders. Surfacing lessons derived from the development process to help build the network as a learning system (Huber, 1991) were an integral part of development work.

Brief History and Context

The community involved in the change effort is small and located in a rural area of Pennsylvania. In general, a conservative social and political climate pervades the community. Within this context, the INSC came into existence in 1993. Several events were critical to its formulation and early development: having someone identify and voice an opportunity for positive development; convening a small group of community members to share the idea; testing and developing support for the idea of forming a network organization; and taking action to engage the broader community.

Identifying an Opportunity

Dr. Benz (a pseudonym) is a retired minister who grew up in the community and returned to town over twenty years ago as a professor at the seminary located there. His early years and time at the seminary provided strong ties to the community and much understanding of it.

His professional experience had taught him that change occurs horizontally through committed laypersons rather than through formal church organizations. And his understanding of the community led him to conclude that the local "ministerium," the organization of clergy that meets to coordinate joint church activities, had no tradition of collaborative action to bring about social change. Consequently, Dr. Benz decided to attempt to create a new organization to link church lay "social issues" committees. He went to the ministerium to gain their understanding of his intention, to avoid alienating clergy from the effort, and to obtain access to the social-concerns committees in the various churches. Then he issued an invitation for each committee to select one or more representatives to attend an exploratory meeting on forming some type of organization.

Convening Individuals and Forming the Network

In early 1993, Dr. Benz convened an "Exploratory Meeting of Social Concerns Committees of Some Rural Town Churches to Look at Possible Cooperation." Eight representatives (including me) of four churches, an Episcopal diocese, and two social-issues organizations (County Human Relations Council and Interfaith Center for Peace and Justice) attended the meeting. Participants gave preliminary expressions of interest and possible directions for cooperation, and tested the existence of common concerns and a willingness to collaborate to address them. Racism in the community emerged as a major concern.

Representatives held a second meeting one month later, in May 1993. Participants agreed that there was a continuing need to meet, and they formed a new organization, the Inter-Church Network for Social Concerns (INSC). Considerable discussion of racism took place, and participants began to talk about the possibility of a meeting or conference on this subject. Representatives expressed general support for the idea and assigned joint responsibility for this potential event to the social-concerns committees of two member churches. Discussion also helped establish primary network functions as identifying, focusing attention on, catalyzing, and helping organize activities and build support on community-wide issues such as racism. Providing information exchange among churches on social-issues activities emerged as another key function. Adopting these functions rather than assuming the role as a primary direct-action organization was crucial to building broad community support for the network.

Developing the Network

The next two meetings in the fall of 1993 gave further shape to the network and its role. Several decisions had substantial impacts in shaping the character of the network. For example, INSC members decided against becoming closely linked to one member organization. Rather, they defined the role of the network as a bridge among existing organizations, not an integral part of any of them.

Discussion of racism in the community continued at these meetings. To advance discussion, Dr. Benz introduced a brief tentative proposal for the INSC to sponsor a community conference. The statement proposed a traditional design with a keynote speaker, reports from the county Human Relations Council, and small-group discussions. This proposal planted the seed for a major network activity: community workshops (see below). Designing, planning, and conducting this activity also helped further define and develop the network and its role in the community.

Community Workshops

Holding a meeting for leaders and members of the community to examine the racial situation was the guiding concept of the first proposal. A second version of the proposal emphasized the historic contribution of the town in establishing and expanding the American vision of equality, and challenged key local citizens to examine the present situation from this perspective: "How is the historic vision of unity and equality faring today in our community?" This theme refocused attention at the ecological level around a key American principle. Network members discussed the proposal and appointed a small group to begin designing and planning the event.

As discussions took place, a new, basic design principle emerged. First, racism in the public school system was chosen as the focus of the meeting.

Second, the original design involved a top-down approach: having leaders from several key local industries, such as banking and real estate, talk about their efforts to improve interracial relationships; initiatives they were taking; forces impeding their efforts; ways the INSC could help improve their efforts. Discussions in several planning group and steering-committee (SC) sessions raised serious questions about this approach. For example, an informal leader of this community flatly stated that minority members would not attend the conference as originally proposed, because they would feel one down to existing leaders and would have too much to lose by participating.

The new design emphasized an open search process (Emery and Emery, 1978; Emery and Purser, 1996; Weisbord, 1992) that would actively involve stakeholders in exploring and defining critical aspects of race relations in the school system. Briefly stated, the revised approach was constituent-centered. This approach was essential, since the exact nature of the problem was unclear, and the willingness of the community to work on it was uncertain. Hence, including representatives of key groups involved in the overall school system in exploring the situation was crucial. Renaming the meeting a "workshop" instead of "conference" symbolized the new approach.

First Workshop

Designing, planning, and making arrangements for the workshop took place over a ten-month period. After several additional planning group meetings, considerable discussion in the steering committee, and further input from minority community leaders, the basic design of the workshop took shape. The design required using an outside facilitator to help coordinate and manage activities.

A greatly modified search process (Emery and Emery, 1978; Emery and Purser, 1996; Weisbord, 1992) guided the six-hour (3:00–9:00 P.M.) Sunday session in early October 1994. Selecting participants in the workshop was a crucial design feature, and the planning group decided on three primary criteria: *stakeholder representation*—key individuals from the teachers, students, parents, school board, school administrators and staff, and citizens groups; *minority community representation*—with a relatively small minority population, the committee paid special attention to identifying potential nonwhite participants; and *balance*—relatively equal representation from various stakeholder groups to ensure different points of view. Gender was a secondary criterion.

Approximately forty-five individuals received written invitations to the meeting three months before the event. This letter explained the general nature, purpose, and scheduling of the meeting, and emphasized the importance of the issue for the community. Follow-up phone calls and a reminder letter one week before the workshop helped inform potential participants and encourage attendance.

The workshop had thirty-one participants, with fairly equal representation from various stakeholder groups. As table 7.1 indicates, workshop activities occurred in the total group and in four concurrent heterogeneous small-group sessions.

Table 7.1
SEARCH PROCESS—OUR SCHOOLS: OPEN AND INCLUSIVE?

Phase 1	*Preconference Work*
	Design workshop; select participants; send invitation letters; make follow-up phone calls; send reminder letters to define discussion areas
Phase 2	*Explore the General Environment—Small Group Work*
	Identify future general economic, political, social, technological, environmental changes. How will these affect the Rural Town School System?
Phase 3	*Define the Current Situation—Small Group Work*
	What words, images, and phrases best describe existing race relations in the public school system?
Phase 4	*Visioning a Desirable Future—Small Group Work*
	What would the ideal rural-town public school system look like?
Phase 5	*Identify Key Issues—Small Group Work*
	What issues must be addressed to move the school system from the current toward the ideal situation?
Phase 6	*Determine Strategy and Plan General Action Steps—Total Group Work*
Phase 7	*Implement Action Steps—Total Group Work*

Having representation of various stakeholders in each small group assured diverse input, as well as communication across stakeholder group boundaries. Following the general phases of the search process, workshop events started with an exploration of environmental factors, examined the current situation, defined an ideal school system, identified issues involved in moving from the present to the ideal, and began to map action steps. The sequence started with the environment to break participants' normal frames and to ground discussion in a broad context.

Responses of workshop participants about the current state of race relations in the school system gave serious cause for concern, bringing up such things as hypocrisy and racism of silence, and a lack of dialogue between racial groups. Identifying key aspects of an ideal school system generated much energy among participants, and they indicated a desire to continue work on the issues identified. At the same time, past failures to make progress made many individuals skeptical. In brief, the workshop appeared to begin a solid foundation for future network development and work, and participants expressed a willingness to attend a follow-up meeting.

Second Workshop

Workshop outcomes were analyzed and typed, and a copy was sent to each participant, along with an invitation to participate in an early December workshop. Sixteen individuals participated in this two-hour second meeting. Workshop activity included restating the top four issues from the October workshop; identifying recent relevant events, such as a school-district retreat initiating strategic planning, which covered several of the topics identified at the October workshop such as how to increase staff and curriculum diversity; and smallgroup discussions on the two top-priority issues. General discussion led to the decision to have workshop participants volunteer as action team members for the school-district strategic-planning process beginning in January 1995. Several participants agreed to sign up and encourage others to do so. Participants also decided to meet again in late spring to assess progress on implementing action steps and to make further plans.

Third Workshop

Thirteen individuals participated in the third workshop on May 21, 1995. Participants reviewed outcomes of the school-system strategic-planning process and noted several accomplishments, especially an action plan on diversity. This plan committed the school district to develop ways of supporting diversity and respect for the inherent worth of all individuals, and defined specific action steps to bring this about, such as recruiting minority-group members. The plan also established a community-diversity committee to follow up, monitor, and evaluate progress.

Participants also shared their expectations about outcomes from strategic planning. Discussion revealed a general feeling of hopefulness, tempered by considerable skepticism based on past failures. For the future, the group agreed to follow through on strategic-planning decisions and to make Martin Luther King Day an official school holiday. Participants insisted on using an existing community group to lead the holiday effort. A network member volunteered to contact the county Human Relations Council to explore its willingness to adopt the holiday issue as a change project.

Action to Bring about Change

This section describes the county Human Relations Council (HRC) work to influence the local school district to adopt Martin Luther King (MLK) Day as an official school holiday. Although this work went beyond the role of the Inter-Church Network, it provides an example of successfully transferring action-taking responsibility from one interorganizational network system to another. Overlapping membership (three individuals, including me, are members of both the INSC and HRC steering committees) and previous shared experiences in designing and conducting the three workshops provided linking pins (Likert, 1967) and helped orient thinking and provide follow-through in devising a strategy and action steps.

Word about the INSC workshops spread through the community. This along with contact by a network member led the county Human Relations Council to call a September 1995 meeting. Two other INSC members and I participated in this exploratory meeting. Participants decided to adopt making MLK Day an official school holiday as a change project. They also agreed to meet again in October to discuss plans.

Developing a Strategy and Early Action

Table 7.2 highlights key action steps in the change process. Identifying the problem, gaining a shared understanding of the issue, and visioning the future occurred during the three INSC workshops. These were also crucial elements in

Table 7.2

**ACTION STEPS IN ORGANIZING TO BRING ABOUT CHANGE
ON A SCHOOL HOLIDAY**

- Identify the problem situation
- Develop shared understanding of issue among constituents
- Create a vision for the future
- Decide to act
- Organize to take action
- Question decision to act
- Reaffirm decision to act
- Define change strategy and first action steps
- Test community attitudes and perceptions
    contact several key community leaders
    feedback and discuss contacts
- Broaden support for change
    develop outline to guide discussions with community members
    contact community members by phone or in person
    feedback and discussion of outcomes at bi-weekly meetings
    define next steps based on learnings from previous actions
    identify additional key organizations, groups, and individuals
- Align action steps with school district schedule for developing school calendar: planning; a mistep; re-planning
- Make informal contacts with key school-board members
- Plan final action steps to influence school-board decision
    write and distribute letter to community members
    write and simulate writing articles and letters in local newspapers
    organize presentations and appearances at school-board meetings
    catalyze and support work of key community groups (e.g., ministerium, Interfaith Center, high-school students)
    stimulate phone calls and letters to school-board members
    coordinate work with minority community
- Student survey
- *Outcome:* School Board approves two-year calendar that observes MLK Day as an official holiday—November 4, 1996

building a strong foundation for the change effort. Still, the HRC had to decide to become involved, learn what was required, and commit itself to organizing and carrying out the change effort.

For more than ten years, various individuals and groups had tried unsuccessfully several times to influence the school board to adopt MLK Day as an official holiday. These unsuccessful efforts made most Human Relations Council steering-committee members highly skeptical about the likely success of the current effort. After lengthy discussion at several later meetings, the steering committee adopted making MLK Day an official school holiday as an action project in late 1995. Despite this official decision, considerable doubt still lingered in the minds of some, perhaps most, committee members many months later.

Based on early work in the fall, the group began to develop its strategy and preliminary action steps. Previous work, contacts with community leaders, and discussion led to adopting a strategy of appealing to the higher community values of fostering diversity and respect for individual and ethnic differences. The philosophy statement included in the school district action plan on diversity adopted earlier in the year captures this theme: "The District will develop a program for the entire school community in order to cultivate respect for the worth and dignity of every person, and to affirm ethnic and cultural diversity, and to combat racism and other forms of discrimination within the school district."

The basic approach was to identify issues, demonstrate, and build support through contacting likely supporters in key constituent groups. In effect, we were building a network of individuals, groups, and organizations. The first action step involved identifying likely supporters in key community groups to test receptivity and begin to build support for the holiday idea. Persons contacted were asked to contact other individuals, organizations, and groups, inform them of the change effort, and ask for their support. Beyond teachers, administrators, and other direct constituent groups of the school district, groups identified included the chamber of commerce, members of a local college faculty, editor of the local paper, local-service group leaders, lawyers, and community opinion leaders. Work placed special emphasis on identifying and involving key members of the minority community through continuous communication with informal leaders.

Group members contacted a few key leaders in community organizations to test support on the holiday issue, identify existing attitudes and perceptions, enlist their help, and discover effective ways of bringing about the proposed change. These contacts provided much encouragement. For example, discussion with the new principal of the high school suggested strong support for the holiday. And the local ministerium expressed support for the holiday and offered to express this view to the school board. These positive reactions from community leaders led the steering committee to reaffirm its decision and spurred us to intensify our work.

Broadening Support

The next action phase involved broadening community support for change. Initially, committee members developed a list of some 30 individuals in key organizations and groups. Contacting these individuals led to expanding the list to more than 50 key individuals (a final list contains 250).

Group members reported the tone and outcome of each contact at biweekly meetings. This action-research practice provided ongoing learning, generated new ideas for further action, and created a feeling of progress among group members. It also educated individuals and rooted the change process in the larger community. Virtually every person contacted expressed support for making MLK Day a school holiday, and many of them volunteered to help. This reaction buoyed our confidence and provided additional motivation.

Final Action Steps

Toward the middle of the summer, it became essential to determine the timing of key decision points in school-board review, discussion, and voting on the holiday issue, and to devise specific ways of influencing the process. We discovered that the process involved three stages: the school-board administrative committee would develop a proposed calendar; the full school board would review the proposed calendar in a closed meeting; and the proposed calendar would be formally presented, discussed, and voted on at an open school-board meeting. Lack of clarity about timing resulted in a misstep, and the administrative committee did not include MLK Day as a holiday in the first proposed calendar. Fortunately, the board returned the proposal to the committee, and the final version included it. This merely meant that the holiday issue would now be up for review, discussion, and action during the fall. So final work to influence that decision had just begun.

The HRC group had been planning final steps to influence the school-board decision for several months and began implementing them in September. Key steps included the following:

• Steering committee member contacts with school-board members to request their support and determine their reactions.

• Presentations and attendance at school-board meetings. The steering committee made sure that at least one member and several representatives from various community groups attended and made presentations at each meeting. This demonstrated our continuing commitment to the issue, supported other community representatives, and provided direct observation of what happened at each meeting (observations were fed back to the entire steering committee for use in planning subsequent steps). The number of presentations ranged from five to twelve per meeting between mid-September and November 4th. Presenters included several ministers, local business persons, minority-group members, parents, teachers and coaches, a doctor, college professors, and interested community members.

• Publicity. Newspapers were contacted to ensure coverage of school-board deliberations and action on the MLK Day holiday. Several steering-committee members wrote articles for two local newspapers. We also encouraged opinion leaders to write articles or letters and facilitated getting these published.

- Triggering and supporting work of key community groups to influence the school board (for example, getting the eleven-member ministerium to write a letter). Several ministers who belonged to the ministerium also made pro-holiday statements at school-board meetings.

- Sending letters to several hundred key community members requesting them to write and phone school-board members, attend board meetings, write letters to the editors of local newspapers, and urge colleagues and friends to give active support to the change effort.

- Two short proholiday skits by a multiracial, multiethnic youth group called Colors of Love—one in early October, the other on November 4th.

- Spontaneous student activity. A high-school senior (an *ex officio* member of the school board) and the president of the junior class set up a card table in the cafeteria during lunch and discussed the holiday issue with students. Later, they conducted a student survey that found very strong support for the change among the 426 respondents, with 88 percent indicating that MLK Day is important enough to be recognized as a school holiday, 77 percent stating that current school activities on MLK Day do not put enough emphasis on what Dr. King achieved, and 72 percent believing that having the day off on MLK Day honored Dr. King more than being in school. They also organized eight student presentations and reported results of the survey at the deciding school-board meeting (November 4th).

A ground swell of support resulted from these and other actions. Approximately forty proholiday supporters attended the November 4, 1996, school-board meeting. Still, several amendments to the holiday motion were made, arguments given against it, and votes on related issues, such as adopting Veterans Day as a school holiday, taken. Finally the board voted. The final result of this change effort was that the school board voted five to four to adopt Dr. Martin Luther King, Jr., Day as an official holiday for the next two school years.

Institutionalizing Change in the Community

Leaders of the change effort—five members of the HRC steering committee plus a key leader of the minority community—had a victory-celebration breakfast in a local diner the morning after the favorable school-board vote. After briefly basking in the glow of victory, attention quickly turned to how to ensure that it would become a permanent part of the school calendar. Given the one-vote margin and the fact that calendars were approved for only two-year periods, there was a real possibility that the decision could be reversed in 1998. Consequently, our attention immediately turned to developing ways of institutionalizing the change within the community. Our goal became to have the change be such an integral part of community events and thinking that in the future, no one would dare consider proposing elimination of the MLK Day holiday. This goal is consistent with that of AR and organization and system development: to make positive intended changes a permanent part of the system (Beer, 1980; Cummings

Table 7.3

ACTION STEPS TO INSTITUTIONALIZE MLK DAY AS A SCHOOL HOLIDAY

November 5, 1996	Identify the need to institutionalize the holiday
January–February 1997	Steering committee assesses change process and identifies lessons learned
February–March 1997	Identify "progressive" potential candidates for school board, contact them informally, and encourage them to run
April 21, 1997	Womens' Issues Committee of YWCA presents award to school board for its leadership in making MLK Day a holiday
May 1997	Forum for school-board candidates
June 10, 1997, to present	Diversity committee activity
MLK Day, January 1998	"Day On" activities
Ongoing	Monitor developments in community to identify threats to MLK holiday and to identify opportunities to advance race relations
May 22, 1998	Joint letter from Human Relations Council and County Council of Community Services to school superintendent
MLK Day, January 1999	"Day On" activities
MLK Day, January 2000	"Day On" activities with local United Way as primary sponsor

and Worley, 1993). Deciding to attempt to make MLK Day an integral part of community activities was the first step in the institutionalizing process.

Table 7.3 identifies key action steps taken to make official recognition of the MLK school holiday permanent in the community. As we planned and carried out these steps, our goal broadened and became, over time, to use our efforts at institutionalizing the holiday to sensitize the community to the principles of racial fairness and justice, and to help educate individuals about how to use these principles to advance other positive work on race relations and diversity in the community.

Identifying Lessons from the Change Effort

A second step in institutionalizing the change involved examining the change process directly and identifying lessons learned from it. Consistent with the AR approach, members believed that the assessment would help develop the network further by raising awareness of important aspects of the change process, increasing understanding of what had taken place, and incorporating lessons in the system. These lessons would then serve as potential resources for future work with the community.

Steering-committee members answered several open-ended questions individually. Answers provided inputs for discussions during two steering-committee meetings. Responses to questions surfaced the following:

plies, cleaning products, educational materials, food, games, arts and
pplies, sports equipment, books, and videos.

mately sixty people of all ages, from children to grandparents, partici-
a community potluck dinner. All activities, including a group sing of
cial-activist songs and youth-group skits, honored the work and
Dr. Martin Luther King. The event brought together many commu-
bers who normally do not interact, thereby extending the network.

' activities gave community members a chance to meet the needs of
participating directly in work that made a difference. High-school
team members, families, students, retirees, and others experienced
ction gained from contributing, sorting, and delivering needed items
social-service organizations. Several local private organizations
d financial support.

s demonstrated the important role of the HRC network. And the
ities helped enrich relationships among many individuals, groups,
ations in the community, thereby increasing its social capital (Cole-

rd, the HRC steering committee conducted an analysis of the "Day
ion. Consistent with the action-research approach, the analysis was
ntifying lessons from the event and making them a permanent part
nembers' shared experience. Members noted that the response was
expected; things had changed; they were making progress. As a
ering committee decided that the event should be repeated the fol-
Members noted Linda's critical role and expressed the need for her
ment. They also felt that it was important to identify members of
' organizing committee early and to define its role and links to the
er community organizations. The importance of documenting the
s, and action steps to help guide future work was noted as well. In
committee members felt that triggering, coordinating, supporting,
with many other groups and organizations through the network
ighly successful "Day On" celebration.
celebration took place on MLK Day, 1999. A seven-person com-
ated and managed the event. The committee used the same net-
of working with and through existing groups and organizations as
sed activity included sending letters to over a hundred social-serv-
ns throughout the county, expanding outreach via broadened
s supported by a corporate gift, and adding two satellite sites in
cations for collecting, sorting, and distributing donated items.
Day On" celebration of Martin Luther King Day was a great suc-
with 1998, more individuals and groups participated in distribut-
ber of needed items to more agencies dispersed throughout the
publicity also made the event more widely known in the com-
this success, the HRC steering committee decided for the future
ry sponsorship of the event to the local United Way organization.

1. Expectations and feelings about the change effort before it began. These
   had ranged from pessimistic (small chance of success but we needed to
   try it anyway) to optimistic (fairly optimistic to greater optimism, feeling
   that eventually right would triumph). Remarks indicated that two members experienced conflict, feeling torn between an in-service day for
   teachers and staff on MLK Day versus an official holiday—something
   needed to be done, but what? Another person expressed having 110 percent commitment because the community had identified the need in the
   May 1995 INSC workshop.

2. Actions, events, and other factors that contributed to success. Most of
   the sixteen specific responses identified the importance of some aspect
   of the network strategy (such as direct contacts with individuals, encouraging them to get involved; selecting people from various key groups to
   contact; presentations to school board by various types of individuals)
   on involvement of a group outside the HRC steering committee (such as
   students or a minority community). Hence, steering-committee members
   indicated that using the network strategy was a key to reaching the
   change goal.

3. Key lessons derived from the experience. Steering-committee members
   stated that they learned the importance of the strategy used, the AR
   approach (series of meetings to plan, assess, and make changes based
   on new information and insights), and the network (using a small tight
   group, the steering committee, to guide the change effort and extend
   influence to other key groups and individuals).

Overall, these responses showed strong support for the approach, strategy,
and action steps developed to bring about change. They also revealed several
important things learned by the HRC steering-committee members. These lessons provided crucial input to developing an approach for institutionalizing the
change in the community.

Ensuring the Support of the School Board

In January 1997, steering-committee members began discussing the future
composition of the school board. They identified eleven potential candidates
thought to be relatively progressive on education issues. At least one steering-
committee member contacted each of these individuals, outlined the seriousness
of the situation, and encouraged him or her to run. Three of these eleven persons
ran for election in the May primary.

The steering committee faced a dilemma in considering further steps on
school-board elections: Overt political activity probably would trigger a backlash
and mobilize the opposition, but doing nothing might result in the elimination of
MLK Day as a school holiday.

Consequently, toward the end of March, the steering committee decided on
an indirect total-community approach: Sponsoring a forum for all school-board
candidates. With less than two months available to plan and hold the event, deci-

sion-making and action occurred quickly. The steering committee held three meetings during the next six weeks to provide support and advice to the candidate forum-coordination committee.

The four-person committee moved rapidly to identify tasks, define key roles, identify individuals to fill the roles, and plan and implement action steps. While the HRC steering committee served as a forum for discussing general questions and providing ongoing support to the committee, the committee operated largely on its own, inviting school-board candidates to participate, publicizing the event, organizing the meeting, and printing programs.

As planned, the candidates forum took place on May 15, 1997, from 7:00 to 9:30 P.M. in the middle-school's small auditorium. All eight school-board candidates participated in the event, which over two hundred community members attended. Spontaneous feedback following the event indicated that those who attended felt that the forum was informative and worthwhile.

At the debriefing session during the next HRC steering-committee meeting, members noted and discussed several lessons learned from the experience of sponsoring and conducting the forum. First, it is good to inform the community. Second, it takes a talented, hard-working leader and a strong, well-organized committee, with clear individual assignments, to make such an event successful. Third, Children First, a network of mothers formed several years earlier to voice concern to the school board on a crucial planning issue, is a latent network that can be activated when needed. Fourth, the League of Women Voters model provided effective basic design and procedure guidelines. In addition, thorough preparation is required; for example, one committee member met with the moderator and timer three times to ensure that they understood their roles and the meeting procedures completely. The steering committee also noted that the planning-committee chair had assembled a detailed notebook on organizing and arranging the forum, which can serve as a resource for future events. The experience confirmed again the value of using a network strategy for planning and conducting events.

Diversity Committee

In June 1997, the district superintendent of schools convened a meeting of a small, diverse group of community representatives. This committee is to assist the school district in following through on the diversity action plan described earlier. Three HRC steering-committee members (including me) are also members of this diversity committee and serve as "linking pins" (Likert, 1967) between the two groups.

So far, the diversity committee has focused primarily on two issues: increasing the number of minority group members on the faculty and staff within the district, and obtaining support for official recognition of a former "colored school" in the community. Much discussion on possible sources of qualified minority group candidates and ways of identifying them and attracting them to the district has occurred. Several recruiting visits to universities within the region have resulted from this effort.

The diversity committee selected two pers[ons in?] recognition of the site of the former "colored [school?] rized the history of this school and identifie[d] recognition. Later, based on a committee re[commendation, agreed to sponsor the installation of an offici[al] the site of the former ——— Street Colored [School?] November 20, 1999, Remembrance Day, whe[n] tion of a local cemetery for African-America[n]

Overall, the committee has helped maint[ain] and racial issues in the school district and th[e] going contact among the school district, the H[RC?] viduals in the community. In this way, it exte[nded] networks.

"A Day On, Not a Day Off"

The HRC steering committee continued [to involve?] and other community members in meaningf[ul] work strategy was to stimulate and provi[de] King's vision and principles. At a late June [meeting, a vol?] unteer coordinator at a local social-service [agency?] the discussion and had many suggestions [based on?] prior experience. Consequently, the steering [committee?] posed design of the event to the next meeti[ng].

Linda presented the basic design prop[osal at a?] meeting in late July. Linda's design includ[ed] conducting a needs assessment of social-s[ervice?] individuals and organizations to donate i[tems to meet?] agency needs; and recruiting students and [others?] to receive, sort, and deliver items to the soc[ial-service agenc?] ities would be organized around the the[me "?] everyone can serve," one of Dr. King's p[rinciples?] Day Off," was designed to connote havin[g people?] engage in helping the less fortunate.

The HRC steering committee formed a [committee to?] activities. Linda chaired the committee, [and handled?] dispersing items for social-service orga[nizations?] Other committee members provided supp[ort by organiz?] ing several other MLK activities, such as [a panel dis?] cussion for children and book on civil rig[hts?]

Several indicators demonstrate the su[ccess?]

- Over two hundred volunteers sorted an[d delivered items to?] agencies, such as a community soup ki[tchen, Head?] Start, and Big Brothers/Big Sisters.

- Groups and individuals donated hundr[eds of?]

and su[
crafts [
- Appro[
pated i[
sixties [
vision [
nity m[
- "Day [
others [
wrestli[
the sati[
to vari[
contrib[

This suc[
shared a[
and orga[
man, 19[

Afte[
On" cele[
aimed at [
of netwo[
greater t[
result, th[
lowing y[
future in [
the "Day [
HRC an[
time line [
sum, stee[
and wor[
resulted [

A sec[
mittee co[
work stra[
in 1998. [
ice orga[
communi[
other cou[

Agair[
cess. Con[
ing a larg[
county. B[
munity. B[
to transfe[

The HRC will continue to support the event, but United Way will become the lead sponsor. This change demonstrated HRC success in recognizing an opportunity, devising a way of capitalizing on it through its network of relationships, and following through with coordinated support during early development and implementation. It also demonstrates flexibility to adjust its role when an activity matures and becomes capable of operating on its own. This change also demonstrates increased institutionalization of the "Day On" event in the community.

Outcomes of the Change Effort

Working to bring about change in the public school system resulted in several identifiable outcomes. As the following list indicates, some of these are tangible and relatively easy to identify; others are less tangible and less evident, but no less important:

• Adopting Martin Luther King Day as an official school holiday.

• Institutionalizing the MLK Day holiday in the community.

• Contributing spillover effects in other diversity and race-relations areas.

• Building a network of relationships among various groups, organizations, and individuals that serves as a reservoir of social capital (Coleman, 1990) for future work.

• Raising the level of awareness in the community of the nature and importance of diversity and of understanding and valuing differences.

All of these outcomes show the impacts of the networks on change; therefore, they are discussed here.

Influencing the school board to recognize MLK Day as an official holiday is the clearest result of the change effort. As table 7.4 shows, this decision stemmed from a long series of network actions that began in early 1993.

Identifying racism as a concern occurred at the initial INSC meeting. Discussion of the topic continued in future network meetings. Next, the INSC focused attention on and triggered exploration of racism in the school system by conceiving of, designing, and conducting the first workshop, "Our Schools: Open and Inclusive?" in October 1994. By involving representatives of all stakeholder groups in an open exploration of the current state of the system versus the ideal state, the workshop laid the foundation for the change and institutionalization work that followed. The third workshop led to clearly identifying making MLK Day an official school holiday as the top-priority change goal. It also resulted in a decision to transfer primary responsibility for leading the change effort to the Human Relations Council. The HRC steering committee then developed around the task. By using a strategy of catalyzing other groups, organizations, and individuals to act, and by coordinating and focusing change activities, an effective network emerged. Carefully planned network activity ultimately led to the school-board decision on November 4, 1996, to adopt MLK Day as an official school holiday. While the outcome was a long time in coming, and at times

Table 7.4

NETWORK(S) INVOLVEMENT IN CHANGE PROCESS

Date	Critical Event	Key Network
April 1993	Racism identified as a concern	Inter-Church Network for Social Concerns (INSC) first meeting
Fall 1993	Proposal for community conference	INSC meeting
Fall 1993–Spring 1994	Continuing discussion of racism and of possible community conference	INSC meetings
Spring–October 1994	Designing and planning first workshop on racism in schools	Planning committee and INSC meetings
October 1994	Workshop—"Our Schools: Open and Inclusive?"	Conducted by INSC
May 1995	Making MLK Day an official school holiday identified as number 1 goal	INSC third workshop
September 1995	Transfer responsibility for bringing about change to Human Relations Council (HRC)	HRC steering committee (SC)
January–November 1996	Strategizing, planning, building network, implementing (and revising) action steps	HRC SC and network
November 4, 1996	School-board decision	Open school-board meeting—many presentations coordinated by HRC SC
November 5, 1996–Present	Institutionalizing the MLK Day holiday	HRC SC and network

uncertain, one thing is clear: Without the concerted change process started by the INSC and organized and conducted during the final stages by the HRC network, the holiday would not have been adopted.

Institutionalizing the holiday in the community became a primary network goal in late 1996. Several indicators show that considerable progress has been made toward this goal. In the fall of 1998, the superintendent stated that the MLK holiday was now official policy of the school district. Thus it would automatically be included in future calendars recommended by the administrative committee to the school board; consequently, the board would have to initiate action if it wanted to eliminate the holiday. Then, in November 1998, the school board unanimously passed the calendar for the next two years with no questions raised about the MLK Day holiday. So at the official decision-making level, short-run success has been achieved.

In the community at large, many individuals and groups have volunteered to donate, gather, sort, and distribute needed items to social agencies in the county as part of "Day On" celebrations. And the scope of the event and enthusiasm that participants display grow each year. Apparently, having an opportunity to join with others to help those in need strikes a responsive chord in many community members. Using the network enables them to act on this motivation. Substantial student involvement demonstrates the special importance of this activity to young people. HRC-network actions initiated, managed, and supported this activity in 1998 and 1999 and have led to its establishment in the community.

Network actions to bring about and institutionalize the MLK Day holiday also have had several spillover effects. One of these is the continuing work of the school district to make diversity goals developed during the 1995 strategic-planning process a reality. Their earlier involvement in the change effort led the school-district superintendent to appoint three HRC steering-committee members to the diversity committee. Committee membership extends HRC linkages and provides another forum for network influence. The diversity committee has helped the superintendent devise a strategy and action steps to hire additional minority group faculty and staff members, and facilitated obtaining official school-board recognition of the former "colored school" in the community. These actions illustrate spillover effects of the network-led change process.

The HRC steering-committee's network strategy of working through existing organizations, groups, and community leaders to bring about recognition of the MLK Day holiday turned out to be an effective approach in achieving the primary change goal. In addition, it built and strengthened community social capital, expanding networks of relationships, norms, and trust that facilitate coordinated community action (Putnam, 1993, p. 167). Organizing and carrying out "Day On" illustrate this phenomenon. Adding Linda, the local United Way volunteer coordinator, to the HRC "Day On" planning group was crucial to the success of the event. She had considerable experience and expertise in organizing volunteer activities and quickly became a key member. This group worked through many existing organizations to make the event a reality—social-service agencies to determine needs; schools, churches, and other community groups to provide volunteers; private corporations and individuals to donate needed items; and various sources to provide publicity. Inviting several additional community organizations, such as the Interfaith Center and the YWCA, to jointly sponsor the event expanded network relationships and built further trust and collaborative norms. Transferring primary sponsorship to the local United Way for 2000 represents a further step in developing overall community social capital.

Linking with Children First is another example of expanding social capital in the community. This network provided a ready list of potential supporters of the MLK Day holiday, and several Children First leaders became active in the change effort. Later, during the institutionalization phase, one member was actively involved in planning and managing the school-board candidates forum. Thus involving Children First built upon the existing relationships within that network, reactivated it by involvement in new meaningful work, and extended its linkages to other organizations, groups, and individuals in the community via working with the HRC network. This enlarged social capital serves as another latent community resource available for future development efforts.

Raising the general level of awareness in the community of the nature and importance of racial issues is another indirect outcome of the change process. The three INSC workshops that triggered the holiday policy change involved representatives from key stakeholders of the school system. Work during these meetings involved having participants identify and share their aspirations for the future, their perceptions of present conditions in the school district, and possible actions to move the system toward the ideal state. The process grounded the change effort in the larger community: School-system stakeholders, not the INSC or HRC, chose the change goal of making MLK Day an official school holiday. And this goal rested on a deep, shared appreciation (Vickers, 1965) of the context for change developed during the three workshops. In addition, the change strategy and action steps have helped educate community members about the importance of appreciating diversity and of having positive race relations in the community.

Two incidents in late 1997 illustrate HRC help in increasing this sensitivity. First, several community members noticed that the "warrior head" used at athletic events conveyed a negative stereotype of Native Americans and asked, "Do we wish to continue to communicate this false negative image to our children?" Following discussion in a steering-committee meeting, one member wrote to the high-school principal, who, in turn, discussed the issue with coaches, teachers, and students. As a result, a decision was made not to use the "warrior head" at future school events. The second incident involved gaining official school-board sponsorship of the "colored school" official wayside marker. The idea for this marker came through the diversity committee as a way of recognizing the historic role of African Americans in the community. Installing the plaque in November 1999 symbolized the growing understanding of minority group members and their involvement in the community for over two hundred years. Both incidents show HRC network involvement in fostering awareness of diversity and a willingness to take action to advance understanding of it.

Conclusions

Experience with the INSC and the county HRC leads to several conclusions:

• Network organizations offer a potentially effective form of organization to engage large-scale community issues. Developing loose linkages among organizations, groups, and individuals who have a critical stake in these issues, and having these linkages center on an identified common purpose, provide a potent way of organizing to bring about change on amorphous problems. Trist's (1983, 1985) socioecological perspective of interorganizational networks is particularly useful.

- Bringing about community change requires solid support within all key constituent groups. In the present case, stakeholders in the public-school system were identified and invited to participate in a broad search process that explored the present situation, defined features of the ideal system, and triggered action to make the ideal system a reality. Positive outcomes of the change process rested on this broad-based, in-depth search process. And the search process complements basic features of interorganizational networks.

- Interorganizational networks offer many members of the community an opportunity to make a difference on issues they consider important. A relatively small number of individuals participate regularly on the steering committees of the INSC and HRC. However, by serving as linking pins to other networks, groups, and organizations, their work is multiplied many times over. And by working through others existing in the community to effect change and eliciting the additional help required on specific projects (such as "Day On" activities and the school-board candidates forum), many others in the community participate. Thus the network concept of temporarily assembling the parties needed to reach specific change goals is crucial. Experience indicates that being involved in bringing about meaningful social change is highly motivating to many community members.

- Bringing about change through interorganizational networks takes considerable time and much focused effort by many people. Over two years elapsed between identifying racism as a concern at the first INSC meeting and adopting the issue of making MLK Day an official school holiday as a specific change goal. Developing and carrying out the change process required an additional seventeen months. However, the slow pace enabled the change to become deeply rooted and broadly supported in the community. In turn, the depth and breadth of support developed during the change effort have provided a solid base for institutionalizing the change. They also have contributed to several spillover effects and to increased awareness of the importance of diversity and race relations in the community.

- Using an AR approach to diagnose, plan, take action, observe outcomes, analyze and learn, and plan anew can be an effective way of bringing about change in a community. This is especially true in situations in which the precise nature of the issue is uncertain and where it is necessary to involve multiple stakeholders in creating action steps that make a difference. Action research enables organizers to act as if they know what they are doing, while providing short-term feedback loops that make it possible to adjust plans and actions based on new information and lessons. It also builds support for change through the process used to bring it about. This process contributed greatly to the success realized in the present case.

- It is possible to carry out the work required to bring about meaningful change on a small budget. None of the work conducted was funded by a grant. Virtually all the activities required to convene, build, and carry out INSC work has been done via *pro bono* contributions of time and in-kind gifts of space, staff, and office supplies. So far, the only notable expense has been the modest professional fee (approximately $500) of the external consultant who facilitated the first workshop. Small contributions from member churches paid for this expense. This experience gives another example of the possibility of bringing about meaningful change with virtually no dedicated resources. Chisholm and Mertel (1997) give a detailed account of change in a state agency conducted with a similar lack of funds.

References

Alter, C., & Hage, J. (1993). *Organizations working together.* Newbury Park, CA: Sage Publications.

Beer, M. (1980). *Organization change and development: A systems view.* Santa Monica, CA: Goodyear.

Chisholm, R. F. (1998). *Developing network organizations: Learning from practice and theory.* Reading, MA: Addison-Wesley.

Chisholm. R. F., & Elden, M. (1993). Features of emerging action research. In M. Elden & R. F. Chisholm (Eds.), *Special issue on action research* (pp. 275–297). *Human Relations, 46*(2).

Chisholm, R. F., & Mertel, P. T. (1997). Stone soup: Doing more with less in a state police department. *Organization Development Journal, 15*(1), 4–21.

Coleman, J. S. (1990). *Foundations of social theory.* Cambridge, MA: Harvard University Press.

Cummings, T. G., & Worley, C. G. (1993). *Organization development and change.* Minneapolis/St. Paul: West.

Emery, M., & Emery, F. E. (1978). Searching. In J. W. Sutherland (Ed.), *Management handbook of public administration* (pp. 257–301). New York: Van Nostrand Reinhold.

Emery, M., & Purser, R. E. (1996). *The search conference: A powerful way for planning organization change and community action.* San Francisco: Jossey-Bass.

Finsrud, H. (1995). How about a dialogue? Communication perspective meets socioecological perspective. In O. Eikeland & H. D. Finsrud (Eds.), *Research in action* (pp. 297–330). Oslo: Work Research Institute.

Hage, J., & Powers, C. H. (1992). *Post-industrial lives.* Newbury Park, CA: Sage Publications.

Huber, G. P. (1991). Organizational learning: The contributing processes and the literatures. *Organization Science, 2*(1), 1–13.

Katz, D., & Kahn, R. L. (1978). *The Social Psychology of Organizations* (2nd ed.). New York: Wiley.

Lewin, K. (1946). Action research and minority problems. *Journal of Social Issues, 2*(4), 34–46.

Likert, R. (1967). *The human organization.* New York: McGraw-Hill.

Putnam, R. D. (1993). *Making democracy work: Civic traditions in modern Italy.* Princeton, NJ: Princeton University Press.

Susman, G. I., & Evered, R. (1978). An assessment of the scientific merit of action research. *Administrative Science Quarterly, 23*, 582–603.

Trist, E. L. (1983). Referent organizations and the development of interorganizational domains. *Human Relations, 36*(3), 269–284.

Trist, E. L. (1985). Intervention strategies for interorganizational domains. In R. Tannenbaum & F. Massarik (Eds.), *Human systems development: New perspectives on people and organizations* (pp. 167–197). San Francisco: Jossey-Bass.

Vickers, G. (1965). *The art of judgement.* New York: Basic Books.

Weisbord, M. R. (1992). *Discovering common ground.* San Francisco: Berrett-Koehler.

PART THREE

Lessons from the Field: Extending
Analytical Findings

8

The Impact of Network Structures on Community-Building Efforts

The Los Angeles Roundtable for Children Community Studies

Myrna P. Mandell

I N RECENT YEARS, THERE HAS BEEN A GROWING INTEREST in community-build-ing efforts in which collaborations are formed among government agencies, the private sector, and/or community groups to solve community problems (Annie E. Casey Foundation, 1995; Stone, 1996). This has occurred because there has been much interest in community-building efforts as a means to develop "a more holistic or comprehensive vision" (Stone, 1996, p. vii) of how to attack problems and develop solutions needed by communities. The literature on com-munity-building efforts recognizes the need for an interdisciplinary focus on "holistic, community-based approaches to the support of children and families and revitalization of the communities in which they live" (Stone, 1996, p. vii). Indeed, it has been pointed out that "most initiatives place an emphasis on build-ing a collaborative process for revitalization; empowering local actors to take on leadership roles in the community; improving systems for assessing and tracking community resources; and promoting a comprehensive view of the social, struc-tural, and economic aspects of community revitalization" (Stone, 1996, p. viii).

In this chapter, we take a look at five such community-building efforts in the Los Angeles area (Los Angeles Roundtable for Children, 1997). Each of these efforts is based on building collaborations among relevant stakeholders in the community. These collaborations do not rely on contracts or government controls to bring about change. Instead, they are based on horizontal partnerships in which control by government is replaced by collaborations in which the public, private, and nonprofit sectors, as well as community members, are equal partners in achieving change (Agranoff, 1992, 1997; Agranoff and McGuire, 1998a, 1998b; Kabra and Khator, 1996; Kickert et al., 1997; O'Toole, 1997). These types of collaborations require the use of different management styles and policy instruments than are used in more traditional public-policy efforts (Mandell, 1999b).

In the symposium on "The Impact of Collaborative Efforts" (Mandell, 1999a), a distinction is made among different types of collaborations. They are viewed as "representing a continuum ranging from loose linkages and coalitions [networks] to more lasting structural arrangements [network structures]" (p. 5). Networks occur when linkages among a number of organizations and/or individuals become formalized. This involves traditional "networking" but is seen as a more formalized means of maintaining linkages with others with whom there is mutual interest. For instance, Medicare requires a network of medical professionals, insurers, and government agencies to coordinate their efforts in reaching their individual goals. Networks may involve simultaneous action by a number of different actors, but each of these actions represents the actions of independently operating organizations (D. Chisholm, 1989; Hanf and Scharpf, 1978; Mandell and Gage, 1988; Provan and Milward, 1995).

Network structures occur when working separately, even while maintaining linkages with each other, is not enough. Individuals representing themselves, public, not-for-profit, and private organizations realize that working independently is not enough to solve a particular problem or issue area. A network structure forms when these people realize that they (and the organizations they may represent) are each only one small piece of the total picture. It is a recognition that only by coming together to actively work on accomplishing a broad, common mission will something be accomplished (Agranoff, 1992, 1997; Agranoff and McGuire, 1998a, 1998b; R. F. Chisholm, 1998; Feyerherm, 1995; Gage and Mandell, 1990; Gray, 1989; Mandell, 1994, 1999b; Mandell and Gage, 1988).

Network structures may include, but reach beyond, linkages, coordination, or task-force action. Unlike networks where people are only loosely linked to each other, in a network structure people must actively work together to accomplish what is recognized as a problem or issue of mutual concern (Agranoff, 1992, 1997; Agranoff and McGuire, 1998a, 1998b; Feyerherm, 1995; Kickert et al., 1997; Mandell, 1988, 1994, 1999b).

Based on the study conducted by the Los Angeles Roundtable for Children (see appendix at the end of chapter), the community-building efforts that were most effective occurred when the participants were transformed into a new whole, taking on broad tasks that reached beyond the simultaneous actions of independently operating organizations. Their effectiveness also depended on the degree to which there was a commitment to a broad mission that could not be achieved without joint and strategically interdependent action by all parties. In other words, the effectiveness of community-building efforts in this study depended on the extent to which they operated as network structures (that is, through a unique structural arrangement).

Although the literature on community-building efforts recognizes the importance of collaborations, it is not clear whether the impact of network structures as a unique means for community-building efforts is clearly understood. This chapter is meant to present the complexities and challenges of these types of efforts, as well as shed some light on how to capitalize and deal with these complexities and challenges.

Very often agencies and the professionals in them make determinations of what communities need and how to provide it to them. Although well meaning, these determinations are "forced" on communities with little understanding of what is actually going on from the community's perspective. Conversely, community leaders and activists try to foster change based only on their involvement with their community and their beliefs of the changes that are needed based on this involvement. Again, although well meaning, by themselves they hold little promise of actually achieving the changes they would like. There is a need to temper what both professionals and community representatives try to do for communities with a better understanding of what is actually needed. The five community efforts presented here are therefore meant to serve as mirrors for both professionals and community representatives to confront their own challenges and opportunities and to learn what is needed from these studies. It is hoped that they will serve to help those involved in collaborative community-building efforts go to the next steps and move beyond practices that may be inappropriate.

The purpose of this chapter is not to discuss why a community should collaborate. Rather, it is meant to serve as a starting point to reshape the thinking of policy makers and community activists in general, on what is meant by "community-building" and what is involved in the ongoing efforts of bringing about changes in communities through network structures. The five efforts in this chapter are works in progress and will continue to evolve over time. Indeed, this chapter can represent only a snapshot in time of the communities involved. What is happening in these communities is very complex, and certainly not static. It is hoped that they will serve to challenge policy makers and community representatives about their own perceptions. The studies, as well as this current chapter, provide a place to start a conversation. It is not intended that they be the final word on the subject.

This chapter first presents an overview of the studies, summarizing information about the communities and giving the initial results, including the impact of network structures on the effectiveness of the community-building efforts in the communities studied. The discussion then turns to the issues and insights learned as a result of these studies, and their impact on established principles and theories of community-building efforts.

The discussion centers on two broad areas of concern. The first deals with a need to rethink and reshape our perceptions of what is meant by community collaborations. In doing so, the emphasis is on our ability to capitalize on the unique features of these types of collaborations. The second deals with the need to adapt to the realities of community collaborations. This applies to practitioners and community members alike and raises issues involving the development of new roles and capacities. The chapter concludes with some food for thought for the development of future community-building efforts.

Background

The Los Angeles Roundtable for Children, according to its brochures, is a "nonprofit education and advocacy organization dedicated to identifying and illuminating the critical issues facing children and families in Los Angeles County." In 1996, the Los Angeles Roundtable for Children decided to initiate a process involving their members in a variety of hands-on learning activities focused on communities in which there are multiple "experiments" under way. These "experiments" involve community collaborations to improve conditions for families and children in their communities. The goal was to learn about change efforts in the various communities and to synthesize what has been learned so that it can be used to inform others in the community, as well as policy makers, decision makers, and so on.

The Los Angeles Roundtable for Children held five meetings focusing on different community change efforts between October 1996 and February 1998. Each of these focused on the efforts of those people who are actively involved in ongoing community efforts. These meetings were not meant to present only success stories of community-building efforts. Neither were they meant to suggest that community-building through collaborative efforts is the only means of achieving change in a community. Rather, they were meant to serve as a starting point for an ongoing dialogue concerning what can be learned from collaborative efforts of communities. The five geographic areas in which the community efforts were selected for study were Pasadena/Altadena, Pacoima, San Pedro, South Central Los Angeles, and South Los Angeles.

Instead of inviting a small panel of select people to speak, however, the Los Angeles Roundtable for Children went to the communities and asked them to bring different constituencies to the table. The usual meeting format thus became dialogues involving parents, community members, professionals, and others actively involved in these efforts.

For each of the meetings held between 1996 and early 1998, it was the community group that selected the participants who were to be part of the presentation. The only guidelines given to each group was a series of questions that they were to cover as part of their presentation. These questions were as follows:

• What kinds of change processes are going on in your community?

• How is success defined?

- What are the key unresolved challenges?
- What are the primary lessons learned?

The participants were asked to submit their responses in writing. Other than this instruction, the presentation was left entirely up to the participants. In addition, audience members were given work sheets on each of the four questions to gather their reactions to the presentations.

The Communities

The following, taken from information provided by each of the community groups, provides a brief summary of the background of each of these community efforts:

Pasadena/Altadena

The Family Community Council (FCC), formerly known as the Pasadena/Altadena Community for Youth Planning Council, began in 1995. The Los Angeles Children's Planning Council provided the necessary support for the development of a local planning council in the Pasadena/Altadena area dedicated to testing the process of developing a comprehensive and integrated plan while examining the barriers to planning and coordination. The FCC includes members of the Pasadena City Council and the Altadena Town Council; representatives of the city manager's office and the chamber of commerce; chairs of existing collaboratives and/or coalitions; representatives of youth and consumer groups; and staff from city and county departments. In all, nineteen public and private partners came together to provide enrichment activities for children, youth, and families, child care, and public safety. Partners are involved in an effort to share information and work toward the common goals of strengthening neighborhoods and stimulating economic opportunities for residents of Pasadena and Altadena.

Pacoima

This effort is an attempt to combine two separate efforts: the Pacoima Urban Village (PUV) and the Vaughn Family Center (VFC). The VFC was started as a joint venture of United Way, the Los Angeles Educational Partnership, and the Los Angeles Unified School District to assist children and families through programs supported by a school-based center. The PUV is a logical extension of the VFC. The village consists of six neighborhoods linked together by a common interest in working together to improve their socioeconomic condition, and designed to have a positive influence on the surrounding neighborhoods. The focal point of each neighborhood is a school-based center. The focus is on a socioeconomic development strategy to help the community become financially independent and self-sufficient. The approach used treats the village as a system of people and programs.

After the initial community study on Pacoima, the relationship between the PUV and the VFC changed. Although there is still a connection between them, they are operated as completely separate entities.

San Pedro

The focus in this area is the Barton Hill Neighborhood Organization, run through the Toberman Settlement House, Inc. The Toberman Settlement House runs a number of human-services programs and has been instrumental in establishing the Barton Hill Neighborhood Organization. The Barton Hill Neighborhood Organization is a community self-help group with over two hundred dues-paying members and dozens of people who participate in the group's activities. It has an elected advisory board that plans membership meetings and keeps the various committees and services running. It provides many services to and for the people in the community, and considers political action to be its primary function. It has been engaged in preventing a number of different commercial developments, which members believe will harm the viability of their community, from moving forward.

South Central Los Angeles

The focus of this effort is on the Community Coalition for Substance Abuse, Prevention and Treatment. The coalition was started as a response to the negative treatment of residents in South Central Los Angeles by the police in their efforts in the war on drugs. The founders of this group were civil-rights and community activists who wanted to start a more comprehensive and relevant response to address what they saw as the real issues in this "war"—namely, attacking the economic problems, the educational disparity, and the overconcentration of liquor stores in South Central Los Angeles. The organization was originally supported by a grant secured through the University of Southern California School of Social Work. When this grant expired, the coalition established a non-profit organization and brought in new money.

The coalition is made up of a number of different efforts, all centered on the problems of drug abuse in their community. These include a youth component (operated by high-school students), a welfare-reform component (part of a larger county effort), and a prevention network (operated through the social-services-agency representatives). The coalition focuses on research and education, and especially on developing the political skills needed to influence the officials in the county who have the power to make changes in legislation affecting this community.

South Los Angeles

This program began in 1995 with a grant from the state for a Healthy Start Program. It is housed in the Norwood Street School, which considers itself a community school. This program is seen as the hub of the community. The Norwood Street Elementary School is located in central Los Angeles. The student body is predominately Latino (96%), and includes 2 percent African Americans, and a 2 percent combination of Asian, Native Americans, Filipino, and white students. The community is characterized by poverty, transiency, and linguistic isolation. The Norwood Family Center is the focal point of Norwood's Healthy Start program. There are programs for parents as well as children. There are fifteen to twenty health- and human-service-provider collaborators. There is a parent center and classes teaching English as a Second Language (ESL), leadership, citizenship, and career development. The idea of the programs is to be systematic and focused on the needs of the community.

The school officials are focusing on developing trust in the community by going to many different programs and meetings in the community and by having an investment in the community. There is a genuine effort to hear and listen to everyone, not to tell them what their needs are. It is believed that the outcomes need to develop from the programs, rather than trying to meet outcomes at the outset, and that making connections is key. There is a need for flexibility and for school officials to think outside the box. The interventions are viewed as being on behalf of children with learning problems who are part of a family. The idea is to have the interventions aimed at the whole child, not just at the learning problems.

Results

The following is a summary of the information obtained from each of the communities based on the four questions that served as a framework for each of the dialogues. The complete answers given by each of the communities can be found in the appendix to this chapter.

1. *What kinds of change processes are going on (in your community)?*

   The emphasis from all four communities was on the changes occurring as a result of bringing together many diverse groups. Empowerment and involvement of parents, teens, churches, social-service agencies, and government organizations were viewed as central to these change efforts.

2. *How is success defined?*

   Although each community had a number of ways they defined success, they all focused on giving power back to the community residents and allowing the community to define success in its own way. A number of achievements were mentioned, including strengthening neighborhoods; peace treaties with gangs; teen-pregnancy programs; the Healthy Start program; and planning for the community by the residents. Each of these achievements represented ways in which there was tangible change in people's lives and improvements to their quality of life.

3. *What are the key unresolved challenges?*

   The predominant unresolved challenges included a lack of resources; building trust in service providers; getting more involvement from the community; conflicts resulting from territoriality, which is threatened by collaboration; and navigating the "political waters" of the community.

4. *What are the primary lessons learned?*

A number of key points was emphasized by all of the communities. These included the need to trust community members to make decisions; building trust between community members and professionals; the need to take risks; and the importance of serious commitment to the process.

Discussions of the Results

After the initial community dialogues were held, a small working group or planning committee was formed by the Los Angeles Roundtable for Children to analyze the results of the study. The committee came up with four questions that highlighted the major concerns revealed by these dialogues. These were based on the information secured by the community panelists and the responses to the presentations by the audience members. These questions are as follows:

- How do the communities in Los Angeles County that consider their work to be community-building efforts define themselves and their goals?
- Who is participating in the community-building efforts going on in Los Angeles?
- What kinds of results are being achieved through community-building efforts in Los Angeles?
- How can we encourage and support community-building efforts?

The planning committee then held meetings with members of the roundtable and panelists from the communities to secure further input on these areas of concern. The following represents the results of these discussions:

- People should and do define "community" for themselves based both on shared geography and on feelings of affiliation with others. Administrative definitions of "community" based on political boundaries or service-delivery regions may be a necessity in an area as large and far-flung as Los Angeles County. The environment and boundaries for community-building efforts, however, should be guided by the perceptions and experiences of community members themselves, rather than administrative definitions.
- Definitions of community should reflect the multidimensional and multicultural nature of Los Angeles. Angelenos' perceptions of both geographic and affiliative communities tend to be quite fluid.
- Participants must include a critical mass of local residents who—based on an initial galvanizing experience and reinforced by a continuing sense of need—are committed to a long-term process of community building. The galvanizing experience can be in response to an immediate threat (such as the possibility of redevelopment) or the result of recruitment into a project planned by professionals (parent involvement in schools). However, over time, as residents

realize their own power through joint action, "professionals" must step back and let the process work at its own pace.

- The pace of community-building efforts must be defined by the community members, and it cannot be forced prematurely by "outsiders" or those who control the resources. Service providers and other professionals are accustomed to planning processes that define goals and outcomes with time lines that respond to the needs of funders. Community members have their own sense of timing, which must be honored. There are roles for everyone in community-building efforts, but they are defined by the personal relationships that are created and by the requirements of the process.

- The results of community-building efforts should be judged by different criteria than those traditionally used in program evaluation. Given the scope of activities, the broad range of participants, and the interactive nature of community-building efforts, the traditional evaluation paradigm clearly does not work. Much more experimentation with how to assess results—including using theories-of-change approaches, qualitative methods, and multidisciplinary teams with leadership from community participants—is clearly needed.

- Understanding the context of the community is as essential in assessing results as it is in helping facilitate community-building efforts. It is important that funders and professionals encourage community members to define success in their own contexts, understanding that key achievements in one community may not be important to residents of another community.

The Impact of Network Structures on the Effectiveness of Community-Building Efforts

Of the five communities studied, three (Pasadena/Altadena, South Central Los Angeles, and South Los Angeles) were most effective, while the remaining two (Pacoima and San Pedro) have had limited effectiveness. While there are different reasons for this in each of the communities, the formation of a network structure as a means for collaboration contributes, in all cases, to the effectiveness of these efforts.

The underlying foundation for the formation of a network structure is a broad vision that supersedes individual problems or issues. The vision is based on a perspective of the community as a whole entity rather than one that focuses only on pockets of problem areas. These studies indicate that although an effort may start with one or more issues or specific projects, to be effective, it must move toward a broader vision based on an understanding of the need to provide "coordinated, comprehensive responses to interrelated needs" (Annie E. Casey Foundation, 1995, p. x). According to a study done by the Annie E. Casey Foundation (1995), "Real changes [in community-building efforts] would require fundamental and deep changes in existing institutions and systems" (p. 1). In effect, the study showed that for community-building efforts to be effective, communities need "to design comprehensive system reforms rather than to add programs" (p. 1).

Although people may get together over one or a number of issues, they cannot just focus on a single problem or even a set of problems without seeing them as part of a total bigger picture. They need to see the community as a total picture and to have this guide what is meant by building communities. This means that action must cut across "a broad front and involve many actors" (Annie E. Casey Foundation, 1995, p. 3). No one group can believe that it is the only critical element needed in the community-building effort. Instead, "a truly diverse array of local stakeholders must be involved early, and . . . this expectation must be communicated as early and as clearly and consistently as possible" (Annie E. Casey Foundation, 1995, p. 5). To accomplish this requires the development of "genuinely collaborative governing bodies that can . . . make binding decisions across . . . systems" (Annie E. Casey Foundation, 1995, p. 2).

A shared vision is usually necessary before these possibilities become a reality. This sort of development often leads to a group of "like-minded" individuals. This does not mean that they are the same in background, or even that they agree with each other on everything. It just means that they share a common understanding of why they need to work together. In addition, therefore, an effective community-building effort requires "core leadership that can articulate the initiative, build the necessary consensus, manage the change process, weather the storms, and continually refine and redesign the effort without losing the community's support" (Annie E. Casey Foundation, 1995, p. 11).

The recognition of this big picture and agreement on being committed to collaboration as an invaluable part of the process has led to the strengths seen in Pasadena/Altadena, South Central Los Angeles, and South Los Angeles. On the other hand, not being able to do this has resulted in the difficulties encountered by the Pacoima Urban Village and the limitations seen in the effectiveness of the Barton Hill Neighborhood Organization (San Pedro).

On one end are the efforts of the Community Coalition (South Central Los Angeles) and the Pasadena/Altadena communities and the South Los Angeles efforts. In these efforts, the groups involved recognized the importance of working together to form a new whole and that their actions were mutually interdependent. In the Community Coalition, for instance, they recognized the need to get the social-service agencies involved in the policies of the coalition. They have formed a prevention network, as part of the coalition, which is an alliance of social-service agencies whose primary focus is on welfare reform. This alliance has also served as a learning device for government representatives of what the community is really like and what this means in terms of developing more meaningful and targeted programs of service delivery.

In the Pasadena/Altadena collaboration, this phenomenon is even more obvious. Government and community residents had a long history of relationships that resulted in government representatives taking the lead in forming the FCC. More important, the government representatives formed the FCC based on inputs from the community and have emphasized the collaborative and equal partnership between government and communities in the way that it was organized and throughout its operation. One of the founding members of the FCC emphasized that no one is excluded from the table. Although this often makes the process messy, it maintains the critical focus on the need to actively involve and support all interested members of the community and government. In Pasadena/Altadena, this includes all human-services providers (both public and private); the cities in the area; representatives of the educational, recreational, and police departments; nonprofit organizations; ministerial alliances; people representing the PTA, the Junior League, and others (large groups of volunteers involved with issues concerning families and children); and county representatives.

In the South Los Angeles effort, the Norwood Street Elementary School, although the lead for the Healthy Start program, never saw itself as being able to act unilaterally. Instead, it has made every effort to provide the community members with a primary role in the decisions made, while at the same time providing whatever guidance and support may be needed to move the community forward as a total entity. It has also actively collaborated on an equal basis with various health- and human-service providers and continually looks to involve others in the collaborative effort.

In contrast, the effectiveness of the Barton Hill Neighborhood Organization has been limited, because the residents have attempted to make changes without involving the active collaboration of public officials and private entities. Instead, they see the government agencies and private businesses more as enemies rather than allies. As a result, although they have achieved some gains for the community, these have been limited in scope. In addition, the community members also see themselves as representing separate groups whose interests do not always overlap. This has also lessened their effectiveness in many instances.

The Pacoima Urban Village (PUV) was originally started based on a vision of a total community effort and included as many diverse stakeholders as possible. The difficulties arose from the parents' group, who are a very strong, vocal voice on behalf of their community. They have very strong opinions as to what their families need and refuse to include any individual or organization who will not follow exactly what their vision for the community is. In many cases, this vision has embraced other sectors of the community (foundations, businesses, and professionals). But overall, the parents do not see the need to incorporate the views of most of the diverse groups that make up the total community. As a result, although the PUV is still a viable collaboration, it has had a number of setbacks, as most of the other stakeholders have dropped out, and those that remain are met with stiff opposition from policy makers and funders alike.

Changing Our Perceptions

Many professionals in the public and not-for-profit sectors view collaborations as efforts to be applied uniformly. They understand the phenomena intellectually, but lack the perspective of what they actually mean in practice. One of the reasons this occurs is the result of learning how to organize and manage in traditional organizational structures. The emphasis there is to maintain order through rules, regulations, and hierarchical authority. Although these views are now being challenged in the literature on "learning organizations" (Daft, 1997; Ghoshal and Bartlett, 1995), we are still concerned with creating order in community collaborations. A network structure, however, is not about creating order, but rather allowing for "ordered chaos." An effective collaboration is not meant to be a "feel-good" partnership (such as giving money to a cause), but partnerships that involve change—both internal and external (Ames and Waddock, 1999; Annie E. Casey Foundation, 1995).

It has become clear from the discussions with these communities that our traditional ways of thinking about how to organize and manage need to be changed in order to fully understand what is happening when communities engage in collaborative efforts to foster change. Just as a perception of depth is the result of having two eyes, and thus two slightly different views of the world, so too do we need to add a slightly different view of how we perceive collaboration and what we mean by community building through network structures.

The difficulty of achieving this is reflected in the Annie E. Casey Foundation (1995) report, which indicates:

> The cross-race, cross-sector, cross-discipline nature of New Futures increased the difficulty of the initiative and starkly revealed the different perspectives of various stakeholders. Business leaders often had a limited appreciation of the real day-to-day conditions of the lives of disadvantaged children. Schools and other public officials frequently reacted defensively, quick to take offense and inclined to confuse calls for change with personal criticism. And low-income residents of the community were often suspicious of the integrity of the process. Communication gaps created by the historical isolation of participants from one another were formidable. The sheer lack of experience that most people have in dealing across racial, class, and cultural lines was as pervasive on most of the collaborative governing bodies as in the communities at large. The diversity of language, style, beliefs and interests— at least in the early stages of the collaborative processes—were considerable and needed to be addressed. (p. 4)

What these observations refer to is the way we are very used to, and comfortable with, operating in professions, governments, markets, and bureaucracies. When policy makers, private business representatives, professionals, and community representatives come together in a network structure, they are therefore used to very different norms of behavior. The realities of network structures, however, are relatively new to us.

Network structures may be organized in a number of different ways (such as a board with a chair or as a task force), but it is not these structural differences that are important. Traditional methods of coordination and control are not what is critical to the effectiveness of community-building efforts through network structures. Instead, it is a certain mindset that reflects an understanding of a network structure as a unique institutional arrangement that is needed to operate effectively in a network structure. This has been referred to as a "program rationale" (Mandell, 1994).

A program rationale is a way of thinking that is distinguished from other rationales, or ways of thinking, in other institutional arrangements (professional associations, private enterprises, public-sector agencies). A rationale represents the mindset that theoretically operates in these different organizational settings based on our perceptions of the characteristics that set each one apart from the others. These perceptions are then reflected in our expectations of what is "appropriate" behavior in different settings. For instance, at a professional meeting, we would not expect our colleagues to follow the regulations of an agency they are also associated with. However, when operating within that agency, we would expect the people in that agency to know and follow the relevant regulations. Similarly, we do not expect supply and demand to control actions in a public-sector agency (hence we move to programs of privatization instead), but we do expect this when dealing with a private business. The strength of each of these community collaborations is therefore based on the extent to which the members operate with a mindset that reflects an understanding and ability to capitalize on the unique features of network structures.

Developing a program rationale in a network structure is similar to rethinking how we view traditional organizations as "learning organizations" (Daft, 1997; Ghoshal and Bartlett, 1995). Although much has been written on this revised perspective of behavior in organizations, and many people are putting these ideas into practice, it is a difficult process to move away from the comfort zone of operating in a traditional organization to operating in a "learning organization." The same is true in a network structure. It is much more comfortable to operate in a network structure as if we were still operating in one of the more familiar institutional arrangements. Unfortunately, this type of behavior will, at best, lead to ineffective collaborations and, at worst, have adverse implications for the continued viability of collaborations for community-building efforts.

To operate effectively, people coming from very different backgrounds must learn how to talk *to* each other, not *around* each other. This requires the ability "to step into each other's shoes" and adjust their behavior based on this changed perspective (Mandell, 1994). This is difficult, at best.

Instead of being "enablers"—trying to implement programs based only on their own guidelines and expertise—a program rationale means that the professionals involved in these efforts need to take on the role of facilitators, allowing the community to set the pace and providing guidance and assistance when asked (Luke, 1995) or the atmosphere in these efforts will be one of distrust and frustration. This is not an easy lesson to learn. The professionals' expertise and support are still needed, but they are needed in a revised form. Instead of trying to create an orderly process, professionals instead must be able to accept a chaotic or, at the least, a very different kind of process. Members who are often used to being in charge must also learn how to operate as equal partners across the board. As indicated in the Annie E. Casey Foundation (1995) study, the problem is compounded by formidable communication gaps and a sheer lack of experience of how to operate in this unique environment.

Rather than viewing organizations as only hierarchies, the literature on "learning organizations" emphasizes a "bottom-up entrepreneurial process" (Ghoshal and Bartlett, 1995, p. 89). This process is seen as not "defining, controlling, or allocating," but rather as "developing and diffusing" (p. 89) the competence that is already there. The same thing is true in community collaborations. Communities need strong leaders, but they find these leaders in community members.

Therefore, just as we are relearning how to manage in "learning organizations," we need to relearn what is meant by collaboration in a network structure and the impact of a program rationale on the effectiveness of such an effort. This relates to the need to adapt to the realities of community collaborations.

Adapting to the Realities of Community Collaborations

Several studies on networks discuss the importance of understanding the unique nature of managing in these settings (Agranoff, 1992; Agranoff and McGuire, 1998a, 1998b; Kickert et al., 1997; Mandell, 1994; O'Toole, 1997). These studies reveal not only the need to emphasize the capacities necessary to manage, but also the need to recognize the changing and critical role played by the nongovernmental participants in these settings. This must be done both from the viewpoint of those professionals dealing with these groups and individuals and also from the viewpoint of these nongovernmental actors themselves. Indeed, much needs to be learned on both sides.

In both cases, people involved in a network structure have to start thinking outside the box. Given the scope of activities, the broad range of participants, and the interactive nature of community-building efforts, this will not be an easy task. Indeed, as evidenced by our comfort levels of operating in institutional arrangements other than network structures, being able to operate effectively in a network structure, which relies on horizontal partnerships rather than hierarchical authority relationships, is a new perspective for everyone involved in the process. To be able to do this requires an understanding of two major areas of concern: political issues, and the difference between organizing and implementing.

Political Issues

Given the complex array of actors in a network structure and the complexity of relationships that are involved, it is critical to remember that actions in a network structure will be highly political. Conflicts, resulting from struggles over power and influence, can occur between members of the community-building effort and interests outside the effort, as well as among members within the community-building effort itself. This is often overlooked because of the emphasis on consensus and joint creative decision-making, but it cannot be ignored.

Given the complexities of getting so many diverse members, with so many differing concerns, to work together, it is not surprising that these issues of conflict exist. Within the membership of a network structure, these conflicts relate to the need to revise our perceptions from being in positions of authority to being in positions of partnership. The difficulty is that in many cases, participants see this as a threat to their existing power base, rather than as an opportunity to add to their power base through joint efforts.

Many of these conflicts are often circumvented by being able to build on what has been called "social capital" (Coleman, 1990). Social capital, as used here, refers to the ability to use interpersonal relationships as a form of human capital (Mandell, 1994). This is built up as people continue to deal with one another and begin to form areas of trust. In Pasadena/Altadena, for instance, the participants have worked with each other over a long period of time and have learned the ways in which they can rely on and trust each other. In others, such as in the Community Coalition, people learn over time that they have common bonds that they can rely on (for example, the social-service agencies have learned that they share the same frustrations as the community members in trying to provide innovative solutions to key problems).

When continuing to work together, people do not need to agree on everything. Instead, they need to build up areas of mutual understanding and trust (Mandell, 1994; Podolny and Page, 1997). Based on these small pockets of trust, people can begin the often difficult process of moving from one step to another in the process. Even more important, by building these areas of trust, each of the different partners can unleash even greater power in the process.

In addition to relying on building up areas of mutual understanding and trust through the use of social capital, there is also a need to legitimate the process. In Bryson's (1995) work on strategic management, he discusses the need for "champions" and "sponsors." Champions are those people who have the energy and commitment to sustain the effort. This role is often taken by the community activists who may also start these efforts. By themselves, however, this is not enough. In addition, the community needs to find and align with sponsors—individuals, organizations, or groups who are in a position to legitimize the effort because they are considered the movers and shakers, or those who have the clout to make a difference.

By being in these positions, sponsors can go a long way toward changing the attitudes and perceptions that the formation of a network structure will result in the loss of power and resources by those involved. This is clearly reflected by the board of the Community Coalition effort. Instead of relying on the activists to get the word out, the coalition sees the board as providing the background and support needed by these activists to make a difference. In Pacoima, the PUV ignored the need to nurture its sponsors. Now it has a long, hard road ahead to recover its former strength and standing with these power brokers. As much as they may want to go it alone, the community members in Pacoima are beginning to recognize the need to at least learn how to maintain a foundation for their efforts, which, of necessity, will include participants outside of the community.

This does not mean that people working in a collaborative effort have to give up on their values or beliefs in what they are doing in order to get the support they need. In the Community Coalition, for instance, the executive director has indicated that although the coalition looks for support from a variety of sources, it will only align itself with those groups and/or individuals who are prepared to accept its values.

Organizing versus Implementing

In an article about the Maine Coalition for Education (Ames and Waddock, 1999), the value of a collaborative effort in educational reform is discussed. It is pointed out that there are three levels in the educational system that must be included in any change process in order for it to be effective:

- The *grass-roots* level (parents and community) provides the foundation on which change at other levels can take place.
- The *educational system* (teachers, training, curriculum, school structures, standards, administrators) provides grants and training resources and changes the way it teaches.
- The *public-policy arena* (laws and regulations) provides mandates for schools (for example, changing systems).

Unless all three levels are included in the process, the effort will be nothing more than a "feel-good" exercise. For real change to occur, not only are community activists (grass-roots level) needed, but also efforts need to be included that will impact on the existing structural systems involved, as well as get changes made in the public-policy arena.

The Community Coalition in South Central Los Angeles made it particularly clear that a critical element in its ability to be effective does not rest only with the many well-intentioned citizens who began this effort. Instead, it rests on a two-ponged attack. One factor is the need to find people to steer activities, who have the technical expertise (such as fiscal, personnel, or legal) to meet the needs of forming and maintaining a viable organizational effort, as well as knowledge of who is important to know and how to reach them. These people helped organize the coalition and serve as members of its board. The board is therefore not a pure grassroots board. Indeed, most of the members do not reflect the youth, neighborhood residents, or social-services agencies central to its programs. Instead, the board reflects the people who have the expertise to put the coalition on the forefront of policy-makers' agendas. Coupled with this is the second factor: The need to develop the skills of community residents in how to deal with and get through the maze of bureaucratic government agencies that are still needed to support their cause. The emphasis at the coalition is on continual education and training of the local residents and youth in the community to be able to influence centers of power that are outside the membership of the coalition (the city council and the media have been particularly targeted).

What this points to is the need to rely on community residents to take on a role that they may not be used to. In this regard, the literature refers to the need to "empower" (R. F. Chisholm, 1998; Daft, 1997; Kirlin, 1995) community residents. In the community studies in this chapter, however, instead of looking to empower the community, the emphasis is on "unleashing" the power and potential that are already present. One of the members of the Pacoima effort, for instance, indicated that empowerment assumes that someone outside the community needs to give power to the residents. Instead, residents in these communities find that they already have power and only need an opportunity for it to be unleashed. In each of the communities in this chapter, the emphasis is on this theme and is reflected by the following comments:

- "Professionals will move back and community leaders will move forward." (Pasadena/Altadena)

- "Partnerships are being built but with the community guiding the decisions." (Pacoima)

- "Community has taken ownership." (Barton Hill)

- "The coalition sees itself as contributing to the development of a future social movement by preparing individuals and organizations to speak and act on their own behalf." (South Central Los Angeles)

This does not mean that each of these community efforts has met with equal success in its efforts. In more than one, the ability of the community members to carry out this revised role has met with failure and/or frustrations, particularly in the Pacoima and Barton Hill efforts. These failures highlight the need to understand the importance of moving a community-building effort from the stage of organizing, or setting it up, to the stage of implementation, or getting things done. Because of an inability to let go of old, established behaviors, community-building efforts get stuck in the organizing stage and are never able to move to effective implementation of their efforts.

Food for Thought

This study of five community-building efforts shows how collaborations can lead to a variety of innovative programs. What these studies show that is even more important, however, is that the emphasis needs to be on including all relevant stakeholders of the community and then allowing them to work through the complex processes that will be unique to each effort.

Because we as professionals are eager to help communities, we look for prescriptions or answers on how to achieve change that will be beneficial to communities. Many of us believed that this study would help provide some of these answers. Instead, this study has highlighted a truth that we often overlook. By their very nature, communities are quite different, and thus they will need to work on change efforts in their own way and on their own timetable.

The people involved in the Pacoima Urban Village, for instance, indicated that what is important is "establishing trust and credibility first, and building teams on the basis of the trust and credibility. The products of such teams have been remarkable because they are the result of merging the talents of both villagers and outside resources." They also pointed out that "adequate services are necessary, but not sufficient. It is only when the services are used and viewed as a means *to help build from within* do we consider the services as an integral part of the evolution process" (emphasis added). The key is to begin to understand that the ways in which people in communities collaborate have a great deal to do with their needs and perceptions and not our own preconceived ideas of what should be done.

The effort needs to evolve out of the *perceptions* of the communities and their perceived needs, not out of the perceptions of the practitioners, requirements of funders, or rules and regulations of public-sector agencies. Conversely, the communities need to understand their position in a total environment and the political realities of how to develop and maintain effective community-building efforts.

All participants need to better understand each other's unique positions and learn how to adapt the collaboration to meet this uniqueness. Practitioners cannot apply a cookie-cutter approach to dealing with communities, and communities cannot expect the same reactions from all public, private, and not-for-profit participants. Communities need to understand, accept, and learn how to work with "political realities." And practitioners and private-sector managers need to understand, accept, and appreciate the potential inherent in community participants.

Today many professionals have begun to question the relevancy of their own roles, and those of their agencies or institutions, to parents and communities. We need to begin to grapple with our relevancy. In many instances parents don't see agencies or institutions as part of the solution or even what they think about. These agencies and institutions have become so narrow in their thinking that they don't even know they have become irrelevant. We have now had the experience of learning from community organizations. The question is how this experience will change us.

The participants of the Pacoima Urban Village noted that "experience has shown that the predominant mode of operation of outside agencies is to impose their paradigm on the community. The consequence is that the techniques and processes introduced by them seldom last."

It is perhaps an eye-opener to those of us in the professions that our interpretations of what is happening or should be happening in communities is not always the realities as perceived by those at "ground zero." The perceptions of the communities themselves shape what is and is not considered "real" within these communities. This includes perceptions of who is "real" in a community (parents and children are, service providers are not) and the difference between what outsiders to the community see as "real" boundaries of a community (geography) and what the community sees as "real" boundaries of a community (sense of community). It also means that definitions of "community" need to be expanded to include place (geography), association (social networks), and administration (service programs).

The term "real" as used here has to do with perceptions of the community. To a community member, "real" is "what is important to me." It does not imply that the feelings or concerns of professionals are not real to community members. Rather, it implies that what will have value or impact or be sought after by a community member may be very different from what someone from outside the community may perceive. It is the difference between the views of someone living in a community and those of a professional trying to administer a program. It is the difference between perceptions and stereotypes.

The following examples of views expressed by community members in the Pasadena/Altadena study express this idea best:

- "Though there is a lot of money for services, there are only a few places in the community that people like me can go to, feel comfortable, and be involved. Most of the time agencies think they know best. They feel they know who I am and what me and my family need. Agencies sometimes think that I am hostile when I get in their face. But all I am trying to do is let them know what is important to me."
- "It felt good being asked to help."
- "Someone listened and knew what families like mine needed."
- "Success is different to different people. Some agencies think that because they have been doing the same thing and getting money for it, they are successful. But this does not mean that people are getting better. Success to me is when I trust an agency and many times that is not easy to trust. Success is when I know that my son is being taken care of at school."
- "Success is when I am getting the best services."

Administrative determinations of what is meant by community and how best to serve a community will often clash with what the residents of that community think. Plans and rules laid down by professionals or funders may do more to hamper the process than to help it. This does not mean they will have to be abandoned completely. Instead, personal relationships, activities, and time lines need to be seen as "real" to those in the community and geared to the realities of the individual communities, or they will be irrelevant or ignored.

Conclusions

This chapter is not about prescriptions of what should be done, but rather about how to reshape our perceptions. This includes understanding the following:

- Network structures are not about "creating order," but rather allowing for "ordered chaos."
- Network structures are not about everyone agreeing with everyone, but rather about agreeing to be committed to the process.
- Network structures are not about professionals "parachuting" into communities, but rather about participating with communities.
- Network structures for community-building efforts are not just collaboration, but a new way of thinking and seeing realities.

There is a need to consider the uniqueness of each effort. Although it is easier to try to build a model of success that fits all communities, this "one-size-fits-all" type of modeling does not take into consideration the myriad of factors and events that take place within the context of a community. The context does count in measuring and defining success or results. The pace of community movement is defined by community needs and cannot be prematurely forced from the outside. Finally, as several of the communities indicated, just getting participants to speak to each other and work together on various goals is considered success in some cases.

This means that we will all experience a level of discomfort and a need to "reinvent" how we communicate with each other and understand the processes that are occurring. Although this will not be an easy process, it appears to be one that will have to occur. Indeed, these community studies represent only the tip of the iceberg of the various movements to develop innovative means of delivering services and revising our views of the roles of the public, private, not-for-profit, and community sectors. It is anticipated that in the future, we will all have to develop new ways of operating to meet the increasingly complex problems we will be facing. Understanding the impact of network structures as a unique means for community-building efforts is certainly a good place to begin this journey.

References

Agranoff, R. (1992). *Intergovernmental policy-making: Transitions and new paradigms.* Unpublished manuscript. School of Public and Environmental Affairs, Indiana University, Bloomington, & Instituto Universitario Ortega y Gasset, Fundacion Ortega y Gasset, Madrid, Spain.

Agranoff, R. (1997). *Partnerships in public management: Rural enterprise alliances.* Unpublished manuscript. School of Public and Environmental Affairs, Indiana University, Bloomington, & Instituto Universitario Ortega y Gasset, Fundacion Ortega y Gasset, Madrid, Spain.

Agranoff, R., & McGuire, M. (1998a). Multi-network management: Collaboration and the hollow state in local economic policy. *Journal of Public Administration Research and Theory, 8*(1): 67–91.

Agranoff, R., & McGuire, M. (1998b). The intergovernmental context of local economic development. *State and Local Government Review, 30*(3), 150–164.

Ames, M., & Waddock, S. (1999). Unum corporation and the Maine coalition for excellence in education. In J. E. Post, A. T. Lawrence, & J. Weber (Eds.), *Business and society* (9th ed.). New York: Irwin McGraw-Hill.

Annie E. Casey Foundation. (1995). *The path of most resistance: Reflections on lessons learned from new futures.* Report of study by the Annie E. Casey Foundation, Baltimore.

Bryson, J. M. (1995). *Strategic planning for public and nonprofit organizations.* San Francisco: Jossey-Bass.

Chisholm, D. (1989). *Coordination without hierarchy.* Berkeley: University of California Press.

Chisholm, R. F. (1998). *Developing network organizations.* Reading, MA: Addison-Wesley-Longman.

Coleman, J. S. (1990). *Foundations of social theory.* Cambridge, MA: Harvard University Press.

Daft, R. L. (1997). *Organization theory and design.* Cincinnati: South-Western College Publishing.

Feyerherm, A. E. (1995). Changing and converging mind-sets of participants during collaborative environmental rule-making: Two negotiated regulation case studies. In *Research in corporate social performance and policy, supplement 1* (pp. 231–257). New York: JAI Press.

Gage, R. W., & Mandell, M. P. (Eds.). (1990). *Strategies for managing intergovernmental policies and networks.* New York: Praeger.

Ghoshal, S., & Bartlett, C. (1995). Changing the role of top management: Beyond structure to processes. *Harvard Business Review,* Jan.–Feb., 86–93.

Gray, B. (1989). *Collaborating.* San Francisco: Jossey-Bass.

Hanf, K., & Scharpf, F. W. (1978). *Interorganizational policy making.* London: Sage Publications.

Kabra, R., & Khator, R. (1996). *Alternative regulation and multi-jurisdictional cooperation.* Paper presented at the Annual Meeting of the American Society for Public Administration, Atlanta.

Kickert, W. J. M., Klijn, E.-H., & Koppenjan, J. F. M. (1997). *Managing complex networks: Strategies for the public sector.* London: Sage Publications.

Kirlin, J. J. (1995, winter). The potential to reframe regional policies and institutions in ways that improve governance and address disadvantage. *Regionalist, l*(1), 55–64.

Los Angeles Roundtable for Children. (1997). *Learning the challenges and opportunities of collaborative efforts: The Los Angeles roundtable for children community studies.* Study of community collaborations in Southern California.

Luke, J. (1995). Catalyst, facilitator, negotiator: The public administrator's role in an interconnected environment. Excerpted from J. Luke, *Catalytic leadership: Pursuing the public interest in an interconnected world.* San Francisco: Jossey-Bass.

Mandell, M. P. (1988). Intergovernmental management in interorganizational networks: A revised perspective. *International Journal of Public Administration, 11*(4), 393–416.

Mandell, M. P. (1994). Managing interdependencies through program structures: A revised paradigm. *American Review of Public Administration, 24*(1), 99–121.

Mandell, M. P. (Ed.). (1999a). *Symposium: The impact of collaborative efforts. Policy Studies Review, 16*(1), spring.

Mandell, M. P. (1999b). Community collaborations: Working through network structures. In M. P. Mandell (Ed.), *Symposium: The impact of collaborative efforts* (pp. 42–64). *Policy Studies Review, 16*(1), spring.

Mandell, M. P., & Gage, R. W. (Eds.). (1988). Management in the intergovernmental system: Networks and strategies. Special symposium. *International Journal of Public Administration, 11*(4).

O'Toole, L. J., Jr. (1997). Treating networks seriously: Practical and research-based agendas in public administration. *Public Administration Review, 57*(1), 45–52.

Podolny, J. M., & Page, K. L. (1997). *Network forms of organization.* Unpublished manuscript. Stanford University, Stanford, CA.

Provan, K. G., & Milward, H. B. (1995). A preliminary theory of interorganizational effectiveness: A comparative study of four community mental-health systems. *Administrative Science Quarterly, 40,* 1–33.

Stone, R. (Ed.). (1996). *Core issues in comprehensive community-building initiatives.* Chicago: Chapin Hall Center for Children.

Appendix
Community Responses from the Los Angeles Roundtable
for Children Community Study

The following are the four questions asked of each of the five communities in the study conducted by the Los Angeles Roundtable for Children and the corresponding answers:

1. What kinds of change processes are going on in your community?

A. Pasadena/Altadena

• Unite the Pasadena and Altadena communities. Family Support Network has helped to unite various agencies. Reason for these processes and approaches is that the community has changed with respect to demographic composition and economic status.
• Bringing together many groups with a long history of activity (some with overlapping membership).
• Family/Community Council with goals of (1) strengthening neighborhoods (building a healthy environment for children and families); (2) economic development and opportunity; (3) economic growth; (4) mobilize individual and community resources (i.e., child care, transportation, etc.); and (5) planning and coordination.
• To fill gaps in services, rather than to create new services.
• To build a sense of community from the ground up (not community development or community organizing) from real people, not social-service professionals.
• Empower the community members and have professionals step back—grass-roots involvement.

B. Pacoima

• Strategies being employed: empowering parents/parents taking charge, trusting in the community/community participation, collaboration between organizations/parents/professionals, organizational structure is becoming stronger but not bureaucratic, building on past experience and lessons learned, clear/common vision is guiding progress, dynamic leadership, creative use of resources available, investments in individuals.
• Equal partnership between parents and professionals.
• Parents guide the process.
• Individual successes.

C. Barton Hill

• Empowerment and involvement in community issues.
• Collaboration (general efforts): getting human-service agencies to work together; involving community members; neighborhood organizing; housing/economic development issues related to neighborhood integrity; parent involvement.
• Collaboration (specific efforts): Healthy Start; the Harbor Area Collaborative (HAC); teen-pregnancy prevention; Barton Hill Neighborhood Organization; tight networking with the faith community.

D. South Central Los Angeles

• The Community Coalition seeks to build an organization with enough power to assist in reversing the perception and reality of South L.A. as a disenfranchised community.
• Establishing a permanent community institution capable of recruiting and training youth, neighborhood residents, and social-service agencies to change public policy and improve the quality of life.

- The coalition sees itself as contributing to the development of a future social movement by preparing individuals and organizations to speak and act on their own behalf.
- The specific problem addressed by the coalition is substance abuse. The coalition analysis of the manner in which substance abuse affects the South L.A. community is symptomatic of the social and economic disinvestment.

2. *How is success defined?*

A. PASADENA/ALTADENA

- Success in general: use participants' own definition of success; don't want to help people "be poor better," but not to be poor; collaboration itself is a success.
- Goal attainment: strengthening neighborhoods; economic opportunities; mobilize community and service resources; create a coordination mechanism for planning, problem solving, and advocacy.
- Collaboration and community empowerment: active involvement of youth, parents, church community, etc.; collaboration among the county, the city, and private foundations; empowerment of the community; "professionals will move back and community leaders will move forward"; obtaining trust from parents and other individuals.

B. PACOIMA

- Unleashing the power that exists in the community toward financial independence and self-governance.
- Peace treaty: San Fernando/Pacoima gangs.
- First Chance employment programs for youth.
- Partnerships being built but with the community guiding the decisions.
- Commitment to development of local leaders.

C. BARTON HILL

- Community has taken ownership.
- Gang-related violence plummeted in San Pedro.
- Teen-pregnancy program.
- Agencies buy into the idea that what parents and children say they want is critical.
- Success in Healthy Start.
- Down-zoned community, which made it less attractive to developers (focus on rehabitation, not development); expanded bus service; denied alcohol license at the 7-11 store; social-security office put in rather than a new motel.
- Building self-esteem.

D. SOUTH CENTRAL LOS ANGELES

- The Community Coalition defines success as the ability to win concrete, tangible change in people s life and in the quality of life in South L.A.
- Utilizing a grass-roots organizing methodology, youth, neighborhood, and adults and social-service agencies concretely address the problem of disenfranchisement in South L.A.

3. *What are the key unresolved challenges?*

A. PASADENA/ALTADENA

- Ensuring involvement/voice of children and families in decision-making process; having all feel that their voices are heard.

- Sharing limited resources among many different organizations and managing those resources on behalf of all.
- Building trust in service providers; building consumer confidence in care for children.
- Responsiveness to demographic changes; coping with interethnic tensions; multiculturalism.
- Forces within the community against change.
- Need for facilitation to make collaboration work.

B. Pacoima

- Additional/better training for teachers and other professionals.
- Insufficient funding/resources.
- Challenges/activities for young people.
- Interagency collaboration (government, schools, churches, etc.) still impeded.
- Need for additional leaders.
- Creating jobs in the community.
- Conflicts among many divergent jurisdictions (government, schools, churches, service sectors).

C. Barton Hill

- Difficulties of gang peace across race lines.
- Personality/ego and territoriality, which is threatened by collaboration.
- Implementation of administrative/professional decisions.
- Too many collaboratives—too many meetings.
- Maintaining funding for programs.
- Biggest challenge is welfare reform.
- Race issue: race-specific versus multicultural models.
- Local employment.
- Making the community teen-friendly.

D. South Central Los Angeles

- External: the public policy that led to social and economic disinvestment in inner-city communities; navigating the perilous political waters of any community is an ongoing challenge.
- Internal: developing and expanding the coalition's capacity to recruit, train, and mobilize larger number of individuals and organizations.

4. What are the primary lessons learned?

A. Pasadena/Altadena

- Bottom-up planning works, but it is a bit messy ("like making sausage").
- Success in a partnership between the community and organizations (not led solely by professionals).
- Real collaboration requires work and facilitation.
- We have to build trust and respect between community and professionals. Take the voice of the people very seriously.
- Quality supervision of youth workers makes them a resource.
- Funding is on the "outside of the circle" with the agencies, but not on the inside with the child.
- Maybe we are not "building" so much as "pulling together" the pieces that are already there.

- Personalize understanding of what is going on in the community.
- Celebrate success.

B. PACOIMA

- Identify strengths in the community.
- Focus on the positive aspects.
- Importance of listening to all sides.
- Being responsive to the community's needs.
- Importance of collaboration/sharing.
- Power of trusting one another.
- Commitment to a vision/strong leadership.
- Need to understand cultural environment/translator necessary.
- Importance of a willingness to take risks.
- Passion is not enough—also need action.
- Need to understand cultural reference of families before expecting change.
- Outsiders will be accepted if they become part of the community.

C. BARTON HILL

- Must address specific barriers.
- Shared goals help keep people going in collaboration.
- True collaboration occurs only when everyone makes resource commitments (so that they have a stake in its success).
- Collaboration works best when individuals bring issues to the table.
- Importance of measurable outcomes.
- Gangs are a community-based institution and must be dealt with as such.
- Community supports its own.
- Every partner does not have to agree with everything.
- Importance of the role of the community organizer—need for enhanced training program for organizers in order to have a future generation of organizers.

D. SOUTH CENTRAL LOS ANGELES

- Social and community change is a process that takes a serious commitment of time and resources. Organizations and individuals must have a strategic viewpoint with clear, tangible goals.

9

Creating Networks for Interorganizational Settings

A Two-Year Follow-up Study on Determinants

Renu Khator & Nicole Ayers Brunson

M ANY ADMINISTRATIVE TOOLS EXIST for management of interorganizational settings. Perhaps one of the most acceptable and adaptable is a network. Networks are defined as "structures of interdependence involving multiple organizations or parts thereof, where one unit is not merely the formal subordinate of the others in some larger hierarchical arrangement" (O'Toole, 1997). Networks are usually flat and informal organizations composed of multiple participants, representing diverse organizations, who are attempting to achieve a goal in which they are all interdependent on each other in some way. The interdependency typically deals with a particular issue, such as water management, air quality, or health risks. Issues can be as abstract and broad as global warming or as specific as management of mental-health institutions. Skok (1995) discusses issue networks, which he defines as being "specialized subsystems of varying structural density, some tightly organized into structures" (p. 326). As an administrative tool, networks serve to form and implement a solution.

In this era of limited fiscal resources and increased complexity of issues, networks are seen as a viable alternative to regulation. Needless to say, their growth and acceptance has multiplied over the years. According to O'Toole (1997), one of the reasons for this growth can be attributed to the decentralization of government from the federal to the state level. Prior decades had created a governmental system where federal mandates were followed by grants and other types of assistance to the states and local governments. In recent years, the number of federal mandates has not declined, but there has been a substantial decline in the amount of funds that follows the mandates. Faced with unfunded mandates, local governments are turning to one another for cost-sharing programs as well as to the private sector for partnership initiatives (Brinkerhoff, 1997; Reeves, 1992; Rhodes, 1997). Networks are particularly beneficial in allowing multiple actors with diverse motives to work cooperatively to achieve a common goal (Gage and Mandell, 1990).

Some networks emerge effortlessly, whereas others are products of a concerted effort. Some evolve over time and are not even visible; others are created at a given time and operate under a formal mission. Some succeed and continue, others succeed and dissolve themselves, and still others fail and eventually disappear. A special symposium on collaborative efforts and networks published in *Policy Studies Review* in spring 1999 makes an attempt to explain these variations. In order for networks to be a viable alternative, it is essential that they share some common ground and that their commonality be transferable in some form or fashion. One of the most challenging tasks for network scholars has been to understand the factors that determine, first, the emergence of a network and, second, its success.

In 1996–1997 we witnessed the emergence of a policy network, in the form of the Tampa Bay National Estuary Program, that produced an interlocal agreement. It was an unique effort that brought fourteen different agencies and local governments together to sign an agreement accepting, among other things, streamline permitting and a joint review of environmental projects. We published the results of this effort in *Policy Studies Review* (Khator, 1999a). Two years after the creation of the network and the development of the interlocal agreement, we surveyed more than forty participants to find out what they thought the network was, why they participated in it, what they considered to be the key achievements, and whether they still found their network to be a viable alternative. In this chapter we report our findings. Elsewhere in this volume (chapter 14), there is also a commentary from one of the key participants to add a nonacademic perspective on the issue of network creation and its usefulness. The discussion of the survey findings is preceded by a brief discussion of network characteristics and the history of the Tampa Bay National Estuary Program network. This survey shall serve to further examine network characteristics and the factors that motivate individuals to participate in them. It is hoped that the results will provide additional insight into and further substantiation of the importance of networks in this time of complex issues that transcend traditional boundaries.

Characteristics of Networks

Networks have a variety of characteristics. To begin with, networks must have some *structural stability*, but structures do not define networks. More often than not, networks go beyond formal linkages and ties (Mandell, 1999a). Networks do not have a formal hierarchical structure. Power is not exerted by formal authority, but rather by associations made within the network, as well as who possesses resources that might be scarce (O'Toole, 1997). Skok (1995) states that power within networks is informal, decentralized, and horizontal. It is possible to have many levels of government involved and for power to still be spread throughout the network, because control is exerted less by legal authority and more by need. Individual participants join the network not because they have to, but because they need the cooperation and expertise of other members to achieve their own goals (Cook, 1977). As Whetten (1977) points out, some networks, especially those that are prompted by legislation, are more vertical than others. Members in such a network accept the authority of one member, and the position of that member may influence the future direction of the network. In most cases, however, networks are formed either by a mediator party that brings the group together with a specific goal in mind or by the voluntary effort of some like-interested people who are brought together by the issue itself. In these networks, *dispersion of authority* is somewhat equal, because all members reserve the right to walk away at any time.

Fulfillment of *self-interest* is an important incentive for autonomous participants to join a network. While commonality of the issue brings people together, it is often the attainment of their own goals that forces them to form a network. Members may or may not agree on the common goal when they enter a network, but they almost always see the network as the best way of attaining their own organizational goals. They see networking as the process by which they have shared access to resources. Thus multiplicity of interests or stakes is an important characteristic of a network. The opportunity to leave a legacy also serves as a motivational factor for some participants to become involved in a network. The chance to be able to provide a lasting solution to a problem that impacts a large number of people is appealing to many network participants.

Networks typically have one major player, often referred to as *champion*, who takes the responsibility of maintaining the momentum of the process. Mandell defines champions as "those people who have the energy and commitment to sustain the effort" (1999b). This major player is also sometimes referred to as a "policy entrepreneur" (converter of a problem into an issue), a social entrepreneur, an issue initiator, a policy broker, a strategist, a fixer (problem solver or coalition builder), a broker, or a caretaker. The scope and intensity of the champion role may vary; nonetheless, networks rarely succeed without a champion.

According to Porter (1990, p. 21), *shared vision* and loyalties play a significant role in forming networks: "There are shared professional values . . . there are shared loyalties to states, cities and counties among mayors, business leaders, citizen volunteers, chamber of commerce members, and philanthropists in the implementation structure. There are shared values of citizens in the dignity of employment and an aversion to the economic devastation." The condition of shared vision is not contrary to the condition of self-interest. They can and do co-exist, because the scope of shared vision is greater than the scope of self-interest. A member from a regulatory agency, for instance, may have the self-interest to make certain that environmental regulations put forward by his or her organization are honored fully, and a member from a local government may have the self-interest to ensure that his or her organization is not put under undue fiscal burden caused by new procedural requirements. Nonetheless, at the macro level, they both have a shared vision of protecting the environment and serving the public good. The process of arriving at a shared vision is easier in all-government networks, but the task becomes challenging when private-sector representatives, whose primary goal is to run a profitable business, join networks.

Emergence and Success of a Network

Cigler (1999) examined nine preconditions to network emergence: occurrence of a disaster, fiscal stress, push from the political constituency, supportive capacity building, support by elected officials, perception of advantage from participation, existence of a policy entrepreneur, focus on visible strategies, and emphasis on collaborative skill building. Though preconditions are not the focus of this study, they are instrumental in defining network goals and consequently network success. This analysis puts many of Cigler's preconditions to the test in our case study of the National Estuary Program. In her three case studies, she found that push from the political constituency was not present in any of them, while supportive capacity building, support from elected officials, and early focus on strategies were present in some of them. Existence of a policy entrepreneur, perceived advantages from the collaboration, and the occurrence of a disaster were common preconditions in all of the case studies.

Just as the emergence of a network depends on a number of factors, so does the success of a network. Success is a fluid concept, and in the context of a network, its fluidity becomes even more apparent. A network can be called successful if it succeeds in achieving tangible results such as the production of a joint document, a binding agreement, or a nonbinding treaty. While tangible results are easy to accept, intangible outcomes also count in the success of a network. Among many intangible outcomes, enhanced understanding among participants, more effective implementation of existing policies, and change of paradigms among stakeholders are the most critical ones.

Ring and Perry (1985) suggest three conditions to network survivability: compatibility, resources, and sociopolitical environment. First, the group as a whole must function cohesively. In order to achieve network goals, participants must be *compatible*, functioning together while at the same time meeting their own organizational goals. Second, it is important to examine whether the ability to acquire the needed *resources* exists. Resources that are typically available in a network are the ability to seek joint funds, creative ideas, expertise, contacts, and access to information. Coleman (1990) refers to this as "social capital." If a network does not provide its members with the ability to acquire needed resources, then there is no need for them to continue in the network. Finally, the social and political *environment* in which a network exists helps determine whether it will be successful in reaching and implementing a consensus. If a network is able to find or construct a conducive environment, it can increase the availability of resources for its members, who, in turn, can strengthen their desire to stay and function in it.

Many factors, including turf protectiveness, assumption of authority by one person or group or nonconducive culture, can make a network ineffective. Turf protection becomes an issue when members fail to set aside their personal agendas and misconceptions in order to come together to build consensus on an issue. Assumption of authority by one member is more likely in legislatively mandated networks; however, it is not unlikely in other types of networks (Whetten, 1977). Most often, a single member or group overtakes the network by the sheer weight of his or her position in the home organization, seniority in the network, experience, or outspokenness. Such efforts, intentional or unintentional, can undermine the nonhierarchical character of the network and dwarf the true spirit of collaboration. It becomes the responsibility of the facilitator, if the network has one, to channel the energies of individual members in a constructive way.

History of the Tampa Bay National Estuary Program

In 1987, amendments to the Clean Water Act provided impetus for the creation of National Estuary Programs (NEP). Those amendments specified that the NEPs were to have a five-year existence, during which they were to develop planning strategies for the estuary they served. The Tampa Bay National Estuary Program (TBNEP) was established in 1991. The main focus of the TBNEP from 1991 to 1996 was to conduct research about the bay's most important issues and indicators. These efforts led to the publishing of a document presenting issues and offering solutions for the restoration and protection of Tampa Bay. Up until 1996, the network of scientists created for the TBNEP was a mandated network, fueled by funding from the Environmental Protection Agency (EPA). It was a focused network where members came together primarily for the resources provided by an external force—that is, the EPA.

In 1996, the TBNEP opted to develop a binding interlocal agreement among its stakeholders, which included six local governments (Hillsborough County, Pinellas County, Manatee County, City of Tampa, City of Clearwater, City of St. Petersburg), three regulatory agencies (EPA, Florida Department of Environmental Protection, Southwest Florida Water Management District), and other agencies with relevant interest in the Tampa Bay estuary and related regional mandate to protect the estuary (Florida Game and Fresh Water Commission, Environmental Protection Commission of Hillsborough County, Tampa Port Authority, Tampa Bay Regional Planning Council, U.S. Army Corp of Engineers). The members' vision was to have a duly signed agreement that could place the responsibility of meeting designated amounts of comprehensive conservation-management-plan goals on each member government. The commitment was envisioned to be binding in the sense that a government could be identified and held accountable for failing to meet its part of the goal. On February 12, 1998, the binding agreement was signed by the participating agencies, except for the EPA and the Army Corp of Engineers, which signed two independent agreements.

The process to arrive at the agreement is an example of a voluntary, self-driven, nonhierarchical network. The incentive of external funding was nonexistent, albeit network resources were plentiful to attract the members into the network. The process included a noninterested party, or facilitator. This facilitator organized the meetings and designed the process that evolved through several phases (Khator, 1999b). In the first phase, the facilitator held individual meetings with each of the stakeholders and consolidated a list of their issues or concerns. Two broad groups emerged from this phase: the regulators, demanding complete and strict adherence to their rules; and the regulated, demanding flexibility and consideration of the net environment benefit for their projects. In the second phase of the process, joint forums between the two major groups were organized, and the groups began to resolve their differences. The third phase of the process began with the emergence of a consensus and involved transforming the consensus into a document.

In our earlier published article (1999a), we noted that the role of historical factors was mixed. While there was a history of a scientific network that initially brought the stakeholders together, the sociopolitical environment was not necessarily conducive. In a similar effort in Sarasota Bay, the culture in Tampa Bay did not make it mandatory that participants implement the scientific study.

The TBNEP network can be classified a successful network because it led to a tangible output. The agreement that was finalized in 1997 and formally signed in early 1998 was the first of its kind for an NEP in the nation. It has been touted as a model document and is being emulated in other NEPs. We nonetheless posed a question about its success to participants, because we feel that from their vantage point, they can better assess its performance.

Survey: Tampa Bay Estuary Case Revisited

In October 1999, a survey to assess participant experience and perceptions of the networking process was mailed to forty-two members who had participated in the process in some way. Although only fourteen members formally represented the effort, more than thirty usually attended the meetings. Many participants were staff members who provided critical support to network members. By virtue of their expertise, opinion, and knowledge, they influenced the process and needed to be included in the survey.

Half the surveys were returned in response to the first mailing. All surveys were returned in unidentified envelopes to keep the responses confidential. In order to understand the context of their responses, the survey asked respondents to identify their position: management, legal, policy maker, or technical. Of the respondents, 39 percent classified themselves as management, 28 percent as legal, 22 percent as policy makers, and 11 percent as from a technical background. This accurately reflects the occupational distribution of the population as a whole, and therefore we were satisfied to proceed with our analysis.

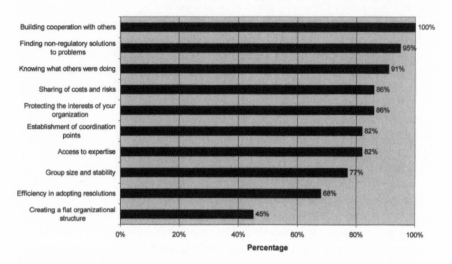

FIGURE 9.1 Factors influencing participation in networks (percentages of respondents identifying each as "very important" or "important").

The majority of the respondents (67%) had been involved in the network for more than two years; only 17 percent were involved for more than one year but less than two years; and only 17 percent were involved for six to twelve months. (Note that some totals may exceed 100 percent due to rounding.) Overall, the range of participant involvement was satisfactory from a survey validity standpoint.

The survey asked the respondents: *"Researchers have identified a number of factors that influence participation in networks. Please indicate how important each of these motivators was for you in your participation in the development of the interlocal agreement."* Respondents were given a list of factors to rate as "very important," "important," or "not so important." The results are given in figure 9.1.

Collaboration emerged as the most important theme in our survey. All of the respondents (100%) considered *building cooperation with others* to be either important or very important, with 83 percent rating it as very important. Considering that a scientific network had been in place for five years, this response is supportive of earlier findings that networks are driven by a shared vision and values. In the case of estuarine water protection, science plays a major role. Managing a bay for its water and sediment quality can be a cumbersome task, especially when the bay crosses over six governmental jurisdictions. However, scientific needs were not the only driving force in the TBNEP network, because 91 percent of the respondents wanted *to know what others were doing* and 82 percent expressed their expectation of *accessing expertise* through the network. While scientists had a network for the previous five years, our study indicates that it was important for policy makers to have the expertise that could allow them to link science to policy making. Respondents also wanted to *share costs and risks* (noted by 86 percent of the respondents) through collaboration. Estuary protection is a classic case of positive cost-risk scenario, because it involves little risk but has great potential for cost sharing. Respondents wanted to work on regional solutions, multi-institutional efforts, and most importantly, streamlined permitting. Streamlined permitting and flexibility were the two most frequently and forcefully made demands by the local governments.

As expected, most of the respondents (95%) also mentioned *finding nonregulatory solutions* to problems as a very important or important factor. More than 90 percent of the respondents chose this as a very important factor in their decision to participate. This confirms Cigler's earlier study (1999), in which she found collaborative skill-building to be a common precondition among all networks.

The most surprising finding was that 55 percent of the members did not find network structure to be an important factor, responding "not so important" to the factor of *creating a flat organizational structure*. Members did not view the dispersion of authority to be an issue, because the Tampa Bay National Estuary Program was not a regulatory body and, as one respondent commented, there was no reason for this network to be anything but flat. Relationships among participants during the sessions also indicated that a certain level of respect and equality existed among participants, despite their serious disagreement over issues. We believe that the preexistence of a scientific network may have diluted the role of this incentive in our survey.

Networks typically have a leader who spearheads the efforts of the network; 64 percent of the respondents identified a champion in the process, although opinions differed as to who the champion was. Since the question defined the champion as someone who keeps the momentum of the process going, some identified the facilitator as that person, while others identified a person with a certain message or vision as champion. In our earlier study (Khator, 1999a), we had noted the definite presence of a champion; however, this survey reveals that participants view champions from their own perspectives. There can be, and often is, more than one champion in a network.

Assuming a decisive role of the champion, the survey asked a follow-up question: *"What characteristics or goals do you feel that this person possessed that led him/her to spearhead the efforts?"* Vision and determination were the most important characteristics, mentioned by 61 percent of the respondents. Twenty-eight percent felt that personal qualities rather than leadership qualities were more critical. The fact that people just could not say no to him or her played a role. Twenty-two percent mentioned forcefulness, and the same number noted personal goals as the driving force for the champion. Our study indicates that it is more important for a network to have multiple people with vision than to have an identifiable champion. Personal qualities of champions, besides being visionaries, are of even less significance. Again, our network had been in existence, albeit in a different form, for several years, and this may have positioned members on a more equal level. This finding is consistent with respondents' lack of emphasis on the flatness of the organization in the earlier question.

Barriers to Networks

Many barriers stand in the way of successful networks. Past case studies identify turf protectiveness, conflicting cultures, personality clashes, budgetary uncertainty, hierarchical structure, and complexity of issues as some key barriers that network participants must overcome. It is because of these barriers that scholars recommend that the assistance of a professional facilitator be sought. Our survey brought some unpredictable results. The respondents found issue-oriented rather than structure-oriented or actor-oriented factors to be the major barriers.

Complexity of the issue itself and *difficulty in developing required actions* were identified by at least 70 percent of the respondents to be problematic or very problematic. Participants acknowledged the overwhelming issue that they were faced with, and this attitude, we believe, explains why the network players sought the assistance of a professional facilitator and exhibited patience throughout the process. *History of noncollaboration* in the Tampa Bay region was identified by half of the respondents as a major barrier. This finding contrasts with the participant perspective offered later in this chapter. While there was a history of collaboration on the Tampa Bay estuary issue, in general, there has been a lack of collaborative history on environmental issues. The perception of noncollaboration may have resulted from an ongoing conflict over water distribution in the Tampa Bay area. During the time of this network building as well as the time of this survey, newspapers have been filled with stories of noncooperation among governments and agencies in the context of water distribution.

Three-fourths of the participants found *turf-protectiveness* and *assumption of authority* by one person or group to be problematic. Most of them did not rank these barriers as very problematic; nonetheless, they found them to be problematic enough for the network. Interestingly, *personality clashes* or conflicts based entirely on likes and dislikes of personal attributes rather than professional standings were mentioned as the least problematic, indicating that the group members worked well together. The network members developed friendships that extended beyond the professional sphere and spilled over into their social lives. Some members had known one another prior to becoming members of the TBNEP network.

We requested participants to identify the strategies or attributes that helped the network overcome these barriers. Some of the commonly cited attributes were the following:

- *Facilitation-related:* keeping the long-range goal in mind, discussion of issues, breaking the issues into smaller steps, and engaging small groups with interest in subissues to resolve them.
- *Participant-related:* common interest, vision of the goal, potential of success, professionalism, hard work, universal acceptance of the value to the program, persistence, patience, feeling of compromise, idea of public good as the ultimate focus.
- *Structure-related:* stability of participants, buy-in by the management.

- *Process-related:* compromise, watering down of requirements, open discussion, good leadership.

Since consensus is the key to network building, we posed a question about the role of various factors in reaching a consensus: *"How important was the role of each of the following variables in reaching a consensus on the interlocal agreement."* All of the respondents agreed that *motivation of parties involved* was either very important or important, with 89 percent finding this to be a very important factor. This finding is consistent with earlier studies, which indicate that actors' motivation is the primary factor in creating flat networks. *Staff support* in providing complete information and *scientific facts* indicating that the problem was serious were identified by 91 percent of the respondents as very important or important. The network was supported by staff members who provided research and information to the group as requested.

The next important factors, with an 82 percent support level for being either very important or important, were *skills of the facilitator* and *role of the champion*. It is interesting that while different respondents identified different champions by name, they thought that whoever they considered to be the champion played a critical role in reaching the consensus. Two other factors that were supported by more than half the respondents included *push from federal and state agencies* and *pressure from peers*. Surprisingly, public pressure was rejected as an important factor by 72 percent of the respondents. The same number rejected the need to find new moneys as an important factor in building consensus. It is worthwhile to note that both of these factors have been touted by previous studies as being important motivational factors in building consensus. The case study of Tampa Bay asserts that it is possible for successful networks to build consensus on the basis of professional and shared values rather than public pressure, as can often be the case in environmental decision-making (Downs, 1972).

Network Performance

The Tampa Bay estuary program's interlocal agreement is an example of a successful network. More than eighteen months later, when asked *"Looking back at the effort, how satisfied are you that the group was able to do the right thing?,"* participants responded with a resounding 100 percent satisfaction level. Eighty-six percent responded that they were very satisfied, while the other 14 percent were somewhat satisfied, and no one thought that the effort was unsatisfactory.

Performance of a network is relative, measured against the organizational goals that the members set forth for their network and the expectations that they individually have when they join it. In the TBNEP network, members had a very well-defined goal: The establishment of an interlocal agreement. More specifically, local governments wanted flexibility in the context of permitting, and regulatory agencies wanted compliance in the context of their individual rules. Streamlined permitting under the rubric of "net environment benefit" afforded the common ground for both camps to achieve their individual goals as well the overall network goal. Similarly, members' expectations were simple: they expected the network to give them access to information and scientific knowledge, expectations that were easy to fulfill, considering that a five-year scientific study had just been completed with the help of funds from the EPA. Members were not consciously looking for equity of access (flatness of the network) or fiscal-responsibility sharing, issues that can force an organization to be politicized.

Conclusions

In this survey study, we tried to answer the following questions: What factors motivate people to work in a network? What factors help them stay in it? What factors help them reach a consensus? And what barriers are confronted by participants? The results reaffirm several observations made by scholars in earlier studies; however, they also shed new light on what works, when, and how.

According to the survey study, networks attract members because they offer an opportunity to build cooperation and share expertise. There is a serious desire on the part of members to find nonregulatory solutions, and this is one of the primary reasons why members engage in the process of network building. The assumptions of self-interest on the part of participants or economic motives on the part of organizations are refuted in our survey. Although these may serve as secondary motives, they are not the primary reasons why members choose to join a network.

While structural compatibility is important to a network, it is not a factor that played a major role in the minds of the TBNEP network players. Our study reflects that members continuously underplayed the role of "flatness" in the network; however, we must analyze the reasons behind this observed nonchalant behavior. A large number of participants in the network were already working in a scientific network and were familiar with one another. The culture that was to dominate the network during the development of the interlocal agreement had already been developed in the scientific network over the past five years. Members had established trust and confidence with one another, even though limited to technical matters only. Our network, in some ways, was an extension of the scientific network. Although there were several new players (attorneys and elected officials, for instance), and the issues confronting the members in the new network were also very different from the science network (strategic versus exploratory), we believe that the foundation for network relations had already been built during the early stages of scientific collaboration. Because of this, the importance of structures in general should not be rejected.

The study reaffirms the belief that champions are critical to a successful network; however, it also notes the possibility that a network can have more than one champion, and that different people can have different champions. In the absence of personality clashes, the multiplicity of champions in our study did not adversely impact the process. However, it must be acknowledged that if network members perceive different people to be champions, and if these champions do not share a common vision, then the survivability of the network can be in jeopardy.

Another important finding of the study is that while the complexity of modern-day issues can encourage members to create a network, the same complexity can overwhelm the members and break a network. Most of the members in our network felt overwhelmed by the complexity of the issue, and some understood that breaking the issue down into smaller steps was important to reach a common ground. The assistance of a professional facilitator in breaking down the complexity of the issue and ensuring an open dialogue is underscored in this study.

Overall, this study suggests that networks must have agility to meet the needs and expectations of their own members. While all networks share some common properties, such as nonhierarchical structure, shared vision, and collaborative attitude, they differ in their goals, histories, and complexity. Successful networks, including the TBNEP, are those that are cohesive enough to find a common objective and agile enough to mold it according to the changing needs of their members. Not all networks are expected to serve the same purpose, and not all should be created alike. It is important for networks to take advantage of their historical contexts (in the TBNEP case, the existence of a scientific network was an important historical context) and develop other needed attributes.

In order to examine the validity and reliability of survey results, we sought the perspective of a staff member. This perspective is found in chapter 14 of this volume as a commentary and offers additional insight into how networks work. The commentary supports the findings in general. We hope that this case study, with its corresponding survey and commentary, enables readers to obtain a better understanding of network functioning.

References

Brinkerhoff, D. W. (1997). *Democratic governance and sectoral policy reform: Linkages, complementaries and synergies.* Paper presented at the American Society for Public Administration, 58th National Conference, Philadelphia.

Cigler, B. (1999). Pre-conditions for the emergence of multicommunity collaborative organizations. *Policy Studies Review, 16*(1), 86–102.

Coleman, J. S. (1990). *Foundations of social theory.* Cambridge, MA: Harvard University Press.

Cook, K. (1977). Exchange and power in networks of interorganizational relations. *Sociological Quarterly, 18*(1), 62–82.

Downs, A. (1972). Up and down with ecology: The issue attention cycle. *Public Interest, 28,* 28–50.

Gage, R. W., & Mandell, M. P. (1990). *Strategies for managing intergovernmental policies and networks.* New York: Praeger.

Khator, R. (1999a). Networking to achieve alternative regulation: Case studies from Florida's national estuary programs. *Policy Studies Review, 16*(1), 65–85.

Khator, R. (1999b). Conflict, bureaucracy and the environment. In R. B. Jain & R. Khator (Eds.), *Bureaucracy–citizen interface: Conflict and consensus* (pp. 61–82). Delhi: B. R. Publishing.

Mandell, M. P. (1999a). The impact of collaborative efforts: Changing the face of public policy through networks and network structures. *Policy Studies Review, 16*(1), 4–17.

Mandell, M. P. (1999b). Community collaborations: Working through network structures. *Policy Studies Review, 16*(1), 42–64.

O'Toole, L. (1997). Treating networks seriously: Practical and research-based agendas in public administration. *Public Administration Review, 57*(1), 45–52.

Porter, D. O. (1990). Structural pose as an approach for implementing complex programs. In R. W. Gage & M. P. Mandell (Eds.), *Strategies for managing intergovernmental policies and networks* (pp. 3–28). New York: Praeger.

Reeves, A. E. (1992). Enhancing local self-government and state capabilities: The U.S. Advisory Commission on Intergovernmental Relations programs. *Public Administration Review, 52*(4), 401–405.

Rhodes, R. A. (1997). From marketization to diplomacy: It's the mix that matters. *Australian Journal of Public Administration, 56*(2), 40–53.

Ring, P. S., & Perry, J. L. (1985). Strategic management in public and private organizations: Implications of distinctive contexts and constraints. *Academy of Management Review, 10*(2), 276–286.

Skok, J. (1995). Policy issue networks and the public policy cycle: A structural-functional framework for public administration. *Public Administration Review, 55*(4), 325–332.

Whetten, D. A. (1977). Toward a contingency model for designing interorganizational service delivery systems. *Organization and Administrative Science, 8,* 77–96.

10

Cross-Sectoral Policy Networks

Lessons from Developing and Transitioning Countries

Derick W. Brinkerhoff
& Jennifer M. Brinkerhoff

THE LAST TWO DECADES HAVE WITNESSED what has been characterized as a worldwide public management "revolution" (Kettl, 1997), which has redefined the basic parameters of government responsibility, operating procedures, and resource allocation. The 1980s and early 1990s focused particularly on redirecting the role of the state away from "rowing"—the direct provision of services—toward "steering," which combines policy guidance, regulation, and contracting for services (Osborne and Gaebler, 1992). As the size and scope of the state have shrunk or been "hollowed out" (Milward and Provan, 1993), the role of nongovernmental organizations (NGOs) and the private sector has expanded (Salamon, 1987, 1989). Governance no longer involves solely public-sector entities. With the addition of new actors and the pressures for more responsiveness to citizen demands, governments are looking for new ways of organizing the task of governance. This search has led to, among other trends, increased experimentation with collaborative and cross-sectoral structures and processes, which have been termed networks. The exploration of networks is expanding at a fast pace (Local Government Management Board, 1995; Mandell, 1999; Osborne and Plastrik, 1997).

Managing governance through networks leads to an expanded set of linkages that connects government to other public agencies, private firms, NGOs, community associations, and so on. Administrative reality is defined by mutual interdependence and negotiated joint action rather than by top-down direction and supervision. As Bogason and Toonen (1998, p. 205) observe, "hierarchical control will be replaced by continuing processes of bargaining among interested parties within most fields of public administration." (See also O'Toole, 1997a, p. 50.) Because of the increased prevalence of networks in public policy and management, it is important to understand them better and to identify their implications for public administration. One source of information and experience comes from beyond the borders of the United States.

The public-management revolution has affected the economies of Eastern Europe, the former Soviet Union, and the developing world, where the failures of government-led development have highlighted the need to scale back the scope and reach of government in the face of excessive state dominance coupled with crippling public-sector incapacity and resource shortages (World Bank, 1997). Also entering the equation have been the increasing number of democratic transitions that have added the voices of formerly silent citizens to the debate. In these nascent democracies, a force for change is the growth of newly empowered citizens' groups advocating a reframed relationship between government and the governed (e.g., Sachikonye, 1995).

This chapter focuses on networks in developing and transitioning countries. It examines three cases of policy networks where governments and civil-society groups are jointly involved, and offers some preliminary lessons relating to the situational variables that constrain/facilitate cross-sectoral networks for policy reform; and mechanisms and processes for bringing together diverse groups to cooperate around a policy issue. The chapter begins with an overview of some of the critical issues related to managing networks involving governments and civil society,[1] highlighting the features of effective networks and the particular challenges for networks in developing and transitioning countries. The next section briefly overviews the three case studies. The last sections analyze the cases and submit conclusions.

Managing State–Civil Society Networks

In broad terms, state–civil-society networks can be defined as cross-sectoral collaborations whose purpose is to achieve convergent objectives through the combined efforts of both sets of actors, but where the respective roles and responsibilities of the actors involved remain distinct. The essential rationale is that these interactions generate synergistic effects; that is, more and/or better outcomes are attained than if the network partners acted independently (Evans, 1996; Lowndes and Skelcher, 1998).

As experience and analysis have demonstrated, managing networks is fundamentally different from traditional public-management's emphasis on hierarchy and control. Networks impose interdependence, yet do not rely upon a central authority. Network partners can and do sometimes have conflicting objectives and seek different benefits and outcomes through networks (Clark, 1997). In addressing these challenges, empirical evidence regarding the relative importance of trust and instrumental rationality is inconclusive (Agranoff and McGuire, 1999). On the one hand, trust is a necessary element of network management. It can reduce transaction costs (Ostrom, 1990), and it is viewed as the prerequisite for the construction of synergy (Evans, 1996). However, others argue that trust among network partners is less important than a shared instrumental view of the network and a corresponding commitment to its objectives (Agranoff and McGuire, 1999, p. 29; Mandell, 1988).

Another issue central to managing networks is how to harmonize and integrate the actions of the network partners so as to achieve the network's shared objectives (see, for example, Machado and Burns, 1998). For individual partners, tensions and possible conflicts can arise from the "insecurity caused by intra-organizational control and the need for intra-organizational implementation of interorganizational compromises" (Börzel, 1998, p. 261). Cross-sectoral policy networks represent another instance where the motivation and management of collective action are central to achieving results, where self-interest and larger purposes need to be aligned (Olson, 1965).

As this brief discussion of some of the issues involved in network management points out, there can be significant obstacles to capitalizing on the synergistic potential of networks. The next section seeks to add some clarity to the analysis of the factors that influence the effectiveness of networks. The additional challenges of managing policy networks in developing and transitioning countries are highlighted.

Clarifying Effective State–Civil Society Networks

The network definition presented above and the discussion of management issues suggest a set of factors that networks need to address in order to function effectively and to contribute to policy implementation. These include specification of objectives and degree of convergence, mechanisms for combining effort and managing cooperation, determination of appropriate roles and responsibilities, and capacity to fulfill those roles and responsibilities.

Specification of Objectives and Degree of Convergence

Logically, the specification of compatible and convergent objectives is the starting point for any network. However, especially in the developing and transitioning country context, this specification is often problematic for a variety of reasons. First is the multiplicity of actors and their broad range of interests. National governments, international donors, international NGOs, local NGOs, and other civil-society organizations all have differing agendas. Development experience is replete with stories of the difficulty of reaching agreement on policy and program objectives. Sometimes the compatibility of objectives is more apparent than real; over time, the hidden agendas often work at cross-purposes with the ostensible ones. The inevitable self-interests of each network actor may interfere with reaching agreement, but self-interest can also be instrumental. Combining self-interested goals with broader, shared goals can enhance the likelihood of success (Kolzow, 1994).

Second is the power differential among the various actors, which arises as a function of differences in resource levels, operational capacity, and political clout. These are particularly salient in cases where international donors are funding the implementation of programs and projects and/or where international NGOs are working with local civil-society groups (Brown and Ashman, 1996). Similarly, national governments are in a significantly more powerful position vis-à-vis local NGOs and communities. The objectives of the relatively stronger partners tend to prevail. But this does not justify any partner's dominance of the network itself, and increasing advocacy calls for partnership on more equal terms (Bratton, 1990; Malena, 1995). In principle, networks are about the nonhierarchical use of power and knowledge (Agranoff and McGuire, 1999; Kajese, 1987).

Third is the tendency for network partners' objectives to shift and potentially diverge over time. Policy implementation is an extended process, and the interests and purposes of the actors involved can change. A classic illustration is when local NGOs initially involved in service delivery begin to want more of a say in policy and resource-allocation decisions (Smith, 1987). Changes of government and staff turnover in government agencies and donor organizations (Perera, 1997) further exacerbate these challenges.

Mechanisms for Combining Effort and Managing Cooperation

Making multiactor arrangements operate effectively is key to the success of any policy-implementation network (Brinkerhoff, 1996a; Machado and Burns, 1998). Managing interdependencies is the *sine qua non* of both policy management and of state–civil-society collaboration. Three interrelated factors that appear critical are discussed here: participation, decentralization, and incentives.

Participation is an important factor for two main reasons.[2] First, from the instrumental perspective of improving the quality of policy formulation and implementation, participation has the following benefits: It leads to better policy targeting—that is, a closer fit between the needs and demands of beneficiaries and the design of policy objectives and modalities. Thus, policy solutions can be achieved more effectively and at a lower overall cost. Participation also can build ownership for policy solutions among beneficiaries and implementors, which can lead to higher use rates of policy goods and services, reduced maintenance and operating costs, and better conformity between policy intent and outcomes. Over time, participation facilitates greater sustainability of policies and programs (Thompson, 1995).

Second, participation is significant from a democratic and good-governance perspective because of its empowerment potential. Increased participation of civil-society groups and beneficiaries in policy-implementation networks can be one of the means by which the accountability, transparency, and responsiveness features of good governance are operationalized and reinforced. Through participation, civil-society partners expand their degree of power not just in the sense of acquiring power that under other policy formulation and implementation arrangements resides solely with government. Empowerment also can lead to a reduction in power differentials and an expansion of power, whereby—as the rationale for networks noted above points out—synergistic potentials emerge and societal problem-solving capacity increases (Brown and Ashman, 1996; Evans, 1996).

Decentralization in its various forms—deconcentration, delegation, devolution, deregulation, and privatization—can be both an enabling condition for the emergence of networks and a means to establish them. Decentralization redefines the relationships between national and subnational entities (regional, state, and local) and between those entities and civil society and the private sector. To the extent that decentralized relationships already exist that support and promote local autonomy and cross-sectoral collaboration, networks can more easily form and operate effectively. In situations where administrative and service-delivery structures remain centralized, networks are a way of experimenting with different forms of decentralization, demonstrating which forms work best under particular conditions, and/or providing operational capacity at the local level in cases where it is nonexistent or weak (Brinkerhoff, 1995). Decentralization can, in effect, create network partners and enhance their capacity, particularly at lower levels of government (Fiszbein and Lowden, 1998).

Incentives are the essential lubricant that makes networks possible. Positive incentives provide the stimulus that impels partners to work together; negative ones discourage them from doing so. Generally, incentive systems must reinforce network identity and the notion of a shared destiny among the partners. This is done when rewards and risks are truly shared. Thus, partners "co-own" network outcomes, including intellectual property and policy-implementation successes, and related credibility, legitimacy, and public trust. More specifically, incentive systems must carefully balance tangible and intangible motivators, recognizing that the relative importance of economic self-interest and value-based motivations may vary from actor to actor (Oliver, 1993).

More specifically, incentives are related to participation in the sense that opportunities for increased participation and empowerment furnish incentives to civil society to enter into networks. Decentralization links to incentives because, as noted above, it changes traditional administrative relationships and encourages new forms of interaction at the local level. Incentives are fundamental to the feasibility of using network mechanisms for policy implementation and to the sustainability of policy outcomes.

Determination of Appropriate Roles and Responsibilities

In the developing world and the former Soviet Union, the state traditionally assumed major responsibility for policy formulation and implementation. Resource constraints, advice and pressure from the international donors and multilateral development banks, international market forces, and citizen demand have all combined to force a fundamental rethinking of the appropriate roles and responsibilities of the state (Frishtak, 1994; Kooiman, 1993; McCarthy et al., 1992; Migdal, 1988; Turner and Hulme, 1997). The expansion of cross-sectoral policy-implementation networks is one result of this process.

In many developing countries, however, the determination of appropriate roles and responsibilities is contested territory, with significant differences in points of view among governments, NGOs, and international donors. For example, governments are often uneasy about the political implications of service-delivery networks with relatively autonomous NGOs, whose grass-roots activities can lead to challenges of state authority (Bratton, 1989b; Ndegwa, 1993). Donor agencies, by favoring programs with NGOs, can exacerbate state–civil-society tensions when governments perceive themselves to be in competition with NGOs for scarce resources (Fowler 1992, 1997). NGOs sometimes view collaboration with government with suspicion, concerned about loss of autonomy or interference. Finally, all actors are on a steep learning curve, testing out and building capacity for new roles and responsibilities, while remaining uncertain as to the appropriate boundaries to this expansion.

Capacity to Fulfill Roles and Responsibilities

Weak capacity on the part of both government and civil society limits the effectiveness of policy networks. The state needs both the willingness and the capacity to respond effectively and appropriately to input from civil society (Brinkerhoff, 1996b; Coston, 1998a; Migdal, 1988). Generally, the institutional capacity of governments varies a great deal and is likely to be questionable in most developing and transitioning government settings. The "New Policy Agenda," whereby donors look to NGOs as implementers of donor-driven development policy (Hulme and Edwards, 1997), has contributed to the weakening of state agencies, as donor priorities have shifted from state capacity building to capacity building of the NGO sector, civil society more generally, and the private sector (Pearce, 1997). Most developing and transitioning governments are also in the midst of radical reforms as they are pressured to pursue political transitions, economic transitions, or both simultaneously. This means that government functions and responsibilities are in flux, a particular regime may not survive through the implementation or even planning of a network, and the morale of government employees is likely to be extremely low.

In addition, the management skills and attitudes that networks require of public administrators are significantly different from those that fit with management in bureaucratic hierarchies. Agranoff and McGuire (1999) review a range of necessary public-management skills and attributes, including assertiveness, knowledge of the organizational landscape, the ability to recognize and tap the comparative advantages of other actors, persuasion and marketing, vision articulation, organizational culture cultivation and management, team building, conflict resolution, coordinating abilities, and transdisciplinary practice. This is a tall order under the best of circumstances; given the limits to capacity noted above, the challenge is particularly daunting in developing and transitioning countries. In addition, network arrangements mean that no single entity is "in charge" in the traditional sense, but many developing or transitioning country agencies remain oriented toward the exercise of control rather than negotiation or influence (Brinkerhoff, 1996a).

On the civil-society side, nonstate actors must possess the capability to insert themselves into the policy-formulation and -implementation process, but in many cases they are weak in these areas. Enhancing the effectiveness of networks is linked to fostering the ability of civil-society groups to address both supply and demand issues. The supply side deals with capacity to handle the managerial and technical tasks involved in implementation networks, including issues of scaling up, responsiveness, and so on (Edwards and Hulme, 1992; Korten, 1990). Demand making capacity relates to advocacy and policy-dialogue functions, as well as policy monitoring and the ability to interact with policy makers and public-sector implementors to promote accountability and transparency.

Both supply-side and demand-side civil-society capacities are problematic in developing and transitioning countries. On the supply side, many organizations are inexperienced and have limited opportunities to cultivate technical and managerial capacity. However, the situation has gradually improved through donor support and linkages with international counterparts.[3] The demand side remains a more entrenched challenge. This is in part due to its reliance on government tolerance for demand-side activities. In many countries, individuals and associations engage in activities to influence others at great personal risk. In newly opened regimes, civil society lacks the history and experience upon which to build demand-side capacity. In some instances, particularly in the former Soviet Union, the absence of any tradition for such activity is a cultural constraint that can inhibit individuals from even considering the possibility of engagement (Coston and Butz, 1999).

Three Case Illustrations

This section briefly presents three cases of state–civil-society networks.[4] Each focuses on economic-policy reform. In each one, civil-society groups interacted with public-sector agencies and officials in a variety of ways, ranging from policy advocacy, to policy analysis, to participation in policy formulation and implementation. Two of the cases are from Africa; one addresses regional livestock trade, and the other concerns the policy environment for private-sector activity. The third case deals with small- and medium-enterprise (SME) policy reform in Bulgaria, one of the East European transition economies.

Sahel Regional Livestock Trade Reform

In the African Sahel, the efficiency of commercial livestock trade is significantly constrained by the prevalence of corrupt practices associated with government regulation of cross-border trade. In 1991, the World Bank and the U.S. Agency for International Development (USAID) jointly financed the formulation of an action plan to improve the efficiency of livestock trade by lowering administrative barriers to intercountry commerce. The action plan's implementation began with a pilot effort in three countries: Mali, Burkina Faso, and the Ivory Coast.

The plan presented an integrated approach to reform that builds upon the convergent interests of government, whose leaders would like to see their economies grow, and civil-society actors, who are the direct beneficiaries of reform. These latter include livestock producers and traders, professional organizations, private transporters, and the consumers of livestock products in each of the three target nations. It addressed a politically charged topic (reducing corruption) in the context of a universally accepted objective: The promotion of regional economic integration. Its proposals to reduce corruption focused upon limiting opportunities for rent seeking through reduction of regulation.[5]

To implement the plan, national coordinating committees were established, made up of government officials from a variety of ministries or agencies and civil-society actors representing stakeholder groups in all three countries. While the network was at first a largely informal, *ad hoc* forum for the discussion and elaboration of a reform agenda, in less than a year the committees obtained legal recognition. Thus the network took on a formal identity.

Progress on the reform agenda took place during a period of major change.[6] The dynamism in the environment required a high degree of flexibility from the coordinating committees, which placed a premium on strategic skills. These are important because progress on reforms often engenders countermeasures aimed at recovering lost revenue or privileges, which then need to be dealt with by the reformers. For example, in Burkina Faso, the suppression of one set of levies was met by efforts to reimpose those same fees under another rubric. Similarly, in Mali, when livestock traders contested the imposition of fees for services provided by customs brokers, the brokers organized an effective political defense of their interests. Unable to obtain suppression of the brokers' levy, livestock traders shifted tactics and organized a campaign to broaden and improve service delivery by customs brokers.

Despite some setbacks, however, the network enhanced the prospects for reform success by ensuring that the principal stakeholders—winners and losers alike—could play a structured role in the policy-implementation process. Although demand making and advocacy were not an explicit focus of the network, the committees have proven to be an effective counterweight to the tendency of African governments to deliberately exclude or marginalize nonelite groups from the policy process.

The West African Enterprise Network

At a 1991 conference that focused on the business climate in West Africa, one of the issues raised was the need to modify the policy environment to make it more supportive of business. Many countries have policies, regulations, and procedures that hamper private-sector operations. African conference participants recommended the establishment of a coalition of the region's private sector to work on advocacy for policy reforms and to dialogue with government officials. USAID initiated a project to set up such a network with the dual objectives of improving the business climate in member countries and promoting regional cross-border trade and investment.

Over the past eight years, thirteen national networks of entrepreneurs and a regional network structure were created. Network members are typically second-generation entrepreneurs, generally educated abroad with a preexisting set of international contacts, who have invested their personal equity in their enterprises. They tend to be innovative, aggressive, and impatient with the pace of change in their countries, and willing to finance their participation in the network out of their own pockets. The Enterprise Network started with 20 donor-selected representatives from eight countries, and grew to comprise around 350 locally designated members in thirteen countries.

Initially the national networks were informal entities, but most of them formalized their status as registered NGOs or nonprofit corporations. As part of their strategic-planning process, each national network identified policy reforms, articulated policy positions, and undertook actions to promote the reforms. In most of the networks, these action plans began with internal mobilization around a policy agenda, followed by lobbying of government and donor officials. Later, however, national networks engaged in partnership activities, such as participation with government officials in joint task forces to explore policy options, organization of policy-debate forums and roundtables, and provision of comment and review of proposed legislation and regulations.

Some national networks are more dynamic than others. Differences emerged in the effectiveness of network leadership, the relative strength of members' participation in planned activities, and the relative progress of country governments toward democratization. The networks in Ghana and Mali have made the most progress. In Burkina Faso, where the government has authoritarian tendencies, the network members proceeded gingerly with the pursuit of an advocacy agenda. The potential of the Enterprise Network has been limited to date by government mistrust both of the private sector specifically and of civil-society groups generally. Organizing autonomously for any purpose has, until recently, been viewed by the state as a possible threat. The state-dominated, corporatist sociopolitical systems that historically dominated postcolonial Africa have impeded the development of formal associational activity (Bratton, 1989a; Moore and Hamalai, 1993).

Small- and Medium-Enterprise Policy Reform in Bulgaria

In recognition of the importance of SMEs to economic growth in the region, USAID sought to improve laws and policies that promote competitive private-sector growth. USAID targeted assistance to creating a policy-dialogue process involving the stakeholders in Bulgaria's SME sector, beginning in early 1997, through collaboration with a new organization, the Bulgarian Association for

Building Partnership (BAP). The BAP developed a SME action plan and a coalition-building campaign that led to a coalescing of support for SME reform nationwide from over fifty private-sector groups. In the meantime, public outrage over the failure of government led to the collapse of the socialist government, and a reformist government came to power in the spring of 1997. The new regime was much more open to change, and subsequently adopted the BAP platform as part of its economic-restructuring package submitted to the National Assembly in the summer of 1997.

The success of the coalition-building campaign and the new openness of the government led to the formation of a SME policy-reform network that linked civil society and the state. A "trialogue" strategy evolved, bringing together three categories of actors. The first two are civil-society entities: business associations and policy research/advocacy think tanks. The third group is composed of members of the public sector: government officials and parliamentarians. The three nodes of the network have pursued a diverse program that concentrates on effective interest aggregation among SME stakeholders; high-quality technical information and policy analysis; and open and receptive public administration.

Interest aggregation progressed significantly with the formation in mid-1997 of a national coalition of business associations, called the National Forum, intended to be a policy-advocacy entity with the capacity to both lobby government and cooperate with it in the development of critical legislation. The BAP, chosen as coordinator, subsequently oversaw the establishment of a working group to develop a strategic plan.

Work on policy analysis has focused on support to local think tanks to undertake analyses and develop position papers. The think tanks work in close collaboration with the members of the National Forum and are carefully building linkages with government that provide them with a seat at the table for policy discussions while preserving their independence. Over the past year, think tanks have participated actively, along with business associations, in the development of the National Strategy for SME Development.

On the public-sector side of the network, the range of actors has included the Public Information Working Group of the Council of Ministers, the Economic Commission of the Bulgarian Parliament, the Bulgarian National Assembly, the Agency for SMEs, the Foreign Investment Agency, and the Agency for Mass Privatization. The unifying theme of their activities is increasing openness, access, and participation. For example, during the summer of 1997, members of the Public Information Working Group undertook a study tour to the United States to increase their capacity in public relations and information dissemination. The Economic Commission organized a roundtable discussion on the Law for Foreign Investment. The National Assembly put together and promoted a handbook containing biographical data and contact information for members of parliament, a list of parliamentary commissions, lists of constituencies and parliamentary groups, and names of assembly leadership.

In the fall of 1997, as part of the process of developing the National Strategy for SME Development, the Economic Commission convened a series of seven participatory regional town-hall meetings around the country to bring together SME stakeholders, government officials, and parliamentarians to discuss policy issues and strategy. These public forums were managed by a joint civil-society–government working group. A team drawn from the working group drafted a policy paper, building on the outcome of the town-hall meetings. The draft strategy was reviewed by a cross-sectoral joint committee in January 1998, revised, and finalized, and then a national summit was organized by the Economic Commission and the Agency for SMEs, attended by nearly three hundred participants from government, civil society, the private sector, and international donors. This type of participatory, structured policy debate was a first for Bulgaria. Following the summit, a small cross-sectoral working group drafted legislation for SMEs, which in July 1998 was submitted to and accepted by the Council of Ministers. Further "trialogue" among members of the network has continued throughout 1999, building on the successes achieved so far.

Situational Variables Influencing State–Civil-Society Networks

The literature and the cases suggest several situational variables that condition both the emergence and the degree of success of state–civil-society networks. Four are reviewed here.

Regime Type

A fundamental variable is the type of regime, which influences the nature of the state, state relations with civil society, and the "space" available to civil society (Fisher, 1993; Frishtak, 1994; Rothchild, 1994). The ability of civil society to play a role in either service provision or mobilization and expression of demand depends on the larger politicobureaucratic setting. As a rule, democratic political systems offer a more supportive enabling environment for state–civil-society networks than authoritarian or limited democratic forms of government (Diamond, 1994). Weschler's (1999) extensive review of policy influence in Latin America and the Caribbean concludes that where there is low tolerance for institutional pluralism, local organizations tend to focus on linking with international donors or other international advocacy organizations to build external pressure for reform. Under conditions of moderate government tolerance, local organizations tend to concentrate on small-scale demonstration of the merits of reform. Only in high-tolerance contexts, as found in relatively democratic regimes, can local organizations fully participate in formulating and openly advocating policy. (See also Bebbington, 1997; Foley and Edwards, 1996.)

The three cases support these observations. The Sahelian livestock coordinating committees depended upon the willingness of the three governments involved to remain open to civil-society participation in the policy-implementation process. The West African Enterprise Network members experienced more or less success in organizing and pursuing a dialogue with the state depending upon the degree of democratization and government openness to citizen input, with Ghana and Mali at one end of the spectrum and Burkina Faso at the other. The effort in Bulgaria began under a government that was relatively unreceptive and unresponsive to citizen involvement; little progress on the partnership was made until a reformist administration came to power. All three cases are characterized by relatively democratic regimes.

However, networks do not have to wait until democratic regimes come to power. Networks can serve as demonstration efforts that help "push the envelope" of the possible. This is one of the ways that sector-specific networks can contribute to encouraging democratic governance (Brinkerhoff, 2000). Further, as Coston points out, "Governments are not monolithic. Regimes of all types may incorporate agencies and actors that are more cooperative or repressive than the overall regime" (1998b, p. 364). This means that though regime type is important, especially for scaling up of networks and for their sustainability, finer-grained assessment is called for to determine the degree of receptivity and responsiveness of the particular public-sector entities that could be potential partners.

Level of Trust

Networks are on occasion uneasy collaborations, both from the government and the NGO–civil-society sides (Coston, 1998b; Farrington et al., 1993). The level of trust among the network partners influences their willingness to initiate a network and to work together over time (Tendler, 1997). Trust is considered a prerequisite for the production of synergy (Evans, 1996). Because initial trust levels are likely to be low, they must be reinforced by accountability and transparency—features that are more common in democratic regimes, and ultimately through experience.

State actors tend to be concerned that the very features that give NGOs and community groups their grass-roots advantages also provide a potential springboard for political activity. In some cases, governments are sensitive to the presence of NGOs in service-delivery and technical-assistance roles as implicit criticism of their lack of capacity to fulfill those roles.[7] In other instances, governments are resentful of the donor-resource flows going to NGOs.

From their side, NGOs and community groups are often suspicious of government intentions. Despite rhetoric to the contrary, NGOs are usually approached for contributing resources and skills to service delivery and project implementation, not for their expertise, analytical perspectives, or representativeness for policy and project design (Clark, 1990; Garilao, 1987). Further, they are rankled by government attempts to monitor and control their activities, often perceiving such efforts as unwarranted interference (Edwards and Hulme, 1992; Fisher, 1993; Ndegwa, 1993). Networks can appear too constricting compared with the relative freedom of independent grass-roots programs.

The trust issue emerges as important in all of the cases. The experience of the national coordinating committees in the Sahelian regional livestock case illustrates a pattern where trust levels rose and fell, and then had to be renegotiated. In the West African Enterprise Network case, the caution exhibited by the founders of the national networks during start-up reflected their concern for building trust with their government interlocutors. National networks formalized their structures into full-fledged NGOs only when they were convinced that government did not perceive them as potential political threats. In Bulgaria, both sides of the network were initially wary of the motives and intentions of the other; the shared experience of collaborating has led to greater trust among the partners.

Legal Framework and Regulation

The presence of a supportive legal and regulatory framework is another important factor conditioning state–civil-society networks. This factor is related to the other two. Nondemocratic regimes tend to have restrictive regulations applying to NGOs and local associations. Conversely, through supportive legal frameworks, democratic regimes can create entities with which to partner, such as through decentralization and empowering local government or through the creation and enforcement of the basic freedoms of association and speech. Oppressive regulations are manifestations of lack of trust in NGOs; they are often implicitly designed to limit political activity by NGOs although ostensibly justified as safeguards against corruption and financial malfeasance (Clark, 1997).

This factor is central to the Sahelian livestock policy case in that a major focus of the network has been to review and revise the legal and regulatory framework for regional trade in order to make it more open and responsive, and less susceptible to rent seeking. It emerges in the Enterprise Network both as a target of the networks themselves and as an influence on the development path of the networks, whose members sought initially to remain small and informal so as to avoid legal and regulatory problems. In the Bulgaria case, the legal framework for SMEs is an explicit focus of the network's joint efforts, along with a new and more participatory approach to policy and legislative development.

Besides laws and regulations applying to NGOs and community groups, the legal framework for the public sector is also critical to the ability of government actors to enter into networks. In the Sahelian livestock case, a key target of reform has been the rules governing how the public sector interacts with private-sector interests and NGOs. In Bulgaria, the new regime has made a strong commitment to new procedures and rules that have increased transparency, shared information flows, and access to public officials.

The Nature of the Policy to be Implemented

The potential for successful state–civil-society networks is also influenced by the characteristics of the policy that the network seeks to implement. Policies vary in terms of the degree of technical expertise required, the time frame within which results and impacts occur, the array of interests affected, and their distributive consequences. These features shape the determination of appropriate roles and responsibilities of the network members and are important for capacity and incentive issues as well (Gustafson and Ingle, 1992). Other policy/issue features can also impact the relative effectiveness and/or ease with which networks can be implemented. Issues that pose the least threat to vested interests, those with implications for fewer government ministries (Mawer, 1997), and those that operate at local levels (Fiszbein and Lowden, 1998) will be less problematic.

While all three cases targeted economic-policy reform, where incentives and interest groupings are relatively more straightforward than in social-policy reforms, each specific policy issue incorporated technical, interest group, timing, and scale features that influenced the ease of implementation. For example, regarding the degree of technical expertise, the civil-society participants in the Sahel livestock policy committees consisted of members of livestock herder and transport associations, marketing groups, and butchers associations. They all possessed in-depth knowledge of the technical issues involved, in some cases to a greater degree than their government counterparts. Thus, civil-society participation in the committees contributed greatly to the success of the reform implementation not simply by representing demands to public officials, but also by ensuring the technical correctness of proposed solutions.

The Sahelian livestock policy case also illustrates the influence of the array of interests and the distributive aspects of policy. Livestock policy touches on a broad range of stakeholders. Because livestock trade is an important component of the economies of the three countries involved, the distribution of benefits and costs is a critical concern. Two important issues over the life of the network arose: How to manage a policy-dialogue process with a large number of participants, and how to keep the process on track when various interest groups—particularly those with vested interests—sought to bend (or in some instances hijack) the process to fit their particular purposes.

The interest-array factor also emerged in the Enterprise Network case in terms of the incentives for organizing around a particular policy agenda. The formation of the national networks required a flexible approach to agenda setting in order to galvanize members so as to stimulate and maintain their commitment to pursuing policy dialogue and network initiatives. Because the civil-society side of networks often involves voluntary collective action, successful policy-implementation networks must pay attention to crafting an agenda and actions that solicit and hold the interests of the nonstate partners, whose contribution is usually noncompulsory and nonremunerative. The complexity of the cross-national component of the Enterprise Network has necessitated informal coordination and linkages (see below).

In the Bulgarian case, the partnership's formulating and vetting of the National Strategy for SME Development illustrate how the technical expertise of the business community was brought into the process. Further, the participatory arrangements ensured that the policy's formulation addressed the panoply of stakeholder interests as part of the development process. Timing was an important factor with respect to credibility of the new regime. The network afforded the government an opportunity to quickly demonstrate its departure from business as usual—specifically, its priorities of responsiveness and inclusion. While a number of government agencies was involved in the network, it was unified in its position and objectives (promoting economic reform and maintaining open and receptive public administration), thus simplifying the network's implementation.

Effective Network Mechanisms and Processes

It is not suggested that the examples summarized here are representative of the full range of state–civil-society network possibilities. Much further analytic work remains to be done. A few concluding points regarding network mechanisms and processes emerge from the discussion.

Ad Hoc *versus Formalized Mechanisms*

All three cases demonstrate a movement from *ad hoc*, informal to formalized mechanisms or structures with increasing complexity, while at the same time maintaining sufficient informal processes to allow for flexibility and responsiveness to changing contexts. This informal approach appeared to be successful in engaging state actors for purposes of policy dialogue, advocacy, and design with civil society. It permitted a "testing of the waters" of cooperation by both sides without committing either one to a formalized path until trust and agreed-upon modes of interaction could be developed.

The Sahelian livestock case began with an *ad hoc* forum for discussion and later became formalized national coordinating committees with legal recognition, once trust levels and potential effectiveness were established. The committees remained flexible in a period of dynamic change and were able to effectively respond to countermeasures to proposed reforms. Similarly, the West Africa Enterprise Network began as a collection of informal associations, which later became formal, registered NGOs. The network is now composed of thirteen national networks and one regional network in West Africa. The Enterprise Network model has been applied to other parts of Africa, with burgeoning networks in East and Southern Africa. Finally, in Bulgaria, the network began with an action plan championed by one organization, which later became a formal policy platform endorsed, promoted, and further developed by a trilateral network. Individual "nodes" have formalized, such as the National Forum for interest aggregation, but the network itself has remained loosely organized. This affords opportunities to converge and diverge for action as needed, as the various civil-society–government working groups demonstrate.

Network Initiation and Evolving Government Receptiveness

It is interesting to note that in none of the three cases reviewed here did the government initiate the partnership. The major impetus for the creation of the networks came from international donors. In the Sahelian livestock action plan and the Enterprise Network, the initiative quickly passed to the civil-society actors involved, and it was they who pressed ahead to define their agenda and make progress. In the case of the Bulgarian SME policy reform, initial donor-supported work with business associations laid the groundwork for the network, and once the reformist government came to power, it was supported by all sides of the "trialogue." The government subsequently initiated participatory regional town-hall meetings, managed by joint civil-society–government working groups.

The cases support Weschler's (1999) findings in that demonstration effects led to increasing opportunities for civil society to engage directly with government through the policy networks in the Sahel and West Africa; and an opening of the regime in Bulgaria led to actual government initiation of direct civil-society–government engagement, though this effort could build on the foundation previously established. The cases confirm the fact that governments in the developing world and in transitional economies are, for the most part, still relatively mistrustful of civil society and tend to retain vestiges of old attitudes concerning the primacy of the state. The state, left to its own devices, does not tend to seek out network arrangements with civil society and in many cases views NGOs at least with suspicion, if not hostility. Democratizing regimes, however, are more disposed to respond to demands from civil-society groups for more involvement and thus may be less likely to resist partnering through networks.

Much remains to be done to move governments to the point where networks become more widely employed for policy implementation and development (Coston, 1995; ODC and the Synergos Institute, 1995; Osaghae, 1994). Further lobbying, education, and experimentation are called for. There continues to be a role for international donors in promoting and funding efforts to engage civil society in policy networks—both in the initiation phase and later in formalizing them and moving toward sustainability (ODC and the Synergos Institute, 1995). These cases, and the literature, underscore the importance of champions to advocate for experimenting with networks (Brinkerhoff, 1996b).

Coordination and Linkages

The success of state–civil-society networks depends upon coordination of effort and effective linkages among the actors involved. Getting groups to work together is not easy, and a significant amount of analytic effort has focused on this question (Alexander, 1995; Börzel, 1998; Brown and Ashman, 1996; Kooiman, 1993). In Bulgaria, the network operates with relatively diffuse linkages among the nodes, each node having a clearly articulated and accepted emphasis. Thus each node concentrates on its own mandate, and the trialogue occurs and is structured as needed through joint civil-society–government working groups. The combination of structure and flexibility has enabled the network to focus on a broad and complex reform effort, while each sector has respected its own and the others' identities and comparative advantages.

The Sahelian livestock and Enterprise Network cases illustrate the complexity of not simply cross-sectoral coordination, but also cross-national. Critical to moving the livestock action plan forward have been the efforts of the national coordinating committees in the three participating countries to orchestrate the efforts of their members to reach agreements, resolve disputes, and implement agreed-upon steps. Similarly, the Enterprise Network supports both individual national networks as well as a regional set of actors to engage in policy dialogue. These two cases suggest the value of informal coordination and linkages as appropriate to deal with a fluid and evolving policy-dialogue process, with multiple stakeholders.

Policy Networks: The Challenge and the Promise

The cases reviewed demonstrate the challenges particular to initiating and implementing networks in developing and transitioning countries. These include a multiplicity of actors, power differentials that put governments and donors in the driver's seat, changing contexts and agendas (which in some cases can lead to enhanced opportunities, as in Bulgaria), unclear sectoral roles and responsibilities, and extensive capacity limitations. Owing to these challenges and the contested nature of respective roles in these evolving contexts and governance models, all of the networks proceeded incrementally, starting from smaller-scale informal efforts and culminating in formalized, sometimes highly technical, collaborative bodies.

Indeed, the cases offer important lessons for initiating and implementing policy networks. These success stories were all heavily impacted by the regime type in which they operated and the corresponding legal frameworks. The degree of openness and government tolerance for institutional pluralism determined initial strategies. While donors played a key role in initiating each of the networks, as trust was built, incentives were clarified, and potential effectiveness was determined, the strategies evolved accordingly, with donors taking a backseat and government and civil-society actors coming to the fore. All of the cases employed an interesting evolution from informal to more formalized mechanisms, while at the same time maintaining a careful balance between formal and informal processes to allow for flexibility and responsiveness. In most instances, economic-policy reform is relatively clear in its objectives and stakeholders. However, the precise micropolicy reforms pursued, the timing, and the scale of reforms were important determinants of opportunities, structure, and the flexibility required for responsiveness.

Besides generating better technical-policy solutions, particularly in situations where state capacity is limited, such as the developing and transitioning country cases reviewed here, state–civil-society networks can promote more responsive, transparent, and accountable government, and can facilitate increased citizen participation in public affairs, empowerment of local groups to take charge of their livelihoods, and capacity to advocate for policy reforms with public officials and political figures. These democracy-enhancing potentials are not automatic, and public managers face complex issues of interest-group pressures, procedural dilemmas, and the "no one in charge" challenge in operating within networks.[8] Such networks, however, are an increasingly common feature of the governance landscape around the world.

Acknowledgment

This chapter draws upon research supported by the U.S. Agency for International Development's Center for Democracy and Governance through the Implementing Policy Change Project, Phase 2. The views expressed are solely those of the authors and should not be attributed to USAID.

Notes

1. The term *civil society* "encompasses a wide range of private associations well beyond NGOs" (ODC and the Synergos Institute, 1995, p. 2). Diamond defines civil society as referring to formal and informal groups of "citizens acting collectively in a public sphere to express their interests, passions, and ideas, exchange information, achieve mutual goals, make demands on the state, and hold state officials accountable" (1994, p. 5). For an extensive overview of the literature, see Coston (1995).

2. There is a huge literature on participation, which is beyond the scope of this chapter to explore. See, for example, the review in Brinkerhoff with Kulibaba (1996).

3. One of the more interesting recent developments with respect to civil-society capacity-building is the International Forum on Capacity Building (IFCB). IFCB is a partnership between developing and transitioning country NGOs, international NGOs, and donors for the purpose of better meeting the capacity-building needs of local NGOs. Information about the IFCB's history, agenda, and regional activities can be found at the IFCB homepage: <http://www.ifcb-ngo.org/index/html>.

4. More extensive discussions of the cases can be found in other sources. On Sahelian livestock policy, see Kulibaba (1996). For more on the Enterprise Network, see Orsini et al. (1996). Regarding Bulgaria, see Brinkerhoff et al. (2000).

5. Rent seeking is the illicit solicitation of unofficial payments by public agents in the performance of their official duties.

6. This included advances toward democratization, public pressure for reform, ongoing structural-adjustment programs, greater public-sector accountability in each of the three countries, and in January 1994, a massive devaluation of the region's common currency, the CFA franc.

7. As one eighteen-country assessment found, African governments are not uniformly receptive to NGO participation in ENR management (Brown et al., 1993).

8. The interplay between democracy and the administrative and implementation issues analyzed here in a developing-country context also emerge in U.S. networks (see O'Toole, 1997b).

References

Agranoff, R., & McGuire, M. (1999). Managing in network settings. *Policy Studies Review, 16*(1), 18–41.

Alexander, E. R. (1995). *How organizations act together: Interorganizational coordination in theory and practice.* Amsterdam: Gordon & Breach Publishers.

Bebbington, A. (1997). New states, new NGOs? Crises and transitions among rural development NGOs in the Andean region. *World Development, 25*(11), 1755–1765.

Bogason, P., & Toonen, T. A. J. (1998). Introduction: Networks in public administration. *Public Administration, 76*(2), 205–227.

Börzel, T. A. (1998). Organizing Babylon: On the different conceptions of policy networks. *Public Administration, 76*(2), 253–273.

Bratton, M. (1989a). Beyond the state: Civil society and associational life in Africa. *World Politics, 41*(3), 407–430.

Bratton, M. (1989b). The politics of government–NGO relations in Africa. *World Development, 17*(5), 569–589.

Bratton, M. (1990). Non-governmental organizations in Africa: Can they influence public policy? *Development and Change, 21*, 87–118.

Brinkerhoff, D. W. (1995). African state–society linkages in transition: The case of forestry policy in Mali. *Canadian Journal of Development Studies, 16*(2), 201–228.

Brinkerhoff, D. W. (1996a). Coordination issues in policy implementation networks: An illustration from Madagascar's environmental action plan. *World Development, 24*(9), 1497–1511.

Brinkerhoff, D. W. (1996b). Process perspectives on policy change: Highlighting implementation. *World Development, 24*(9), 1395–1403.

Brinkerhoff, D. W. (2000). Democratic governance and sectoral policy reform: Tracing linkages and exploring synergies. *World Development, 28*(4), 601–615.

Brinkerhoff, D. W., with assistance from Kulibaba, N. P. (1996). Perspectives on participation in economic policy reform in Africa. *Studies in Comparative International Development, 31*(3), 123–152.

Brinkerhoff, D. W., Coletti, W., & Webster, R. (2000). *Small and medium enterprise policy reform in Bulgaria.* Implementing Policy Change Case Study No. 7. Washington, DC: U.S. Agency for International Development.

Brown, L. D., & Ashman, D. (1996). Participation, social capital, and intersectoral problem solving: African and Asian cases. *World Development, 24*(9), 1467–1481.

Brown, M., Rizika, J., Cawley, J., Amstadter, I., Clark, J., & Prendergast, J. (1993). *Non-governmental organizations and natural resources management: An assessment of eighteen African countries. Executive summary.* Washington, DC: World Learning, CARE, World Wildlife Fund. PVO-NGO/NRMS Project, March.

Clark, J. (1990). *Democratizing development: The role of voluntary organizations.* West Hartford, CT: Kumarian Press.

Clark, J. (1997). The state, popular participation, and the voluntary sector. In D. Hulme & M. Edwards (Eds.), *NGOs, states and donors: Too close for comfort?* (pp. 43–58). New York: St. Martin's Press.

Coston, J. M. (1995, March). *Civil society literature review: Democratic governance and civil society's theoretical development, contemporary conceptualization, and institutional, economic, and political implications.* Washington, DC: U.S. Agency for International Development, Global Bureau, Center for Democracy and Governance.

Coston, J. M. (1998a). Administrative avenues to democratic governance: The balance of supply and demand. *Public Administration and Development, 18*(5), 479–493.

Coston, J. M. (1998b). A model and typology of government–NGO relationships. *Nonprofit and Voluntary Sector Quarterly, 27*(3), 359–383.

Coston, J. M., & Butz, J. L. (1999). Mastering information: The birth of citizen-initiated voter education in Mongolia. *International Journal of Organization Theory and Behavior, 2*(1&2), 107–139.

Diamond, L. (1994). Rethinking civil society: Toward democratic consolidation. *Journal of Democracy, 5*(3), 4–17.

Edwards, M., & Hulme, D. (Eds.). (1992). *Making a difference: NGOs and development in a changing world.* London: Earthscan Publications.

Evans, P. (1996). Government action, social capital and development: Reviewing the evidence on synergy. *World Development, 24*(6), 1119–1132.

Farrington, J., Bebbington, A., Wellard, K., & Lewis, D. J. (1993). *Reluctant partners? Non-governmental organizations, the state and sustainable agricultural development.* London: Routledge.

Fisher, J. (1993). *The road from Rio: Sustainable development and the nongovernmental movement in the third world.* Westport, CT: Praeger.

Fiszbein, A., & Lowden, P. (1998). *Working together for a change: Government, business and civic partnerships for poverty reduction in LAC.* Washington, DC: Economic Development Institute of the World Bank.

Foley, M. W., & Edwards, B. (1996). The paradox of civil society. *Journal of Democracy, 7*(3), 38–53.

Fowler, A. (1992). Distant obligations: Speculations on NGO funding and the global market. *Review of African Political Economy, 55,* 9–29.

Fowler, A. (1997). *Striking a balance: A guide to enhancing the effectiveness of NGOs in international development.* London: Earthscan Publications.

Frishtak, L. L. (1994). *Governance capacity and economic reform in developing countries.* Technical Paper No. 254. Washington, DC: World Bank.

Garilao, E. D. (1987). Indigenous NGOs as strategic institutions: Managing the relationship with government and resource agencies. *World Development, 15*(supplement), 113–120.

Gustafson, D., & Ingle, M. (1992). *Policy characteristics analysis.* Technical Note No. 3. Washington, DC: U.S. Agency for International Development, Implementing Policy Change Project.

Hulme, D., & Edwards, M. (1997). NGOs, states and donors: An overview. In D. Hulme & M. Edwards (Eds.), *NGOs, states and donors: Too close for comfort?* (pp. 3–22). New York: St. Martin's Press.

Kajese, K. (1987). An agenda of future tasks for international and indigenous NGOs: Views from the south. *World Development, 15*(supplement), 79–85.

Kettl, D. F. (1997). The global revolution in public management: Driving themes, missing links. *Journal of Policy Analysis and Management, 16*(3), 446–462.

Kolzow, D. R. (1994). Public/private partnership: The economic development organization of the 90s. *Economic Development Review, 12*(1), 4–6.

Kooiman, J. (Ed.). (1993). *Modern governance: New government–society interactions.* London: Sage Publications.

Korten, D. C. (1990). *Getting to the 21st century: Voluntary action and the global agenda.* West Hartford, CT: Kumarian Press.

Kulibaba, N. (1996). *Good governance in sheep's clothing: Implementing the action plan for regional integration of the livestock trade in West Africa's central corridor.* Case Study No. 3. Washington, DC: U.S. Agency for International Development, Implementing Policy Change Project.

Local Government Management Board. (1995). *Public/private/voluntary partnerships in local government.* London: Local Government Management Board.

Lowndes, V., & Skelcher, C. (1998). The dynamics of multi-organizational partnerships: An analysis of changing modes of governance. *Public Administration, 76*(2), 313–333.

Machado, N., & Burns, T. R. (1998). Complex social organization: Multiple organizing modes, structural incongruence, and mechanisms of integration. *Public Administration, 76*(2), 355–386.

Malena, C. (1995). Relations between northern and southern non-governmental development organizations. *Canadian Journal of Development Studies, 16*(9), 7–29.

Mandell, M. P. (1988). Intergovernmental management in interorganizational networks: A revised perspective. *International Journal of Public Administration, 11*(4), 393–416.

Mandell, M. P. (Ed.) (1999). Symposium: The impact of collaborative efforts: Changing the face of public policy through networks and network structures: Foreword by the editor. *Policy Studies Review, 16*(1), 4–17.

Mawer, R. (1997). Mice among the tigers: Adding value in NGO–government relations in South East Asia. In D. Hulme & M. Edwards (Eds.), *NGOs, states and donors: Too close for comfort?* (pp. 243–253). New York: St. Martin's Press.

McCarthy, K. D., Hodgkinson, V. A., Sumariwalla, R. D., and Associates. (1992). *The nonprofit sector in the global community: Voices from many nations.* San Francisco: Jossey-Bass.

Migdal, J. S. (1988). *Strong societies and weak states: State–society relations and state capabilities in the third world.* Princeton, NJ: Princeton University Press.

Milward, H. B., & Provan, K. G. (1993). The hollow state: Private provision of public services. In H. Ingram & S. R. Smith (Eds.), *Public policy for democracy* (pp. 222–237). Washington, DC: Brookings Institution.

Moore, M., & Hamalai, L. (1993). Economic liberalization, political pluralism and business associations in developing countries. *World Development, 21*(12), 1895–1912.

Ndegwa, S. N. (1993, May). *NGOs as pluralizing agents in civil society in Kenya.* Working Paper No. 491. Nairobi: University of Nairobi, Institute for Development Studies.

Oliver, P. E. (1993). Formal models of collective action. *Annual Review of Sociology, 19,* 271–300.

Olson, M. (1965). *The logic of collective action.* Cambridge, MA: Harvard University Press.

Orsini, D. M., Courcelle, M., & Brinkerhoff, D. W. (1996). Increasing private sector capacity for policy dialogue: The West African enterprise network. *World Development, 24*(9), 1453–1466.

Osaghae, E. (Ed.). (1994). *Between state and civil society in Africa: Perspectives on development.* Dakar, Senegal: Council for the Development of Social Science Research in Africa.

Osborne, D., & Gaebler, T. (1992). *Reinventing government: How the entrepreneurial spirit is transforming the public sector.* Reading, MA: Addison-Wesley Publishing.

Osborne, D., & Plastrik, P. (1997). *Banishing bureaucracy: The five strategies for reinventing government.* Reading, MA: Addison-Wesley-Longman.

Ostrom, E. (1990). *Governing the commons: The evolution of institutions for collective action.* Cambridge: Cambridge University Press.

O'Toole, L. J. (1997a). Treating networks seriously: Practical and research-based agendas in public administration. *Public Administration Review 57*(1): 45–52.

O'Toole, L. J. (1997b). The implications for democracy in a networked bureaucratic world. *Journal of Public Administration Research and Theory, 7*(3), 443–461.

Overseas Development Council and the Synergos Institute. (1995, September 26–28). *Strengthening civil society's contribution to development: The role of official development assistance.* Washington, DC: Report on a Conference for Official Development Assistance Agencies.

Pearce, J. (1997). Between co-option and irrelevance? Latin American NGOs in the 1990s. In D. Hulme & M. Edwards (Eds.), *NGOs, states and donors: Too close for comfort?* (pp. 257–274). New York: St. Martin's Press.

Perera, J. (1997). In unequal dialogue with donors: The experience of the Sarvodaya Shramadana movement. In D. Hulme & M. Edwards (Eds.), *NGOs, states and donors: Too close for comfort?* (pp. 156–167). New York: St. Martin's Press.

Rothchild, D. (1994). Structuring state–society relations in Africa: Toward an enabling political environment. In J. A. Widner (Ed.), *Economic change and political liberalization in Sub-Saharan Africa* (pp. 201–229). Baltimore: Johns Hopkins University Press.

Sachikonye, L. (1995). *Democracy, civil society and the state: Social movements in Southern Africa.* Harare, Zimbabwe: Southern African Political Economy Series Trust.

Salamon, L. M. (1987). Of market failure, voluntary failure, and third-party government: Toward a theory of government–nonprofit relations in the modern welfare state. In S. A. Ostrander (Ed.), *Shifting the debate: Public/private sector relations in the modern welfare state* (pp. 28–49). New Brunswick, NJ: Transaction Books.

Salamon, L. M. (1989). The changing tools of government action: An overview. In L. M. Salamon (Ed.), *Beyond privatization: The tools of government action.* Washington, DC: Urban Institute Press.

Smith, B. H. (1987). An agenda of future tasks for international and indigenous NGOs: Views from the north. *World Development, 15*(supplement), 87–93.

Tendler, J. (1997). *Good government in the tropics.* Baltimore: Johns Hopkins University Press.

Thompson, J. (1995). Participatory approaches in government bureaucracies: Facilitating the process of institutional change. *World Development, 23*(9), 1521–1554.

Turner, M., & Hulme, D. (1997). *Governance, administration, and development: Making the state work.* West Hartford, CT: Kumarian Press.

Weschler, J. S. (1999). Non-governmental organizations and policy influence in Latin America and the Caribbean. *International Journal of Organization Theory and Behavior, 2*(1&2), 141–166.

World Bank. (1997). *The state in a changing world: World development report 1997.* New York: Oxford University Press.

11

Will the People Really Speak?

A Networking Perspective on Hong Kong as It Attempts to Build a Democratic Political Infrastructure

Robert W. Gage

I N THIS CHAPTER, A MACRO ASSESSMENT of democratization in Hong Kong to date is attempted using a networking perspective. To accomplish this objective, two broad categories of change are discussed. The major focus of the chapter is on changes that have occurred in the political/administrative sector and the interesting constellations of activities and networks that are attempting to vie for a voice in governance. Changes that either support or are dysfunctional to democratization in the political system are also examined, including socio-cultural and economic system changes.

The discussion of the network perspective is relevant for the public-administration community, theoreticians and practitioners alike. Among the proponents of the networking approach, O'Toole argues that the emergence of networks in public administration is more than a passing fad, and that "public administration should attend to network-focused research efforts" (1997, p. 50). Others have viewed the study of networks as a critical part of research in governance, in human-services delivery, in interorganizational relationships, and in intergovernmental relations (Drucker, 1995; Gage and Mandell, 1990; Heclo, 1997; Kickert et al., 1997; Knoke and Kuklinski, 1982; Provan and Brinton, 1995; Scharpf, 1993).

For purposes of this chapter, networks are viewed generally as "structures of interdependence, involving multiple organizations or parts thereof, where one unit is not merely the formal subordinate of the others in some larger hierarchical arrangement" (O'Toole, 1997, p. 45). Networks typically exhibit some structural stability and extend beyond formally established linkages and policy-legitimated ties. The networking approach taken in this chapter acknowledges these properties of networks and the relationships in network interactions as relevant and useful for analysis. Its objective is to demonstrate that this approach is helpful to the analysis of changing relationships in Hong Kong, which have resulted in new networks that have facilitated the growth or led to the disintegration of existing networks.

In chapter 2 of this book, Agranoff and McGuire pose some important questions for scholars who have been concerned with the state of research and theory in this area. This chapter is intended, in part, to respond to Agranoff and McGuire's cogent arguments. The setting in contemporary Hong Kong, as it has moved from the point of transition from British rule to Chinese sovereignty and to the present, provides an excellent laboratory for research on networks as they are formed, transformed, or dismantled. The development of new networks in Hong Kong in three sectors—social/cultural, economic, and political—is described and analyzed. While the emphasis in this chapter is on the contemporary significance of *political* networks in Hong Kong, because of their importance to the issue of democratic institution building, social/cultural and economic networks are also part of this analysis. They will be discussed first, since they provide a contextual framework for political networks in contemporary Hong Kong.

From the standpoint of empirical analysis and generation of hypotheses, this chapter focuses on an interesting question posed by Agranoff and McGuire. These authors ask whether there are critical functional equivalents to traditional management processes that can be identified in the knowledge base of network management. They propose a grouping of network-management behaviors as critical functional equivalents to POSDCORB. Given the intensity of networking activity in Hong Kong since the transition to Chinese rule in July 1997, much of what this chapter will deal with has to do with what they refer to as "activation." I shall focus on activation of networks in this chapter, seeking to describe and better understand the emerging patterns of network structures and interaction evident in Hong Kong.

The chapter first presents a background and history of democratization in Hong Kong. It then gives an analysis of networks that are in the phase of activation in the sociocultural and economic sectors. Networks in these two sectors have evolved in ways that support new patterns of centralization of governance in Hong Kong. The remainder of the chapter is an analysis of political networks, including an examination of certain critical developments that are dysfunctional for the development of democratic institutions.

Background: Key Elements of the Structure for Democratization in Hong Kong

The Legislative Council (LegCo)

Much of the attention that has been given to democratization in Hong Kong has focused on the electoral structure prescribed by Hong Kong's new constitution (the Basic Law) and its Legislative Council, referred to as LegCo. Today LegCo is an important component of the political structure, but there are other components too, such as the local government structure and the growing number of political parties, that must be considered in the analysis of political networks in contemporary Hong Kong.

LegCo, as the former colonial legislature was called, was disbanded summarily when Hong Kong became part of China, and a provisional legislature was then appointed. Hong Kong's Basic Law provided for a ten-year transition period (from 1997 until 2007) in which a new Legislative Council, reestablished by elections in the Hong Kong Special Administrative Region (HKSAR), was to be elected in three separate phases.

Initially only twenty of the sixty LegCo seats were elected from geographically defined constituencies through direct elections, while thirty were elected from so-called functional constituencies composed of elite business and professional groups, and ten were chosen by a "specially" constituted eight hundred member election committee, composed of political and economic elites. These elections, the first to take place after Hong Kong became part of China, took place in May 1998 and the first elected Legislative Council under Chinese rule was seated.

The Basic Law provides for an increase in the number of directly elected seats in the second and the third phases of democratization during this initial ten-year transition period. In the second phase, an election, expected this year, will have twenty-four directly elected seats, while the functional constituencies will retain thirty seats and the election committee will choose only six seats. In the third phase, an election, expected in 2004, will have thirty directly elected seats, equaling the number elected from functional constituencies (National Democratic Institute for International Affairs, 1997, p. 5). In this third phase, the election committee will not choose any LegCo seats.

Thus it would appear that the electoral structure provides for gradual, but only partial, democratization in LegCo governance. Half the LegCo seats will eventually be directly elected. However, with its overarching powers, the executive has established special commissions and executive departments, creating new networks that have circumvented not only LegCo, with its limited powers, but local government and the traditional career civil service as well.

Local Government

Another key element of the government structure in Hong Kong is local government, which has three components. In the mid-1980s and the 1990s, directly

elected seats were introduced into political institutions at the territorial, municipal, and district levels. These institutions are the Regional Council; the Municipal Council, which has been responsible for the traditional municipal services;
and the district board. Representatives from municipalities constitute the body
called the Urban Council. Representatives from new towns and rural areas constitute the Regional Council when functions extend from urban into rural areas.

The evolution of these local government institutions has been complex, with
many reform plans and provisional institutions surfacing as political parties and
public-interest groups attempted to implement democratization proposals of the
former British governor Chris Patten, and as provisional institutions under
Chinese rule took their place on the local government scene. There have been
interesting proposals for vertical and horizontal mergers of these local government institutions, which are leading to considerable change and the activation of
new intergovernmental networks, whose spheres of activity have been limited by
the reticence of the chief executive to decentralize in the HKSAR government
(Lo, 1999, p. 301).

Political Parties

A third element of governance in Hong Kong are the many political parties,
which received impetus under Patten's democratization proposals, particularly
during the last years of British rule. The plethora of political parties and groups
that have assumed roles in public affairs in Hong Kong have been closely monitored by researchers and scholars. Their data on activities of parties such as the
Democratic Party, the Democratic Alliance for the Betterment of Hong Kong, the
Liberal Party, the Association for Democracy and People's Livelihood, and data
on activities of groups such as the Trade Union, the Kaifong, mutual-aid committees, charitable associations, and religious groups or churches provide a rich and
detailed account of citizen interaction and the coalescing of network structures
(Chan and Kwok, 1999; Hong Kong Transition Project, 1998a, 1998b, 1998c).

Observers of the contemporary scene in Hong Kong today are struck by the
scope of change that is under way. It is marked by the emergence and intersec-
tion, if not the collision, of many new networks. This leads to the question of the
contribution that network theory can make to the understanding and explanation
of what has happened in Hong Kong in the 1990s and what might be expected in
the future.

History

The return of Hong Kong to Chinese sovereignty at midnight on June 30, 1997,
represented a departure from a trend for former British colonies, such as India
and South Africa, to pursue independence and self-governance after colonial
rule. Hong Kong's return to China also was viewed by many as a test of Deng
Xiaoping's "one country, two systems" model. This added a further element of
experimentation and drama to the event.

The significance of the event cannot be gainsaid. For the millions of Chinese who witnessed the countdown to the handover date on a massive clock in Tiananmen Square, the return of Hong Kong was a matter of national pride and sovereign right. To the Chinese government, it could set a precedent for a next step, the return of Taiwan to the mainland. For the people of Hong Kong itself, the change has been the most immediate and significant.

As Hong Kong approaches its third full year under the Basic Law, it seems posed to test the "one country, two systems" model in numerous ways. These tests have in a very real way been postponed by the turmoil caused by the Asian economic crisis, which led to immense financial pressure on the Hong Kong economy. For the first time in a nonwar environment, Hong Kong's economy shrank considerably (Hong Kong Transition Project, 1998b, p. 2).

One effect of the Asian economic crisis, which admittedly did lead to dissatisfaction with certain aspects of the performance of the HKSAR government, was that the visibility of the economic crisis may have diverted public attention from democratization and other issues significant for long-term governance in the HKSAR.

Sociocultural and Economic Change

This section looks at changes in symbolism, basic values, and cultural emphases in Hong Kong and their impacts on assimilation and networks.

Symbolic Importance of the Posture of Beijing as the Sovereign

In Chinese culture, perhaps more than in other cultures, there is a tendency to personalize government. "Beijing" becomes an almost anthropomorphic symbol, an incarnation of China's human leadership. Thus the distant Chinese capital takes on lifelike characteristics and is ascribed emotions. This immediate personalization has significant meaning in the context of an authoritarian government such as China's. The routine and extensive penetration of its power and authority in the lives of Chinese citizens is accepted in China, but is strange and can be quite terrifying to easterners who are unaccustomed to it.

The presence of mainland China, just beyond the borders of Hong Kong, has always been prominent for the Hong Kong people. There are ways in which Hong Kong was totally dependent on the mainland for decades before the handover. For example, 85 percent of the fresh water for Hong Kong lies in reservoirs just beyond the Hong Kong borders inside China. A simple act of turning off this resource would quickly bring a rebellious Hong Kong into line. Obviously the Hong Kong people have not been able to go too far in risking the displeasure of the mainland government.

Personalized oversight, real or imagined, has become an effective means of assimilation and control in Hong Kong's new institutions and networks. Officially, the Chinese government has pledged noninterference in Hong Kong's affairs. However, with progressively greater integration of Hong Kong's governmental, business, and social sectors into China's polity, more networks are being established. Consequently, there are more "listening posts" for surveillance by the personalized, anthropomorphic "Beijing." The oversight of the Chinese government actually can and has become self-policing to a significant degree. One behaves at variance with "approved" ways at greater and greater risk as assimilation progresses.

Values and Self-Censorship

Public values in any polity are the mainstay of its cohesiveness. They shape the direction and intensity of political action among groups and constituencies, and determine the cohesiveness and alignments of networks. In Hong Kong, there was considerable value fragmentation among the populace as the transition process continued toward the date of the handover. Value diversity can be a strength, and the strength of our own polity can be traced in some respects to the diversity of its strong immigrant groups. However, diversity, such as that in Hong Kong, can also pose a difficult challenge to nation building for political leadership.

Uncertain National Identity. The Hong Kong population is ethnically 95 percent Chinese, but only 25 percent identified themselves as "Chinese." Twenty-four percent thought of themselves as "Hong Kong Chinese," and the largest portion, 44 percent, thought of themselves simply as "Hong Kong People" (Hong Kong Transition Project, 1997). The uncertainty of the Hong Kong people about their own identity makes them more susceptible to the campaign for acceptance of traditional Chinese values being conducted by the HKSAR government.

Networks, as typically loose structures of interdependence, depend for their viability and cohesiveness upon common values and mutually accepted mega-goals (Mandell, 1990, p. 40). The Chinese are masters at building networks (*guangxi*). Chinese use of informal and traditional networks, which are at the foundation of business and economic practices, has contributed to their reputation as inscrutable and difficult for Western businessmen. They know the critical importance of common values and symbolism to building networks and exerting influence through them.

Reinforcement of Traditional Values and Self-Censorship. Chief Executive Tung Chee-Hwa's speech to the Asia Society annual dinner, shortly before the handover, sought to reinforce common values within the new jurisdiction. He highlighted differences between values of North American and Asian executives, and pointed out that traditional Chinese values, which "have been with us for thousands of years and are as relevant today as they have ever been," are "held dear." According to Tung, these values are "trust, love, and respect for our family and our elders; integrity, honesty, and loyalty towards all; commitment to education; a belief in order and stability; *an emphasis on obligations to the community rather than rights of the individual*; a preference for consultation rather than confrontation" (Tung, 1997, emphasis added).

These values help explain the benign paternalism enunciated by Tung. By pitching himself as a fatherly figure bent on practicing benevolent rule, he has appealed to the Hong Kong people. Despite the popular prehandover rhetoric about the need for democracy, a 1997 survey found that 69.7 percent of the populace concurred with the view that "a good government treats the people as though they are its children" (Lau, 1998). Tung's statements clearly advocate subordination of individual rights to community rights and have a broad symbolic significance for defining appropriate behavior.

The power of traditional values also has been reflected in the discussion of self-censorship in the Hong Kong press (Halligan, 1997). The problem of self-censorship also extends into academic circles. In the new institutional networks, five university presidents were co-opted by the preparatory committee, which oversaw all aspects of the transition for China. The problem, in the opinion of some professors, is that some academic administrators have tried too hard to please the Beijing government. In this case, "academic freedom will be lost before China lays a finger on it" (Lee, 1997). Self-censorship acts to discourage expression that is suspected to be "inappropriate" under Chinese sovereignty.

Value Change, Language, and Education

Education of the young is an obviously important mechanism for socialization to new regime values. Tung moved quickly in this arena to assert the importance of teaching in Chinese rather than English as the primary language. Patriotic educational efforts were increased. In addressing a conference on youth affairs, Tung said that young people's exposure to Chinese and Western culture had often left them lost and confused when it came to nationalism. In response, the Hong Kong Education Department devised a civics syllabus for secondary students on aspects of the Basic Law and the situation in China.

Economic Change: Impacts on Economic Networks in the Pearl River Delta

Hong Kong's Visibility. The visibility of Hong Kong as the economic success story of the Pearl River Delta began to diminish before Hong Kong's return to China. There are at least two important factors in this reduced visibility. The first is the rapid development of the city of Shenzhen, which is immediately across the border from Hong Kong. It is an interesting example of successful assimilationist policy by the Chinese central government, undertaken by former Chinese paramount leader Deng Xiaoping. Shenzhen was built from a small village into a metropolis of more than ten million inhabitants in less than ten years. It was built in an essentially rural environment with labor conscripted from the People's Army. Now Shenzhen is an economic powerhouse in the Pearl River Basin, a formidable economic hub in its own right, along with Canton (now Guangzhow) and Hong Kong. The growth of Shenzhen gives Hong Kong less economic visibility today.

The second factor is infrastructure development. Many infrastructure integration projects have been completed in the past decade integrating Hong Kong with the mainland. Several six-lane superhighways linking Hong Kong to the iron-producing interior of China have been completed. One especially noteworthy project was new rail service from Beijing to Hong Kong (Kwok, 1997).

Other Challenges

The independence of Hong Kong's economic networks is now challenged in other ways as well. As a British colony, Hong Kong had achieved stature as an international financial center—indeed, fourth in the world after London, New York, and Tokyo. Extensive networks, domestic and international, were especially visible in the financial and economic arena.

Red Chips. Red chips are mainland China-funded companies that are being registered and operate in Hong Kong and sell stock on the Hong Kong stock exchange. They are neither fully private nor fully public. The Chinese government still controls these companies, although red chips have some measure of private ownership (Chua, 1998). As the British withdrew from Hong Kong and more red chips expanded into Hong Kong's economy, more Hong Kong employees working for these companies have become susceptible to mainland political mobilization and control (Chua, 1998, p. 3). To maintain Hong Kong's separateness, if not autonomy, Chua points out that it will be "increasingly necessary for Hong Kong to find a solution, acceptable to both Beijing and the international community, to effectively regulate the red chips" (1998, p. 3). The independence of the Hong Kong stock exchange, and its networks that depend for survival on free exchange of information, is threatened by the penetration of red chips.

International Financial Center. The position of Hong Kong as an international financial center and the independence of the Hong Kong stock market are under pressure from other directions. Peter Churchouse, managing director of Morgan Stanley in Hong Kong, pointed out before the handover that in the longer term, China clearly was positioning Shanghai to become its international financial center (Churchouse, 1997). This prediction seems to be on target. On its seventieth anniversary, Shanghai formally introduced its new stock exchange, touted to have Asia's largest trading floor, capable of seating 1,608 traders (Peng, 1997, p. 3). The power of the financial networks associated with Shanghai's new stock exchange has been enhanced.

Tourism. Tourism is a vehicle for open exposure of a people to external influences and ideas. It also reflects choices in destinations that foreign nationals freely choose as desirable. Tourism in Hong Kong not only decreased after the handover, but it also reflected increased ethnocentrism. In the aggregate, the slump in Hong Kong tourism cannot be attributed solely to the Chinese takeover. The extent of Asian economic problems that were then emerging and the fact that Hong Kong, as a tourist destination, is expensive, must be included. However, the aggregate tourism decrease has meant less exposure to external influence. Perhaps more important, the decrease in Japanese tourists, which was the largest, reflects a possible element of ethnocentrism. There have been long-standing problems in international relations between China and Japan. Newspaper editorials suggested that hotel prices in Hong Kong to Japanese are much higher than prices for other tourists because of these problems (*South China Morning Post*, 1997).

Chief Executive Relationships with Business Elites. Chief Executive Tung Chee-Hwa, a former businessman, took over a powerful bureaucratic machine when he assumed office. Under the British, there had been a tradition for political power to be concentrated in the executive, with an appointed group of elites, in the Executive Council, who advised the chief executive. There also had been a parallel structure of statutory bodies directly answerable to the chief executive. In 1997, there were fifteen policy and resource bureaus, seventy-one government departments and agencies, and a number of statutory bodies. The government employed over 180,000 civil servants.

While a comprehensive review of the HKSAR government's expanded role in business and economic affairs is beyond the scope of this chapter, expansion has been noteworthy, and some of it will be discussed. The trend contrasts with the more noninterventionist role of the British colonial government in economic affairs. According to Tang (1999), "a large number of government departments or other public corporations have been set up to regulate the economy, to provide more support to local industries and to ensure the territory's compliance to international agreements" (p. 288).

The establishment of organizations such as the Hong Kong Industrial Technology Centre Corporation, the Hong Kong Industrial Estates Corporation, the Software Industry Information Center and Cyberspace Center, as well as legislation to permit development of a captive insurance industry and a mortgage corporation are indicators of the increased visibility of the HKSAR government in business and economic affairs.

Furthermore, as Tang (1999, p. 290) points out:

> Under Tung's leadership, businessmen and professionals have been able to dominate the Executive Council again. Among Executive Council members, only Tam Yiu-Chung, a trade unionist and member of the pro-Beijing Democratic Alliance for the Betterment of Hong Kong, comes from a grass-roots background.
>
> Beijing loyalists and those from the business community were also able to dominate the provisional legislature. . . . Political parties and other groups such as the Democratic Alliance for the Betterment of Hong Kong, the Hong Kong Progressive Alliance, and the Liberal Party, which have had good relations with the leadership in Beijing during the territory's transition, became dominant forces in the legislature.

With more pro-Beijing business elites gaining political influence, and as China becomes a leading investor in Hong Kong, the political framework has become much more dynamic. Tang (1999, p. 295) concludes that the dominance of the bureaucrats is being challenged by the pro-Beijing elites, while Chinese mainland enterprises are becoming more important in the SAR, and the Hong Kong state has become more proactive in the economy.

Political and Governmental Change

Preparatory Committee, Chief Executive Officer, and Provisional Legislature

As new institutions emerge, actors change and new networks are formed. In Hong Kong, important institutional changes occurred immediately before the handover and during the first year of Chinese sovereignty. The appointment by the Chinese government of the four hundred-member preparatory committee was one such change. The selection by the preparatory committee of Tung Chee-Hwa, a Harvard-educated Hong Kong businessman, as Hong Kong's future chief executive was another. These actions created an institutional foundation for new formal networks and also brought future top-level leadership into position as key network actors.

Interestingly, many of the network relationships used by the Hong Kong branch of the former Communist Chinese Press Agency (*Xinhua*), which were somewhat covert, were now either brought into full public view and formally acknowledged by the preparatory committee or abolished. Equally significant and somewhat controversial was the appointment by the preparatory committee of the Provisional Legislature. It replaced, by Chinese fiat, the colonial Legislative Council (LegCo) on July 1, 1997. These new institutions took center stage for the formation of formal networks within the HKSAR government. Networks that had existed among former LegCo members were formally dissolved. Some did continue informally, and some began to function through the many political-party structures.

Senior Civil Service

Relationships were also changing among network actors in the Senior Civil Service, becoming fraught with tension and politicization as the handover date approached. In a detailed survey, Cheng and Lee (1993, p. 921) observed:

> Until the 1980s, civil servants in Hong Kong were described as typically belonging to the classical Weberian model. They have been illustrated as "complacent and technocratic" as well as "introverted, conservative and apolitical." This study reveals that, in the 1990s, senior civil servants in Hong Kong are in the process of evolving from "classical bureaucratic" to "political bureaucratic." Most of the interviewees agreed to the premise that "greater interference from politics in bureaucratic life is acceptable" (95 percent) and "more considerations have now to be given to political factors when making a policy" (86 percent).

The tenor of uncertainty and the expectation of politicization that permeated the directorate-level staff of the Hong Kong Senior Civil Service changed relationships in senior civil-service networks. Tension in the ranks of the directorate-level relationships was reflected in speculation about relationships at the top levels of the HKSAR government. In particular, the relationship between Chief Secretary for Administration Anson Chan Fang On-Sang (Hong Kong's senior civil servant under the British and in the new government) with Chief Executive Tung Chee-Hwa was singled out repeatedly by the press (Wong, 1997; Yeung, 1998).

The People's Liberation Army (PLA)

The entrance of an elite garrison of the People's Liberation Army (PLA) into Hong Kong, which replaced the British military, gave the handover a demeanor of resolute finality. The British military network was replaced by another, one whose commanders reported directly to PLA commanders in Beijing. The grooming of this elite garrison of People's Liberation Army troops was covered closely by an apprehensive press. Their entry from across the border was accomplished in a very definitive, yet peaceful manner. The presence of these new network actors sent a military message that was as unambiguous as the naval blockade of Taiwan by China, earlier in 1997. This time, the message was that, for China, the return of Hong Kong was a serious matter of national right and honor.

Finally, the handover ceremony itself, the raising of Hong Kong's new flag (colored red, representing the motherland of China, with a bauhinia flower in the center), and the departure of colonial governor Christopher Patten were accomplished with appropriate fanfare and symbolic dignity.

There followed a period of intense diplomacy, networking that was equally symbolic for establishing Hong Kong's new leadership in the world community. Chief Executive Tung Chee-Hwa traveled extensively abroad to met with world leaders: U.S. president Bill Clinton, British prime minister Tony Blair, Japanese premier Ryutaro Hashimoto, president of the European Commission Jacques Santer, and others (*South China Morning Post*, 1997). Full-page articles and editorials in the Hong Kong press carried the message of Tung's policy meeting with the U.S. president (Yueng and Beck, 1997). The full press coverage in Hong Kong seemed to be aimed at establishing Tung's legitimacy at home as well.

Hong Kong's Delegation to the National People's Congress

Election of thirty-six Hong Kong representatives to the National People's Congress (NPC) completed the new institutional structure for the HKSAR government. The election of Hong Kong's delegation to the NPC, nominally the highest power organ of Chinese government, established a major channel by which Hong Kong people would participate in China's national affairs. These elections were held on December 8, 1997, under close scrutiny of a senior NPC official from Beijing and a selection panel, the bulk of whose members came from the Beijing-appointed preparatory committee for the Hong Kong transition (Yeung, 1997).

Evolving Relationships of Hong Kong's Chief Executive

The relationship of the central government to the HKSAR government is clear: It is one of superior to subordinate. According to Burns (1999, pp. 85–86):

Although the relationships are not specified in detail in publicly available written documents, the Chief Executive has reported directly to Qian Qiqian (a Politburo Standing Committee Member . . .) and to Le Peng, also a Politburo Standing Committee Member. Together with party secretary-general Jiang Zemin, they form the core membership of the CCP Hong Kong Work Leading Small Group, which made China's policy on Hong Kong.

It is important to note that the Chinese central government easily has had more resources to pursue its policy objectives in Hong Kong than the British did under colonial rule. "Chief among the resources of the Central Government is the Chinese Communist Party and its united front network in the territory. Through this network, which includes newspapers, community groups, groups of entrepreneurs, think tanks and so forth, the CCP is able to mobilize public opinion to support Central Government policy on Hong Kong" (Burns, 1999, p. 86).

In many ways, the rhetoric about Hong Kong's independence under the "one country, two systems" model is just that—rhetoric—and it should be recognized as such. Hong Kong is clearly subservient to Beijing. This does not mean that there is no conflict or disagreement between the Hong Kong government and the central government. What it *does* mean is that the conflict, under Chinese rule, is not open to public scrutiny. Thus, Burns (1999, p. 84) points out, unlike colonial governors, who, because they were outsiders, were heavily dependent on the civil service, the present Hong Kong chief executive comes to his post with extensive resources.

As a lifelong member of the Hong Kong community, he is embedded in a dense social network. Thus his former position as the CEO of one of the largest shipping companies in Asia means that he is intimately familiar with the political, economic, and social problems of Hong Kong. When he took office, he came with policy preferences based on his life experiences. He also came to the position with views about the efficiency and effectiveness of the public sector in general, and the Hong Kong government in particular. The chief executive's relationship with the civil service is therefore a complex one (Burns, 1999, p. 84).

The official policy of Tung's government has been to ensure continuity between the higher civil service and the chief executive. At the time of transitions, Tung decided to reappoint virtually all principal officials who had been serving in the colonial government since 1995. Burns (1999, p. 82) also indicates that continuity is evident in other key institutions and processes, such as the Civil Service Bureau, the Senior Civil Service Council, and many others.

Finally, the chief executive has acted to strengthen relationships with the Provisional Legislature (LegCo). He selected "three Provisional LegCo members [Leung Chun-Ying, Tam Yiu-Ching, and Henry Tang Ying-Yen] to serve on his Executive Council, the body that advises the CE on major policy decisions. . . . Executive Councilors, it was thought, would sell their policies to the LegCo" (Burns, 1999, p. 83).

It also appears, despite political rhetoric to the contrary, that the Provisional Legislature has continued to effectively monitor the government. Burns (1999, p. 84) notes that: "The Public Service Panel [of LegCo] met frequently and cross-examined civil service managers on their policies. From July 1997, the panel met monthly . . . and discussed many of the same sorts of issues that has been considered by the colonial legislature."

Thus members continued to challenge the government, asking for more information and justification of particular policies, and making suggestions for more effective implementation of policies. He concludes that "in no sense, then, may we describe the legislature, at least in the area of civil service management, as a 'rubber stamp'" (Burns, 1999, p. 84).

It may be concluded from this analysis that the chief executive has moved decisively to ensure the integrity of the HKSAR government. These initiatives stand in sharp contrast to his handling of local government and political parties.

Local Government

Not accidentally, the two principal tiers of local government in Hong Kong, the municipal council and district boards, today remain without clearly defined political responsibilities. The municipal council basically has been responsible for a wide range of municipal services, such as environmental protection, liquor licensing, sports and recreation services, and arts and cultural activities. Because of the growth in rural areas and numbers of new towns, urban services increasingly had to be extended to rural areas, giving rise to a similar council organization called the regional council, which has jurisdiction in the more rural areas. In discussing change in urban governance and the flux introduced into existing networks, Lo (1999, p. 299) points out that on July 1, 1997, the HKSAR government replaced the municipal council and regional council with provisional councils, and that fifty members were then appointed to each of these provisional councils by Chief Executive Tung Chee-Hwa.

Likewise, the eighteen district boards, which were established originally in new towns, especially for environmental, recreational, and cultural activities, were replaced by provisional district boards, and the formerly elected members were replaced by a total of 468 members, each appointed by the HKSAR chief executive.

What is of central interest, from the standpoint of network activation, is the flux and confusion that would have been introduced by the complete reestablishment of each of these major local-government institutions (municipal councils, regional councils, and the district boards). But in the subsequent HKSAR local-government-reform plan, the problems of flux and confusion were further compounded. The essence of this plan illustrates how, by horizontal and vertical mergers, existing networks would be dismantled, leaving power in the hands of the central government.

From October to December 1997, the principal assistant secretary for Constitutional Affairs, John Leung Chi-Yan, visited each of the eighteen provisional district boards, the provisional municipal councils, and the provisional regional councils to consult members on their views about a horizontal merger between municipal councils and regional councils while retaining district boards, and a vertical merger between district boards and municipal councils.

In June 1998, the HKSAR government gradually revealed its intention of disbanding the municipal councils, retaining the existing eighteen district boards, and centralizing the administration of food safety and environmental hygiene (Lo, 1999, p. 315).

What is apparent from an examination of the reform documents and proposals is the attempt at centralization by the HKSAR government. Another indicator was the cursory treatment in the reform plans for other local institutions and networks. As Lo (1999, p. 315) reported: "A hallmark of the consultative document and report reviewing district organizations is their cursory treatment of the District Management Committees, while simultaneously ignoring the role of Mutual Aid Committees, Owner's Corporations and Area Committees."

Political Party Networks and Elections

Any contemporary discussion of political parties and elections in Hong Kong must be couched in the realization of how much power is actually wielded by political parties in the new system. This means that it must be recognized that in 1997, sovereignty over Hong Kong was transferred from a multiparty Western democracy to an authoritarian single-party system. It also means that under the "one country, two systems" model adopted by China, in the long term there will be severe limits placed on the extent to which democracy, as it functions in a multiparty Western system, will be allowed to flourish in Hong Kong. This should not be surprising, however, since the political culture of British colonial rule, while it appeared to cultivate democratic governance, was in reality quite an autocratic colonial executive form of government in which the royal governors retained most of the significant political power. This is not an example of which the British can be particularly proud.

Nevertheless, the hopes of many in Hong Kong to build a democratic political system were encouraged as Patten's reforms were aired in the last years of his governorship. The development of the political-party structure and the many political networks that were spawned then flourished in this pretransition climate.

The electoral structure in Hong Kong is complex, and at the outset, one is impressed with the broad scope of political activity that occurred in the past decade.[1] The focus of this analysis will be on activation of political networks that were developing during the 1998 elections, since they were the first to be conducted for LegCo under the auspices of the HKSAR.

Election results for LegCo were reported by Chan and Kwok (1999, p. 62). The 1998 elections returned sixty LegCo councillors, twenty by geographic (direct) election, thirty by functional election, and ten by election-committee election. For direct elections, summarized in table 11.1, the geographic boundaries were completely redrawn from the 1995 elections. Instead of the twenty single-member constituencies of 1995, Hong Kong was divided into five multimember constituencies in 1998, each returning between three and five candidates.

For the functional constituency elections (thirty LegCo seats), there were fundamental changes also. Nine former constituencies were canceled and given new designations for the 1998 elections. Furthermore, the functional vote of the

Table 11.1
1998 LEGCO RESULTS FOR DIRECT ELECTIONS

Political Parties/Groups	Number of Seats	Percentage of Total Seats
Democratic Party	9	15.0
Democratic Alliance for the Betterment of Hong Kong	5	8.3
The Frontier	3	5.0
Citizens Party	1	1.6
Association for Democracy and People's Livelihood	0	0
Liberal Party	0	0
Neighborhood and Workers' Service Center	1	1.6
Independents	1	1.6
Others	0	0
TOTALS	20	33.3

working population was canceled, reducing the size of this electorate from 2.6 million to about 233,000.

Finally, the 1998 election-committee membership was changed. The new election committee, which elected ten LegCo seats, was made up of a group of eight hundred individuals coming from four sectors, instead of directly elected district-board members.

The major point to be made about political networks involving just these groups alone is that most of the political networks in and among the major political parties were unlikely to survive such widespread change. Networks that had existed in the old system were challenged and were functioning on precarious financial bases, and there was hardly time for *activation* of new networks into viable functional entities.

Conclusions

Change can be expected when a change of sovereignty occurs. Change can also be a strategy to dismantle active and growing political organizations, and many such organizations had been encouraged and were growing during the last years of the Patten government.

China and the HKSAR government have often advocated stability and the importance of "not killing the goose that lays the golden eggs," referring to Hong Kong. Yet the extent to which "stability" will be allowed may inadvertently permit the growth of some democratic institutions in the future. It can and will be judged as the elections of 2000 and beyond are actually conducted.

Surveys conducted by the Hong Kong Transition Project revealed that satisfaction with government performance was at a low of 37 percent in June 1998, compared with 73 percent in February 1997 (Hong Kong Transition Project, 1998c). These comparatively low levels of satisfaction supposedly indicate that there was great concern in Hong Kong about government performance and also the economy. However, the HKSAR government's frustration of efforts to build viable local political networks is likely to be a part of this problem.

Notable as a counterbalance to the significant citizen concerns during this period were two interesting trends that are important from the networking perspective: the decreasing citizen contacts with provisional (appointed) members of the legislature and other governmental bodies, and increasing participation in elections, signing petitions (signature campaigns), answering surveys, and donating to political parties.

The networking approach taken in this chapter has brought several benefits to this analysis. One is its deliberate inclusion of a wide range of factors—contextual, institutional, cultural, and value related—into one comprehensive viewpoint. While the corroboration of the actual impact of new networks in institutions, hinted at in this chapter as a preliminary analysis, must await further research, a direction and focus for that research have been established by this analysis. The broad scope that can point the way to future research is certainly a good argument for using the networking perspective.

Future research is needed on network activation and other network management behaviors proposed by Agranoff and McGuire in this book (chapter 2) such as framing, mobilizing, and synthesizing. Attention also needs to be given to leadership in networks (Coe, 1990; Rossy and Mandell, 1992). Such concepts as partnerships, linking communication, championing, and evocative leadership provide a potential for future empirical research.

Acknowledgments

The author would like to acknowledge the encouragement of Professors Ian Scott and John Burns, both of whom served as chairpersons of the Department of Politics and Administration at Hong Kong University. Both were helpful in my securing an appointment as visiting scholar at the Robert Black College, Hong Kong University, during a sabbatical leave in 1997. In addition, Michael DeGolyer, director of the Hong Kong Transition Project at Baptist University, Kowloon, provided longitudinal data, extending into the Special Administrative Region (SAR) period, that was important to completing this work.

Note

1. For an in-depth discussion of political activity, see the Hong Kong Transition Project report (1998a) and Chan and Kwok (1999).

References

Burns, J. P. (1999). The Hong Kong civil service in transition. *Journal of Contemporary China, 8*(20), 67–87.

Chan, E., & Kwok, R. (1999). Democratization in turmoil? Elections in Hong Kong. *Journal of Contemporary China, 8*(20), 47–65.

Cheng, J. G. S., & Lee, J. C. Y. (1993). The changing political attitudes of the senior bureaucrats in Hong Kong's transition. *China Quarterly, 47,* 912–937.

Chua, A. C. H. (1998). Whistleblowing, red chips, and the provisional legislature in Hong Kong. *Public Administration Review, 58*(1), 1–7.

Churchouse, P. (1997). SAR to become hub of southern China. *South China Morning Post (International Weekly), V*(38), 8.

Coe, B. A. (1990). Open focus: A model of community development. *Journal of the Community Development Society, 21*(2), 18–35.

Drucker, P. F. (1995, March 30). The network society. *Wall Street Journal, Europe,* 8.

Gage, R. W., & Mandell, M. P. (Eds.). (1990). *Strategies for managing intergovernmental policies and networks.* New York: Praeger.

Halligan, F. (1997). Hollywood's Tibet films left out in cold. *South China Morning Post (International Weekly), VI*(29), 6.

Heclo, H. (1997). A government of strangers. Washington DC: Brookings Institution.

Hong Kong Transition Project. (1997). Hong Kong: Bridge to the future. 13/4 Briefing, June, 51pp. <http://www.hkbu.edu/~hktp>.

Hong Kong Transition Project. (1998a). Will the people speak and what will they say? May, 43pp. <http://www.hkbu.edu/~hktp>.

Hong Kong Transition Project. (1998b). A year of great significance: Hong Kong in economic crisis. November, Section 1, Democracy and political development, 20pp. <http://www.hkbu.edu/~hktp>.

Hong Kong Transition Project. (1998c). A year of great significance: Hong Kong in economic crisis. November, Section 4, Performance and policies, 20pp. <http://www.hkbu.edu/~hktp>.

Kickert, W. J. M., Klijn, E.-H., & Koppenjan, J. F. M. (1997). *Managing complex networks: Strategies for the public sector.* London: Sage Publishers.

Knoke, D., & Kuklinski, J. H. (1982). *Network analysis.* Newbury Park, CA: Sage Publishers.

Kwok, S. (1997). Through-train delayed by well-wishers. *South China Morning Post (International Weekly), VI*(6), 3.

Lau, S.-K. (1998). Social malice on rise as values abandoned. *South China Morning Post (International Weekly), VI*(40), 6.

Lee, R. (1997). Academics face a test of their own. *South China Morning Post (International Weekly), VI*(9), 11

Lo, S.-H. (1999). Democratization without decentralization: Local government in Hong Kong. *Journal of Contemporary China, 8*(21), 297–318.

Mandell, M. P. (1990). Network management: Strategic behavior in the public sector. In R. W. Gage & M. P. Mandell (Eds.), *Strategies for managing intergovernmental policies and networks.* New York: Praeger.

National Democratic Institute for International Affairs. (1997). *The promise of democratization in Hong Kong.* NDI Hong Kong Report No. 2. Washington, DC.

O'Toole, L. J. (1997). Treating networks seriously: Practical and research-based agendas in public administration. *Public Administration Review, 57*(1), 45–51.

Peng, F. C. (1997). Shanghai exchange celebrates birthday. *South China Morning Post (International Weekly)*, *IV*(37), 3.

Provan, K. G., & Brinton, M. H. (1995). A preliminary theory of network effectiveness: A comparative study of four mental health systems. *Administrative Science Quarterly*, *40*(1), 1–33.

Rossy. G., & Mandell, M. P. (1992, April 12–15). A leadership framework for building commitment and effective implementation in program networks. Paper presented at the National Conference of the American Society for Public Administration, Chicago.

Scharpf, F. W. (1993). *Games in hierarchies and networks.* Boulder, CO: Westview.

South China Morning Post (International Weekly). (1997). Tung takes message to world. *VI*(19), 1.

South China Morning Post (International Weekly). (1997). Editorial. *VI*(27), 10.

Tang, J. T. H. (1999). Business as usual: The dynamics of government–business relations in the Hong Kong special administrative region. *Journal of Contemporary China*, *8*(21), 277–295.

Tung, C.-H. (1997, May 15). Untitled speech by HKSAR chief executive, Mr. Tung Chee-Hwa at the Asia society annual dinner. *Keynote Speeches of Officials*, HKSAR, 397.

Wong, F. (1997). Guess where the buck stops? *South China Morning Post (International Weekly)*, *VI*(25), 11.

Yeung, C. (1997). Two systems face to face. *South China Morning Post (International Weekly)*, *VI*(32), 6.

Yeung, C. (1998). Anson soothes Beijing. *South China Morning Post (International Weekly)*, *VI*(40), 11.

Yeung, C., & Beck, S. (1997). Tung wins U.S. hearts and minds. *South China Morning Post (International Weekly)*, *VI*(23), 1.

12

The New South Wales Demonstration Projects in Integrated Community Care

Michael Fine

P EOPLE WITH COMPLEX CARE NEEDS are being increasingly supported to remain longer in their own homes. This has been facilitated in Australia by the growth in the number and range of publicly funded community-support services through the Home and Community Care program (HACC) (AIHW, 1993, 1999; Fine, 1995, 2000). The joint federal/state-funded HACC program was established in New South Wales in 1986, building on the base of preexisting services, such as Home Nursing, Meals on Wheels, and Home Care, originally funded under a series of earlier government programs. As these services expanded with additional public funding, a range of newer services, including case-management services, community transport, social day-care services, and other specialized care and support services were added over the following decade. But this growth has not been without its problems. As the provision of complex care has become a task undertaken by small, generally specialized community-based agencies, so has the division of labor required to provide care changed. Instead of bureaucratically coordinating labor within a single organization, as occurs within a residential institution, community care entails a division of labor between different organizations requiring collaborative efforts among them. Attempts to improve links between services have seen a variety of different approaches being trialed (Fine, 2000). One of the main causes of this appears to be the fragmentation of service provision, which can be confusing and frustrating for consumers and the cause of unnecessary inefficiencies for service providers.

These concerns led in 1995 to the establishment of a series of demonstration projects in the state of New South Wales. These were intended to enable local communities to develop and test approaches to enhance the effectiveness of service provision to people remaining in their own homes by improving linkages among existing services. Following a public process in which submissions of interest were invited from across the state, demonstration projects proceeded in eight areas. Four of these are rural and regional areas: Ballina/Byron Bay, Orange/Cabonne, Tamworth North-West, and Wagga Wagga. The others (Baulkham Hills, Manly Warringah Pittwater, Ryde/Hunters Hill, and Sutherland) are part of metropolitan Sydney. Table 12.1 provides an overview of the projects, their funding over three years, and the main initiatives they undertook to achieve their goals.

The Evaluation and Its Findings

The evaluation was undertaken using documents and other accounts of project developments, together with the collection and analysis of quantitative service-provision data collected from all projects over three years. In four of the projects, a more in-depth process evaluation was undertaken. Interviews were conducted with service managers on two or more occasions, and questionnaire-based surveys of staff and of new consumers were conducted in 1997 and 1998. The remainder of this chapter addresses the main findings and recommendations that emerged from the evaluation.

How the Projects Worked

A key feature of the demonstration projects was their local character and the emphasis placed on local initiative, participation, and control. Each project began from a different starting point and had different operational circumstances with which to contend. The organizational arrangements, populations, number of local government areas serviced, and departmental regional boundaries involved also varied significantly among projects. Some projects were also inherently more ambitious than others and therefore took on a greater risk of falling short of their goals. Given these differences, it is all-the-more interesting that one of the most striking features from the perspective of the statewide evaluation was the similarity of experiences of the participants in each of the separate projects.

The projects adopted an approach based on the development of links between services in a collaborative, consensus-building way. Steering committees were formed in which representatives of local community-support agencies jointly assumed a mutual or collective responsibility for the project and functioned as a voluntary forum for the discussion of ideas and for joint decision-making across the different agencies and authorities involved. If any of the participating agencies

Table 12.1

AN OVERVIEW OF THE DEMONSTRATION PROJECTS' FUNDING, PERSONNEL, AND MAIN INITIATIVES

Area (Population)[a]	DP Funds 1995–1998	Project Personnel[b]	Main Initiatives	
Ballina/Byron Bay (pop. 62,267)	$30,000	HACC DO[c] and consultant	Assessment and referral initiatives	Directory, first phone-call strategy
Baulkham Hills (pop. 119,545)	$54,000	Consultant	Assessment and referral initiatives	Directory, computers, care coordination, staff training
Manly Warringah Pittwater (pop. 212,014)	$77,000	Consultant and working parties	Assessment and referral initiatives	Computers, staff training
Orange/Cabonne (pop. 45,908)	$32,000	Members of steering committee. "Team approach"	Assessment and referral initiatives	Directory, policy and procedures manual, "at-risk" meetings, promotion of GP strategy, staff training
Ryde/Hunters Hill (pop. 104,644)	$47,000	Council officer and consultant	Applied research approach	Directory, promotion of GP links, staff information, care-coordination policy
Sutherland (pop. 194,105)	$55,000	Project worker and working parties	Assessment and referral initiatives	Quality Improvement (QI) manual and training, care-coordination guidelines, plans for information service
Tamworth North-West (pop. 74,538)	$44,000	HACC DO[c] and consultant	Assessment and referral initiatives	"At-risk" and SCAN committees, directories, training
Wagga Wagga (pop. 55,519)	$25,000	Consultant	Assessment and referral initiatives	Flip charts and directory, single information line, protocols for agency cooperation
ALL PROJECTS	**$364,000[d]**			

Notes: [a]Population of area/region in 1996 (Australian Bureau of Statistics).
[b]Key project personnel, in addition to members of local steering committee and working parties.
[c]HACC DO: Home and Community Care Program Development Officer.
[d]Figures rounded to nearest thousand.

was opposed to a particular initiative proposed, it would unlikely have been successfully implemented, with subsequent initiatives serving only to accentuate the fragmentation of local services. Hence attempts to develop consensus were fundamental to each of the projects. Associated with the collaborative, voluntaristic character of the projects was the absence of major structural reform. Projects focused on improvements in communication and cooperation among services.

Types and Outcomes of Initiatives Undertaken

Most projects undertook a broadly similar range of initiatives and strategies. These initiatives commonly consisted of specific measures to improve links among different services, each of which was capable of being introduced as a part of the procedures of each of the independent agencies.

One set of reforms, concerning processes for the assessment and referral of community-care clients, stands out for its near-universal advocacy. Assessment and referral represent strategic processes that serve as a gateway to the provision of assistance, with a common approach among services serving to enhance access for consumers and help them obtain a more appropriate and comprehensive package of care than would otherwise be available.

Other important outcomes of the initiatives successfully introduced by the projects included the following:

- Significant improvements in the levels of communication and cooperation among services.
- Improved access for consumers to services.
- Enhanced systems of referral documentation.
- The introduction of common policies and procedures for the coordination of care for individual clients, largely through "at-risk" committees in rural and regional areas and case-management-type care-coordination approaches in the metropolitan areas.
- Expanded opportunities for consumer participation.
- The trialing and introduction of computerized information systems.

A full list of achievements of the demonstration projects is set out in table 12.2. These achievements were broadly in line with the projects' aims at the commencement of the program, although in some instances, efforts were being made to extend or refine the initial plans following early practical experience.

Measuring the Projects' Achievements

Drawing on the literature on the coordination of community care (Fine, Thomson, and Graham, 1998), a schema for charting the extent of the projects' achievements in implementing initiatives that would enhance collaboration among services was developed. This views service integration as a continuum, extending

Table 12.2

SUMMARY OF DEMONSTRATION PROJECT ACHIEVEMENTS

All Projects

- Broader networking, and development of a team approach.
- Increased communication and trust among services.
- Improved understanding and knowledge of other services.
- Increased awareness of services and improved access and referral for consumers.
- Increase in appropriate referrals.
- Publication and distribution of service directories.

One or More Projects

- Model and tools for integrated assessment and referral developed and adopted.
- Referral protocol adopted.
- Policy and procedures manual: improved and refined procedures—consistent across services.
- Reduced paperwork.
- Improvements to Meals on Wheels services.
- Protocols for agency cooperation.
- Consumer representation strategy: Consumer and Carers Forum.
- Quality improvement approach adopted, QI training held.
- Improvements in computer skills and hardware availability; services connected by e-mail.
- Development of software for referral, etc. (CIARR).
- Training workshops held on assessment and referral protocols, computers, etc.
- Conduct of Care Coordination trial.
- Improved coordination and referral mechanisms through implementation of "at-risk" committees for older people and SCAN committees for younger disabled people.

from the autonomous operation of services at one extreme to complete integration into a single system under a unified authority with a common financial system at the other. The schema also draws attention to the *level of integration*. This identifies activities at three levels: the macro level of policy, planning, and financing decisions, undertaken by the commonwealth and/or state governments; the meso- or middle-service level, involving relationships among services within a region and the relationship between one service and another in the local area; and the micro level, which concerns the interpersonal relationships among different service staff and between staff and consumers. This third level involves the direct relationship between the personnel that constitute a service and the individuals they assist (Fine, 2000; Powell, 1997; Waldvogel, 1997; Webb, 1991).

Applying this schema in a general fashion across all eight areas, it is possible to graphically represent the extent of coordination in the demonstration project

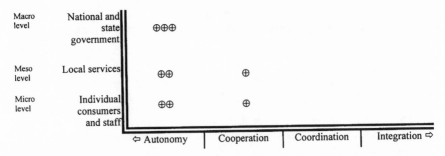

FIGURE **12.1** Baseline representation: Extent of coordination at different levels at the commencement of the demonstration projects.

areas at the time of their commencement, the projects' baseline, as in figure 12.1. At the micro level, individual consumers were confronted with an array of specialized but autonomous service providers. Evidence from consumers and service providers suggests that the staff from each service worked independently of the others in most instances, with little sense of teamwork evident. There were, nevertheless, cases where some limited coordination arrangements were operative, and some of the projects were conceived as a way of building on this existing foundation. At the meso level, services generally acted with considerable independence, maintaining their own identity and entry requirements, and imposing their own rules and regulations about the days and hours they worked and the sorts of clients they accorded priority. Most services were located in their own premises, in many cases in premises that were difficult to find and often quite isolated from other community services. The nature and extent of fragmentation among community support services could be said to be reflected in the fragmentation evident at the macro level. Both commonwealth and state governments were responsible for policy initiatives in the field of community care. In the state of New South Wales, until 1996–1997, the HACC program was administered by no fewer than five separate departments, as well as a highly autonomous statutory authority (HCS). The primary orientation of services tended to be a vertical one, toward the funding departments, rather than a horizontal one promoting the development of links with other services at the local level.

Applying the same schema to represent the outcomes of the demonstration projects, the picture after the initiatives had been developed and implemented resembles that depicted in figure 12.2. At the level of the state government, changes in the administration of the HACC program have reduced fragmentation in planning and finance. The HCS is now also more closely linked to ADD planning processes. There continue to be fragmentary tensions at this level, however, due to changes initiated by the commonwealth government, as well as continuing tensions arising from state and regional administrations. These developments, both positive and negative, were outside the direct influence of the demonstration projects.

Initiatives at the level of the local services undertaken as part of the projects

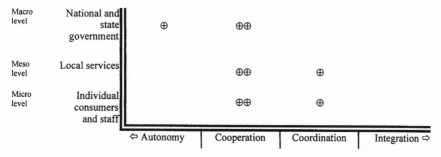

FIGURE 12.2 Outcomes of the demonstration projects and related developments at the conclusion of the evaluation.

served to significantly enhance the level of collaboration among local services. They were no longer acting autonomously, and directories were developed that provided information about all services in the community, presenting a relatively unified picture to potential consumers. Other initiatives, such as information lines, common assessment and referral procedures, successful and partially successful moves to introduce common computerized information systems, and joint staff-training sessions, also contributed to the development of closer links between what remain legally autonomous agencies. But the participatory, collaborative decision-making process of the demonstration projects was, itself, perhaps the single most-important factor contributing to better ties among services. This situation is best described as a move from autonomy to cooperative relations among services. Some evidence of coordinated relations among services emerged with the success of such initiatives as the assessment and referral protocol developed by the Orange Cabonne Interlink project. Some developments in other areas held the promise of achieving similar and possibly greater degrees of coordination in the near future.

Developments in the care provided to individual consumers were perhaps the most exciting outcomes. "At-risk" committees, for example, served to coordinate arrangements for clients with complex care needs in a number of regional and rural regions. Care-coordination policies, although initially less successful, were also evidence of closer cooperation among previously independent services in some of the urban areas. Aspects of the assessment and referral policies adopted by most projects were also based on close cooperative relations among staff from different agencies. (A report has been published documenting all of the strategies and approaches used in the demonstration projects. This can be secured from the New South Wales Ageing and Disability Department in Australia or from the author.)

Lessons from the Evaluation

One of the important lessons from the projects is that it is necessary to allow sufficient time for any changes in service provision to develop from initial proposal through to final implementation. The time taken should be regarded as a form of investment, since the various parties involved are given the opportunity to become involved, develop an understanding of the issues confronting them, and work toward a solution that they endorse as their own.

The importance of allowing sufficient time is particularly important if the collaborative approach is to be given a real chance to work. In several cases, implementation of important measures had just commenced, or was about to commence, after three years, at the conclusion of the evaluation. As a member of the coordinating committee of the successful Tamworth North West Project pointed out:

> The project did not commence implementing its agreed objectives until early 1997 [a year after it started]. By June 1997 it had made little headway in changing services' work practices. Even now [three months after the conclusion of the evaluation], . . . the Coordinating Committee sees the project as only just starting to impact. We see that it has an ongoing continuous improvement role and intend to continue the process indefinitely.

It was widely stated that while the projects had proved time-consuming and at times had been somewhat frustrating for active members of the steering committee, the collaborative approach had been a success and would be continued, in one form or another, into the future.

An analysis of annual service-provision data covering the period of demonstration projects shows that these achievements were not at the cost of service efficiency. In some projects, modest gains in service efficiency were achieved. This was well in excess of the expectations of the projects' steering committees at their commencement.

The collection of official service statistics for the evaluation, however, proved to be flawed. Because service statistics provide a retrospective view of activities, evidence of significant changes in the work practices of participating services would be most likely to show in statistics covering the final year of the project or in subsequent years. Problems also arose because many services had not submitted returns required to understand trends over time. Such difficulties were particularly acute in services from the health sector. There was also evidence of inconsistencies among services and in some of the data items provided by a single service collected over time. The problems with basic data, at a time that measurement of activity is being increasingly emphasized, underline the need to improve the collection and analysis of community-care data. Without this, the achievements and value of community services cannot be readily demonstrated.

What Helped?

The collaborative, locally based approach of the demonstration project was seen by the steering committees and other participants to have a number of strengths as well as weaknesses. The evidence suggests that the factors that enabled the projects to succeed with so few resources were derived very much from the capacity of those in a local community to work together for a common purpose.

In doing so, their ability to draw on the resources, support, and guidance of major public institutions and of other sources of expertise, such as experienced consultants, was of crucial importance. Some of the main factors that facilitated the development and successful implementation of initiatives are discussed below.

Local Participation and Commitment

The participatory, community-based process of management was cited as an enabling factor and a strength by participants in all projects. The involvement, ownership, and participation that the approach engendered was said to have been an important strength behind the achievements. Aspects of the process were described positively in terms of the common purpose or common goal of services to improving services for consumers, and the commitment of participants to achieving improvements. This in turn was frequently linked to preexisting goodwill associated with such aspects as the sense of community and common purpose in service delivery and the level of ownership of the project by participants.

HACC Development Officers

The work of HACC development officers in areas such as Tamworth North-West and Ballina/Byron Bay was of fundamental importance and sorely missed in others where, for various reasons, it was not forthcoming.

Local Leadership

Another important feature of the most successful projects was the emergence of an effective and representative team of local leaders. These may be thought of as "community-sector entrepreneurs," a group of people who together have taken on the task of renegotiating and invigorating service provision at the local level. Where leadership was less united, or where strong leadership did not emerge at crucial times of the trial, difficulties were experienced in maintaining the project on any path of progress.

Extra Funding

Not surprisingly, another factor enabling projects to succeed was the availability of extra funding, placed at the disposal of the local steering committees responsible for the demonstration-projects program. While the amounts of funding available were small, they were sufficient to be able to be put to good use. Having funds with which to be able to undertake modest initiatives appears to have had an empowering effect on those participating in the projects, that in many ways outweighs the modest purchasing power the limited funds may otherwise have been seen to have if administered through more formal channels.

Policy Partnership

The development of a working relationship between project personnel and government officers was another matter widely praised by service providers. It was pointed out on a number of occasions that the demonstration project represented a new form of partnership in the development and implementation of policy. It was a partnership in which local staff members were made responsible for major decisions, but their work was able to benefit strongly from the ready availability of ADD staff from central office at different stages of the projects.

Support of Major Services

The commitment, support, and expertise of major services, particularly the Area Health Board, Home Care Service, and local government, were also extremely important in a number of projects. Two of the most outstanding examples in this regard were the projects in Manly Warringah Pittwater and Orange/Cabonne. The success achieved in Tamworth North-West also owed much to the early support offered by the Area Health Service and HCS.

Consumer Involvement

Consumer involvement was important, not just because it was itself a desired outcome, but also because it helped keep the momentum of projects going.

Impact of Broader Initiatives

The capacity to draw on links with other state and national community-care initiatives, such as the CIARR and the development of the common assessment framework, were also important in this regard. Projects benefited significantly from the support of both government and the community, where it was forthcoming.

Use of Consultants

The use of a skilled consultant at the local level enabled a number of projects to develop and elaborate plans from the general proposals first advanced by the steering committee. Although the small amounts of funding available to the projects were insufficient to enable them to appoint an extra person on a salaried basis, those chosen as consultants had the skills and knowledge of issues regarding community services to provide advice. While capable of bringing a degree of external objectivity and discipline to the exercise, those who were successful in the task also proved to be dedicated and able to act in ways that gave sympathetic expression to the general vision of the projects' participants.

Obstacles and Problems

The projects also faced a number of obstacles to the achievement of positive changes. Just as a number of the strengths and advantages of the approach were understood to be the products of the local, participatory approach adopted, many of the difficulties experienced reflected the approach adopted. Difficulties included insufficient time and resources available to move the process along at a quicker pace; fragile consensus for change; and policy uncertainty and external factors.

Insufficient Time and Resources

The amount of work required and the lack of staff time often meant that projects progressed at a slower pace than most participants would have desired. The delays arose in part as a consequence of the collaborative decision-making approach, as well as from the fact that the projects involved, as one participant remarked, "additional workload for service providers without additional resources."

Fragile Consensus for Change

It was a difficult and time-consuming task trying to keep large numbers of less-involved key services committed, especially with frequent staff changes. Building a consensus based on mutual understanding and commitment to a common course of action is particularly difficult in the interorganizational field. This reflects differences in power and resources of participating organizations, as well as differences among the individuals concerned and the varying levels of enthusiasm, commitment, and support from employers and organizations.

Policy Uncertainty and External Factors

A commonly cited cause of problems and delays for the projects was the uncertainty of developments with the Home and Community Care program and, more generally, with the future of government-funded services in Australia.

Other problems identified included those over geographic boundaries; the need for training of existing and new staff; and those arising from the entrenchment of service gaps and duplications that the resources and influence of the projects were not able to overcome.

Conclusions

The collaborative processes of the projects provided a common basis that was lauded for encouraging a high degree of support for the projects and the reforms proposed. These were seen, in the words of one participant, as fostering the development of a trusting and cooperative environment. Others pointed to the enthusiasm and dedication elicited from participants, the commitment of new and existing members to the process, and the goodwill encouraged by the participatory style of the committees and working parties. These remarks are all the more significant when measured against the sense of jealously guarded autonomy evident among many of the services at the beginning of the project in a number of the areas.

Other closely related features that were seen as beneficial were the use of a multidisciplinary focus by the projects and the strength of a local center of control. The availability of someone, either a permanent staff member or consultant, to expedite work was another key advantage. The importance of key project personnel who provide leadership to the projects is one of the clearest lessons to emerge from the evaluation.

There were also weaknesses evident in the projects' mode of operation. Most key participants were engaged in the direct provision of services to consumers on a full-time basis, and their capacity to devote significant amounts of time to the project have proven to be very limited. This has clearly slowed down the rate of progress. There was also a feeling that the limited financial support available acted as a constraint on their rate of implementation. It was suggested by some participants that this perhaps also signaled a lack of commitment of the state government to the project. Problems related to the administration of community-care services by government departments were also cited as weaknesses by project participants. The uncertain support offered by area health boards in a number of projects, and the lack of involvement by the Department of Community Services in one project, were experienced as major difficulties. What was described at one point in the program as "the collapse of direction from ADD and the Department of Health" was also demoralizing and served to undermine the momentum that had been developing. Other related problems concerned the complexities of higher-level departmental administration of community services, problems with the lack of fit between different regional and service administrative boundaries, and difficulties with the involvement of both disability- and aged-care services.

In summary, the achievements of the projects were impressive, especially when considered from a cost-effectiveness perspective. These initiatives, of importance to those involved in the projects at a management level, were also valued by other direct-care staff and by new consumers who had only recently commenced using services. Some evidence also suggested that they had the potential not only of improving access and quality of care for consumers, but also, over time, to achieve measurable increases in service efficiency. With only modest funding at their disposal, the projects helped develop a degree of cooperation among services that had previously seemed elusive.

The evidence examined for the evaluation confirms that the approach adopted by the demonstration projects provided a practical, value-for-money strategy for making significant improvements to the provision of community support services in New South Wales. However, it is clear that the success of the approach could be improved significantly if efforts were successful to overcome the problems of fragmentation inherent in the current administration of community support at the state and national levels. A greater sense of partnership among departments responsible for planning and funding services and those at the local level charged with actually providing care is also desirable.

Acknowledgments

This chapter, by Michael Fine, is based on the Final Evaluation Report by M. Fine, C. Thomson, and S. Graham. The evaluators would like to acknowledge the assistance of the evaluation liaison officers for the projects, members of the projects' steering committees, the managers and staff of participating services, the consumers who helped us with surveys or attended interviews, and all others who made this evaluation such an exciting and gratifying project to work on. We are also grateful for the contribution of staff from the Ageing and Disability Department and the Department of Health, to colleagues at the SPRC, and to Anna Howe and Terry O'Brien.

References

Australian Institute of Health and Welfare (AIHW). (1993). *Australia's welfare 1993: Services and assistance.* Canberra: AGPS.

Australian Institute of Health and Welfare (AIHW) (1999). *Australia's welfare 1999: Services and assistance.* Canberra: AIHW.

Fine, M. D. (1995). Community-based services and the fragmentation of provision. *Australian Journal of Social Issues, 30*(2), 143–161.

Fine, M. D. (2000). Coordinating health, extended care and community support services: Reforming aged care in Australia. *Journal of Aging and Social Policy, 11*(1).

Fine, M., Thomson, C., & Graham, S. (1998). *Demonstration projects in integrated community care.* Final Evaluation Report, Report for the NSW Ageing and Disability Department, Sydney.

Powell, D. G. (1997). Working together: A conceptual framework for integration. Unpublished manuscript. Centre for General Practice Integration Studies, School of Community Medicine, University of New South Wales, Sydney.

Waldvogel, J. (1997). The new wave of service integration. *Social Service Review, 71*(3), 463–484.

Webb, A. (1991). Coordination: A problem in public sector management. *Policy and Politics, 19*(4), 229–241.

PART FOUR

Lessons from the Field: Views of Practitioners

13

Neighborhood Networks in Worcester

Partnerships That Work

Richard Ford, Laurie Ross, & Mardia Coleman

F OR SEVERAL YEARS, WORCESTER'S (Massachusetts) Oak Hill Community Development Corporation (CDC) had been struggling to develop a positive neighborhood identity and to build feelings of unity in an older and declining urban neighborhood. Historically, Worcester has been an entry point for immigrants seeking employment in its numerous textile, abrasive, shoe, steel fabrication, and wire factories. Today most of these older industries are closed or greatly reduced in scope. Yet the immigrant flow continues, creating a strain on the city's infrastructure. This transitioning economic base and Worcester's persistent reputation as home to dozens of new immigrant communities has created selective pockets of poverty throughout the city. While the Oak Hill CDC had been effective in housing initiatives, it had been less successful in organizing residents to solve thornier problems such as youth gangs, lack of security, landlord–tenant disputes, and ethnic tensions, especially between the older generations of Eastern European origin and newer arrivals from Southeast Asia and the Caribbean.

Given similar situations across many Worcester neighborhoods—both resource rich and poor—priorities for neighborhood development are rekindling. Issues, especially those focused around youth and safety, have led to a variety of new community-based groups. While neighborhood organizations are not new in Worcester, the shape and style of the new generation are quite different from before. First, they are not primarily ethnic in character nor do they flow out of traditional urban neighborhood centers such as churches or social-service providers. Second, they are not political groups that define neighborhood organizing as getting money from city hall. Third, the organizations tend to focus on partnerships, networking, and consensus building rather than on confrontational tactics. Although many of the older techniques are still useful, their use has been substantially reduced compared to earlier years.

In their place, new partnerships and network-building tactics are emerging. A brief example from Oak Hill will illustrate these new elements (Allen et al., 1999; Ross et al., 1999; Ross and Coleman, forthcoming). In its search to move beyond housing and focus energies and resources on neighborhood development, the Oak Hill CDC hired two consultants. Their task was to help the community prepare a vision statement that would build consensus around the neighborhood's highest priorities. The consultants adapted community-based planning tools for network building that have been working effectively in Asia, Africa, and Latin America for the last decade. The approach, known as Participatory Rural Appraisal (PRA), engages all constituencies in a community and establishes neutral ground upon which all groups—male and female, poor and rich, empowered and marginalized, informal and formal, professional and lay—can hammer out priorities that all elements of the community can support (Ford et al., 1990; Ross and Coleman, forthcoming). The result of the process is a community-based action plan that sets in place the following:

• A detailed statement of what needs to be done.
• Which members of the community will do which things.
• What needs cannot be met from resources within the community.
• Who will seek external partners to attain these additional resources.

The core partnership is formed from elements within the community. A second-level partnership emerges between the community group or groups and the external partners. The combination of the bilevel partnership creates an effective network to implement the neighborhood's action plan.

In the case of Oak Hill, the action plan identified housing–landlord relations, youth, safety, and community building as its highest priorities. With a group of teenagers forming the core of the alliance, the partnership decided to rehabilitate a neighborhood park that had been trashed over the years and harbored drug traffic and wayward youth. The action plan called for converting this neighborhood liability into a community asset.

An informal alliance of the youth group, known as Teen Inspirators on the Move (OTM), the CDC, the consultants, a university department, the city Office of Planning and Community Development, the mayor, the Parks Department, and the city councillor who represented the Oak Hill area each played a role in making the dream become reality. Although it took two years, the teens persevered, working through the network's constituent members. They joined with other community groups to plan the park of their dreams, worked with city agencies to adjust the park plan to meet legal and environmental specifications, raised the money (a total of $60,000), and saw the plan through to a fully rehabilitated park.

In similar Worcester-partnership exercises, the partners have included parent councils, business leaders, neighborhood crime-watch groups, churches and interfaith organizations, and social-service agencies. The specific organizations that join these continually evolving networks depend on geography, the development issue at hand, and the individuals at the table.

Functions of a Neighborhood Network

Reviewing the work of Worcester networking activities reveals six functions that can be performed more effectively through networks (citizen–city–private sector–research organization) such as the Oak Hill park collaboration than with individual agencies acting unilaterally. These functions include accountability, physical development, social development, neighborhood planning, networking and information sharing, and organizational capacity building and staff training. All six functions for facilitating networking are well known in community-development circles. Three—neighborhood planning, networking, and capacity building—are highlighted here because of Worcester's particular emphasis on local planning and building capacities among neighborhood organizations.

Neighborhood Planning

The Oak Hill community-based planning illustrates the role of planning in both physical and social development. The plan that produced Oak Hill's teen-planned park rehabilitation also developed other priorities, including housing, security, landlord–tenant relations, and better information access for newcomers to the neighborhood. The Oak Hill consultants who had amended PRA tools for U.S. urban planning were highly creative in their adaptations. For example, in an African village, the standard procedure to stimulate interest in planning is to call a village meeting to identify a community's assets and problems. Tools such as a sketch-map exercise would help community members locate the best and worst parts of their community and explain why. In a U.S. urban neighborhood, if two consultants called such a meeting, no one would come.

The consultants opted for an alternative approach. They prepared a dozen flip-chart-size maps of the neighborhood, mounted them on cardboard sheets, and took them to frequently visited businesses in the neighborhood: the supermarket, liquor store, coffee shop, hair salon and barbershop, and the twenty-four-hour store where lottery tickets are sold. There they placed the maps on easels. As people passed by, the consultants asked if they would help by locating the neighborhood's best and worst places. Some ignored the question and kept walking. Others explained that they did not live in the neighborhood. Yet some stopped. Over a three-week period, about two hundred people drew on the maps, explained their reasoning, offered suggestions about how to solve the area's problems, and perhaps most important, left their names and addresses and promised that they would come to a community meeting to discuss these issues with other neighbors.

Armed with a new address list, the consultants synthesized the multiple maps into a compilation of the neighborhood's perceived assets and problems. They mailed it, along with a meeting invitation, to the two hundred people who responded. They also sent the invitation to key city and neighborhood figures. Instead of a handful of die-hard residents, the planning meeting had a turnout of eighty people, including the chief of police, several church leaders, local businesspersons, several city-department heads, and a good cross section of residents.

The meeting distilled a large assortment of needs down to a manageable list of four, one of which was youth priorities. It was from this process that the Oak Hill teen group first thought about the park. It was follow-up work from this meeting that built the multiple-constituency park-planning team. Neighborhoods can act as effective multiple-constituency entities for planning and action. The key is a planning process that mobilizes the neighborhood's information and resources in ways that encourage outside partners, such as city departments, to join forces with the neighborhood. When this chemistry works, the resulting network is almost certainly going to be effective.

Networking and Information Sharing

Worcester executive directors, community organizers, economic-development staff, and members of resident-led neighborhood organizations have always had impromptu and informal opportunities to meet and discuss their successes and struggles. These meetings were made more formal in 1996, with formation of the Neighborhood Forum, hosted by the Greater Worcester Community Foundation. All members of the Worcester community with interest in neighborhood development are welcome to attend. The forum now holds a regularly scheduled monthly opportunity to discover ways to promote the health, viability, and livability of Worcester's neighborhoods. The forum draws a relatively diverse group of people from resident-led organizations—CDCs, city government, hospitals, universities, the banking community, an environmental group, and other housing and social-service organizations. Regular attendees from city government include representatives from the DA's office, the Office of Planning and Community Development, the Probation Department, and two elected city councillors. Other city employees may come, depending on the issue.

Creation of the Neighborhood Forum represented a shift beyond primarily a "bricks and mortar" focus to consider a more holistic and comprehensive view of neighborhood development. While the forum has only an informal mission statement, it suggests that its purpose is to bring diverse people together who share an interest in exchanging experience and information in neighborhood planning and development. It provides a splendid opportunity for potential net-workers to get to know each other. About forty attend each month. While the Neighborhood Forum is not the only reason why Worcester neighborhood action is shifting from confrontation to networking, it is a strong force in regularly bringing people together who cut across the many constituencies—public, pri-vate, civic—of neighborhood planning.

Organizational Capacity Building and Staff Training

A recent role for Worcester's neighborhood networks is capacity building and training for staff and members of neighborhood-development organizations. Organizations had long been aware that they would benefit from training in areas such as membership development, community organizing, conflict mediation, action planning, and fund raising. While some organizations could afford to hire trainers and/or send staff to workshops, the majority could not. In cases of smaller groups, they did not necessarily know how to get help when institutional shortcomings surfaced. It also became clear that neighborhood organizers and residents were tired of going to prearranged workshops in which so-called experts came and told residents how to be neighborhood workers. During dis-cussions at the Neighborhood Forum, people began to see trends in the types of struggles they were confronting. Several forum sessions were then designated to introduce groups to community-development and -training theories and models, models in which residents were themselves simultaneously teachers and students with important experience and expertise to share. These sessions sparked a great deal of discussion and resulted in a survey of the forum membership to assess interest in more formal training sessions.

While these training discussions were going on, Clark University received a grant to bring seasoned community organizers and planners from Kenya to Worcester. The plan was to see if adaptation of African community-planning tools that had worked so well for the Oak Hill planning exercise might be expanded. The Neighborhood Forum, several CDCs in Worcester, and several community groups jointly sponsored the Clark effort, called Neighborhoods Taking Action.

Community-development experts from Kenya's Egerton University partici-pated in Worcester planning workshops to share their experiences and tech-niques. Later, Worcester residents traveled to Kenya to enroll in a three-week course in community-based planning. During these workshops, both in Worces-ter and Kenya, much information was shared. But organizations felt that work-shops were not enough. They preferred expanded training sessions, some of which would focus on peer-to-peer sharing of experience, while others would rely on professional trainers in community organizing and management. At the moment, Worcester neighborhoods are hoping that the training will add new energy and strength in community participation and networking to the neighbor-hood groups that have already begun to flourish.

Lessons Learned

Based on Worcester's neighborhood experience, four important lessons become clear about successful neighborhood collaboration and networking. Increasingly, Worcester leaders advocate formal methods of participation, because they see the results. Worcester has long been plagued by haphazard and ineffective revitalization efforts that city and business leaders, who often feel they alone know what is best for the city, have initiated. However, they have sometimes been proven wrong. Leaders throughout the city are learning that neighborhood and community members should have a say in how their city is developed. Although a participatory model can take longer to accomplish, the end result has proven to be more enduring.

Committed and Charismatic Individuals

The lessons of participation and networking would have little impact were it not for a driving energy for neighborhood improvement on the part of a select group of residents. A number of neighborhood leaders invest hours in meetings, organizing, writing proposals, and talking with city and business leaders—all on a voluntary basis and usually on top of raising families and working regular jobs. Concerned members of the community contribute to the Greater Worcester Community Foundation to support the continuing work of neighborhood grants, training sessions, neighborhood improvements, and seed money for new ideas. City employees, teachers, and administrators work far beyond the normal day to ensure that the work of the neighborhoods will continue. Two city councillors, on their own time, regularly attend the meetings of the Neighborhood Forum, as well as many of its sponsored activities. Perhaps the most interesting dimension about committed individuals is that the phenomenon is contagious. Good work begets even better work. Although the energized neighborhood volunteers are still a small minority of the city's population, they are growing.

Committed Institutions

Strong institutional support has set an important tone for the community. The Greater Worcester Community Foundation makes known its desire to fund participatory models of neighborhood development, as well as to direct training resources toward teaching participatory models. BankBoston (recently merged with Fleet Bank) and Clark University also are well known for their long-standing commitment to fund neighborhood initiatives. These institutions raise community awareness and expectations around collaboration. At a neighborhood organizational level, a participatory model of collaboration will not even be attempted unless there are leaders who are committed to these models. Certainly the Oak Hill CDC would never have pursued a participatory community-planning initiative, or devoted financial resources and staff time to the Teen Inspirators, were it not for its leadership and broad support for such models.

Additionally, the city's schools frequently collaborate with a variety of organizations and institutions to provide a much wider array of after-school programs than the schools themselves could offer. Thus, because of the strong history of collaboration and networking that exists in this city, a variety of professional-level art, theater, photography, pottery, computer, language, music, dance, sports, and other personal-growth opportunities are routinely provided to Worcester's youth and families.

Networking Rather Than Confrontation

Perhaps the most important lesson of all is that neighborhood energies and popular participation are having impact because of the philosophy of networking. Whereas in earlier times, a neighborhood or other special-interest group could make its weight felt through demonstrations and confrontational politics, that spirit is slipping away. Although confrontations are still important tools and major demonstrations may still be necessary to emphasize needs or priorities, they are no longer the first line of attack. Regular meetings of the Neighborhood Forum bring many diverse partners together on a continuing basis, so confrontations are headed off well before they become crises. Training and experience with systematic participation demonstrate that networking works. While every situation does not lead to a win-win solution, many do. Without question, the networking that pervades so many situations in Worcester occurs because of skills in using participatory tools, committed individuals and institutions, and an ambience that is sustained through institutions such as the Neighborhood Forum. Although many of these circumstances grow out of the unique social, economic, political, and institutional settings of Worcester, many are generic and can be adapted to other urban situations.

Conclusions

This short chapter suggests that principles and tools for networking and community participation are now available to enable community groups to join with city and other public agencies to form coalitions. These coalitions differ from earlier modes of community organizing, utilizing networking rather than conflict. Networking suggests that government agencies and neighborhood groups share common values and goals that are cooperative rather than conflict based. It is a promising principle to consider as a hallmark for urban planning and action in the new century.

References

Allen, K., et al. (1999). *Neighborhoods taking action: Linking community action and local participation in Kenya and Massachusetts.* Program for International Development, Clark University & PRA Programme, Egerton University.

Ford, R., et al. (1990). *Participatory rural appraisal handbook: Conducting PRAs in Kenya, program for international development.* Clark University, World Resources Institute, PRA Programme, Egerton University, & Kenyan Environment Secretariat.

Ross, L., Coleman, M., & Hall, R. (1999). *Students, schools, neighborhoods: A SPARCS action curriculum for community change.* Worcester Public Schools, Program for International Development (Clark University) & Jacob Hiatt Center for Urban Education (Clark University).

Ross, L., & Coleman, M. (Forthcoming). Urban community action planning inspires teenagers to transform their community and their identity. *Journal of Community Practice.*

14

Reaching Consensus on the Tampa Bay Estuary Program Interlocal Agreement

A Perspective

Richard Eckenrod

I N SPRING 1998, local government and agency partners of the Tampa Bay
National Estuary Program approved an Interlocal Agreement that commits
them to achieving the goals set forth in Charting the Course, the comprehensive conservation and management plan (CCMP) for bay restoration. Those
signatories are Hillsborough, Manatee, and Pinellas counties; the cities of
Tampa, St. Petersburg, and Clearwater; the Southwest Florida Water Management District; and the Florida Department of Environmental Protection. Additional signatories include the Florida Game and Freshwater Fish Commission;
the Environmental Protection Commission of Hillsborough County; the Tampa
Bay Regional Planning Council; Florida Marine Research Institute; and the
Tampa Port Authority. The U.S. Environmental Protection Agency entered into a
separate memorandum of understanding with the new TBEP, and the U.S. Army
Corps of Engineers entered into a joinder agreement with the new entity. The
Interlocal Agreement ensures consistent, timely, and cost-effective implementa-
tion of the CCMP by reducing duplication of effort and focusing attention on the
most pressing problems facing the bay. In return, participants in the Interlocal
Agreement are eligible for a streamlined permitting process for projects that pro-

vide a net environmental benefit, further the goals of the bay management plan, and are otherwise in compliance with agency rules and regulations.

Key elements of the Interlocal Agreement include the following:

• A commitment by signatories to accomplish the goals of the CCMP. The agreement includes a specific time frame for accomplishing each of the goals for bay improvement. TBEP partners will reevaluate and refocus these goals every five years, or more often if warranted.

• Effecting of the commitment through action plans prepared by each party and updated periodically.

• A commitment from regulatory agencies to exercise reasonable regulatory flexibility within their discretion to streamline the permitting of projects included in the action plans prepared pursuant to the CCMP.

• Reorganization of the Tampa Bay National Estuary Program as an independent alliance of government entities (under chapter 163, Florida Statutes) charged with overseeing implementation of Charting the Course. The new entity, called the Tampa Bay Estuary Program, is directed by a nine-member policy and a supporting management board composed of signatories to the agreement.

• A formula for funding the administration of the new entity.

Factors Contributing to Success in Reaching Consensus

The following are among the factors that, in the judgment of the author, contributed most to successfully reaching unanimous consensus on the Interlocal Agreement. No order of importance is implied.

• Requirement of federal grant for an implementation plan.

• A history of cooperation in the Tampa Bay region on environmental issues.

• Preference of regulated parties for a voluntary, as opposed to a regulatory, approach to reaching goals for bay restoration.

• The regulatory flexibility extended to regulated interests as an inducement for participation.

• Peer pressure—the fear of appearing uncooperative in the eyes of peer groups and the public in an effort with broad public and political support.

• Protection of organizations' interests.

• Continuity of service and ownership of participants in a process based on principles of watershed management.

• A desire on some people's part to leave a legacy.

• An understanding among policy makers that a healthy bay is important to the economy of the region and to their constituents.

• Affordable implementation.

Requirement of Federal Grant

Tampa Bay was accepted into the National Estuary Program in 1991 and became eligible for $1 million in federal funds over the next five years. The so-called Management Conference Agreement under which the federal funds were accepted required the development of a comprehensive conservation and management plan (CCMP), with certain elements prescribed by EPA. Among the required elements was a plan to implement and finance the CCMP.

History of Cooperation

For nearly twenty years, the Tampa Bay region has enjoyed an exceptional degree of cooperation among government, academic, industry, and citizen-interest groups on matters of bay management and protection. The first Bay Area Scientific Information Symposium (BASIS), held in 1982, set the stage for managing Tampa Bay as an ecosystem—a diverse array of biological communities interacting with their chemical and physical environment, all under the influence of man's activities.

The recommendation of bay-area scientists and resource managers to begin managing the bay as an integrated system led to the creation of the Tampa Bay Study Commission. The commission culminated in 1985 with the adoption of "The Future of Tampa Bay," the first comprehensive management plan for Tampa Bay. To foster implementation of the management plan, the Agency on Bay Management (ABM) was created as an arm of the Tampa Bay Regional Planning Council. As an alliance of approximately fifty individuals representing local governments, agencies, industries, and public-interest groups, the ABM provides a forum for discussion and action on a wide range of bay-related and other environmental issues in the Tampa Bay region.

Through the lobbying efforts of the ABM, Tampa Bay was named as a priority water body in the Surface Water Improvement and Management (SWIM) Act adopted by the Florida Legislature in 1987. The act called for SWIM plans to be developed for each priority water body named in the act or selected by the water-management districts designated by the legislature as the implementing agencies. And the act provided significant state funding to begin restoring Tampa Bay and other priority water bodies. The Resource-Based Water Quality Advisory Committee was formed within the Agency on Bay Management to advise the SWIM program as it developed a more detailed management plan for the bay. The process of developing the SWIM plan further strengthened working relationships among the diverse group of bay-area scientists and environmental managers serving on the water-quality advisory committee.

This backdrop of regional cooperation on bay-related issues greeted the Tampa Bay National Estuary Program when it was kicked off in 1991. The president's finding of Tampa Bay to be a water body of national significance, and the infusion of $1 million per year in federal funding to support development of a comprehensive conservation and management plan, attracted even more policy leaders and high-level managers to the arena. The dialogue among stakeholders over the next five years leading up to adoption of the Interlocal Agreement benefited immeasurably from the solid foundation of intergovernment cooperation forged over the preceding ten years.

Voluntary versus Regulatory Approach

Local governments and other parties to the Interlocal Agreement are generally opposed to purely regulatory approaches to achieving environmental objectives. A survey of environmental managers conducted by the Estuary Program during development of the CCMP revealed a widespread belief that additional regulations were not needed to achieve the goals for bay restoration. Participation in the first place of some parties in the Estuary Program may have been spurred in part by a desire to ensure that the program followed a nonregulatory approach to resource management.

Regulatory Flexibility

As an inducement to regulated parties to join the agreement, regulators agreed to extend reasonable regulatory flexibility within the limits of their regulatory discretion for projects that were part of action plans approved by the policy board. The regulatory flexibility specifically included permitting-process flexibility; expedited permitting processing; alternative monitoring and reporting requirements; coordinated permitting and inspections; and cooperative inspections that provide an opportunity for informal resolution of compliance issues before enforcement action is initiated.

The agreement also included commitments from regulatory parties to participate in a streamlined permitting process when requested by other signatories and to consider granting variances or waivers or changes to their rules for projects that demonstrate consistency with the goals of the CCMP.

Peer Pressure

Leading up to discussions of the Interlocal Agreement committing participants to implement the CCMP, two important factors were at play. First, a widespread consensus had developed over five years on the scientific validity and feasibility of achieving the goals for bay restoration adopted in the CCMP. And not only the EPA, but also the many stakeholders who had invested much time and effort in developing the CCMP expected it to be implemented. A compelling leader on the Estuary Program's highest level committee, the policy committee (later the policy board), envisioned very early in the program that the planning phase of the program should culminate in a formal written agreement among all parties to implement the CCMP. That individual frequently and forcefully reminded other committee members of that objective, and it grew to be widely accepted by the group.

The broad acceptance of the CCMP and its goals within the community as a reasonable and cost-effective approach to improving the quality of Tampa Bay would have made it difficult for any of the participants to refrain from entering the agreement.

When the U.S. Environmental Protection Agency and Army Corps of Engineers balked at signing the primary agreement and opted to sign an ancillary memorandum of understanding and joinder agreement, respectively, other parties were initially concerned. In time, the group accepted the alternate approach for the federal agencies. Had the primary agreement provided for long-term funding support from the EPA, the agency's absence from the primary agreement probably would have created more concern. The Corps of Engineers' involvement in implementing the CCMP is minimal compared with that of other participants, making the corps' absence from the primary agreement easier to accept.

Protection of Organizations' Interests

Although it was never verbalized to the author, it is likely that one of the motivations for organizations to be represented in the Estuary Program was to ensure that the interests of their local government or agency were protected. This concern may have been greater in the early stages of the Estuary Program, when regulated parties were uncertain what role regulatory agencies would assert in what was supposed to be a voluntary, nonregulatory program. However, after a five-year track record of mostly amiable cooperation in developing the bay management plan, suspicions about other parties' motivations were probably reduced.

Two regulatory programs—the National Pollutant Discharge Elimination System (NPDES) as applied to storm-water runoff, and the Total Maximum Daily Load (TMDL) requirements of the federal Clean Water Act—generated a good deal of discussion in the period leading up to and during negotiations on the Interlocal Agreement. An unsuccessful attempt was made in the year preceding the start of discussion on the agreement to adopt a resolution regarding the impact the Interlocal Agreement would have on these programs. One of the key sticking points was reaching agreement on how actions required in NPDES permits for storm-water management issued to local governments by the EPA would be linked to implementation of the CCMP. Local governments were equally concerned about whether the TMDL for nitrogen being developed by the Florida Department of Environmental Protection would impose another set of requirements on them over and above their commitments to the Estuary Program to control nitrogen loading. Ensuring satisfactory resolution of these issues probably helped keep regulated parties at the table.

Continuity of Service and Ownership in the Process

There was a remarkable degree of continuity among membership of key committees, particularly the management board. Fourteen of the sixteen members of the management board who were appointed to serve on it in 1991 were still active on it when the Interlocal Agreement was finalized in early 1998. It was not unusual for policy and management board members to express frustration over the fate of many long-range planning documents that too often just occupied shelf space. They pledged that the CCMP would not meet a similar fate. The expenditure of considerable time and effort surely fostered among most of the members a feeling of ownership in the CCMP and a desire to see the product of their labor successfully implemented.

Leaving a Legacy

To at least one member of the policy board, adoption of the landmark Interlocal Agreement was an important element of his legacy to the Tampa Bay community. As chairman of the powerful Southwest Florida Water Management District, his leadership and influence over the consensus-building process was of inestimable importance.

Economic Sense

To some participants, cleaning up and protecting Tampa Bay to sustain the economic vitality of the region was a stronger motivating factor than preserving the environment for its own sake. And while it may not have been a primary motivation for all of the participants, they all understood that the economic well-being of the region depended on the quality of the bay and the environment in general.

Affordable Implementation

A study conducted by the Estuary Program revealed that over $260 million is expended each year by governmental entities in the Tampa Bay region on projects that directly or indirectly advance the goals of bay restoration. Approximately $160 million of that amount accounts for collecting, treating, and disposing of domestic wastewater. It does not include expenditures by industry for environmental controls and monitoring. The estimated increase in cost each year to implement the CCMP was less than 1 percent of the total expenditures. Had implementation costs been significantly greater, resistance to the Interlocal Agreement likely would have been proportionately greater.

Overcoming Barriers to Consensus

Several barriers were encountered in the course of reaching consensus on the Interlocal Agreement. They and the measures taken to overcome them are discussed below.

Professional Facilitation

Many of the potential obstacles to successfully reaching consensus on the Interlocal Agreement were avoided through a well-designed and competently facilitated process. Identification of stakeholder interests through interviews with individual parties helped identify most significant issues and avoided pitfalls late in the process. Development of a detailed framework for the agreement based on the interviews helped organize and focus the discussion on key unresolved issues.

Cracking the Governance Nut

One of the most difficult issues consistently encountered by national estuary programs is deciding what public or private entity will administer the program as it moves from the planning phase into implementation. At the core of the issue is what agency, local government, or other entity will receive and manage the program's funds, and who will be vested with decision-making authority, including decisions on expenditure of program funds. Many estuary programs continue to struggle with this issue years after the adoption of CCMPs.

In the case of the Tampa Bay program, the choice boiled down to two alternatives: leaving the structure of the program substantially the same, with funds coming to a regional planning council that provided administrative support for the program, or creating a new, completely autonomous legal entity with a board of directors that would ultimately be responsible for establishing program policy and making decisions on program spending. Two subcommittees were formed to evaluate the options. One group consisted of attorneys representing the governmental bodies that would be signatories to the Interlocal Agreement. Their task was to identify and evaluate legal and policy implications of creating a new legal entity versus maintaining the existing governance arrangement. A second group was created to determine what the impact on staff employment benefits would be if they were to become employees of a new entity.

The recommendation of the legal review group was almost unanimous to create a new legal entity as provided for under chapter 163, Florida Statutes. The regional planning council attorney supported the status quo option. The other subcommittee determined that there would be adverse impact on staff benefits associated with creation of a new entity. Whereas the regional planning council was not pleased with the governance decision, the council recognized the overriding importance of the Interlocal Agreement and agreed to be a signatory.

Inducement to Regulated Parties

Extending regulatory flexibility to local governments and other regulated parties was an important incentive for participation of regulated interests in the agreement. The flexibility covered permitting, monitoring, and inspection activities and included consideration of variances and waivers from state regulations. The agreement also included a special section on streamlined permitting.

During negotiations on the agreement, regulated parties indicated that regulatory flexibility was necessary for their participation in the agreement. A good deal of effort was devoted to negotiating satisfactory terms. Although regulatory flexibility may have provided some inducement at the time for regulated parties to join the agreement, to the author's knowledge, none of the parties has sought to take advantage of the provisions since the agreement took effect in March 1998.

Positive Involvement of Attorneys

Consistent involvement of attorneys representing various groups throughout the negotiating process was an important factor in overcoming certain barriers. The crucial role played by attorneys in resolving the governance issue was described above. In that case, a group of fourteen attorneys worked cooperatively to overcome a major potential obstacle. And when the process bogged down over how the agreement would interface with the Florida Legislature's recently adopted Ecosystem Management Act, a group of four attorneys representing regulators and regulated parties was assigned the task of redrafting the ecosystem-management provisions of the agreement. The group's work product, representing balanced points of view, was then ready to be accepted by the management board. For the most part, attorneys participating in the process sought ways to facilitate consensus, not obstruct agreement. The process would not have reached a successful conclusion without the constructive participation of attorneys.

A Champion for the Agreement

It is difficult to judge which of the foregoing factors was most important in overcoming obstacles to reaching consensus on the Interlocal Agreement. But there is little doubt that the strong leadership provided by a vigorous champion for the Interlocal Agreement advanced the consensus-building process more than any other single factor. The individual who championed the agreement not only was instrumental in overcoming obstacles encountered along the way, but also conceived the idea of the agreement, drafted the majority of it, and served as its principal advocate throughout the consensus-building process. His effectiveness as the champion was enhanced by his ability to appreciate the interests of all stakeholders in the process and to conceive compromises that preserved the integrity of the agreement. When obstacles were encountered, he wisely appointed task forces, with differing viewpoints appropriately represented, to work through the problem. To minimize the appearance of a conflict of interest, he relinquished his position on the Estuary Program's policy board, on which he represented the governing body of a powerful water-management agency in the Tampa Bay region.

15

Thoughts on Motivational Problems in Networks

Nina Burkardt

C HAPTER 6 IN THIS VOLUME (by Lisa S. Nelson) poses several important questions for practitioners in natural-resource-management fields. The discussions of what motivates people to participate in decision-making, and what factors encourage continued involvement, are ongoing and continue to puzzle natural-resource managers and others interested in collaborative planning or decision-making.

In our work, we have seen interorganizational networks in their very early days of formation and those at a more mature state. We have seen networks formed to address a single issue, like the licensing of a hydropower project, or a more complex and long-term issue, such as coordination of diverse land-management responsibilities on a broad geographic scale for a long period of time. We have seen networks formed with intent and those that seemed to spring up with less clarity of purpose. While each situation is unique, it is possible to make a few observations along the lines of Nelson's work on interorganizational networks.

An interesting example of a voluntary network formed through mutual motivation is the Canyon Country Partnership in southeastern Utah. This group was formed in 1994 as a forum for public-land managers, county commissioners, representatives of state agencies, and others with an interest in the impacts of tourism and recreation on public lands in the area. Because approximately 95 percent of the land in this region is publicly owned, with management responsibilities dispersed across several federal and state agencies, coordination among various jurisdictions is essential but occurred only on an *ad hoc* basis prior to establishment of the partnership. By the early 1990s, southeastern Utah was facing a crisis as tourism increased exponentially and land-managers' budgets remained flat.

The original intention of the partnership was to provide a forum for consensus-based decision-making, but it became apparent that value differences among various interests were too great to accommodate consensus. Rather than dissolve, the partnership reexamined its mission and determined that focusing on the process of information sharing was a more realistic goal than the products of consensus-based decision-making. This seems to illustrate some of the risks of public participation. With the expectation that substantive resource-management decisions would indeed be made, local and regional interest groups attended partnership meetings. The partnership, however, determined that it lacked the capacity to guide the group toward resolution of what have proven to be intractable conflicts. While there is always pressure to move beyond process and produce results, networks need to be cognizant of their legal, financial, and practical limitations.

The Legal-Institutional Analysis Model (LIAM)

Another use of a network is to attempt to resolve conflicts bounded in time. In such cases, the network might form for the purpose of addressing a particular set of circumstances and then disband. Under this scenario, participants tend to have a much shorter time frame and may be suspicious of an emphasis on process. We observed some of the dynamics of network formation when we conducted a workshop using the Legal-Institutional Analysis Model (LIAM). This is a computer-based model developed by a group of social-science researchers in the U.S. Geological Survey that allows participants in a natural-resource conflict to analyze the likely behavior of other organizations involved in the problem. It is most effectively used in the early stages of problem solving, so that parties can come to a shared vision of the scope of the problem and the intensity of the disagreement. The main players in an emerging interorganizational network are identified during the workshop. Indeed, many of the potential players participate in the workshop.

Our most recent experience with a LIAM workshop occurred during the summer of 1999. The Wyoming Department of Fish and Game approached us because the department had to write a state management plan for the grizzly bear, to implement if the bear is removed from the endangered species list. This is a highly contentious issue, and the disagreements over the scientific status of grizzly bear recovery, coupled with value differences among those interested in the issue, are enormous and complicated. The long list of stakeholders in this instance includes state and federal fish and game agencies, national park managers, environmental- and wildlife-interest groups, ranchers, outfitters, county commissioners, congressional delegates, and others. At the end of the two-day workshop, the group agreed that a collaborative decision process was preferable to other options, but articulated a number of concerns noted by Nelson. In particular, the group feared that the decision would be dominated by the traditional, more powerful network members and that the appearance of collaborative decision-making would merely be a smokescreen for behind-the-scenes deal-making. Most of the workshop members were experienced in collaborative processes and exhibited a fair dose of skepticism. On the other hand, organizations had an incentive to participate in the network, because decisions about bear management must be made, with or without the involvement of all potential network members.

Organizational and Participant Preferences

Nelson notes that there are sometimes differences between organizational and participant preferences in collaborative decision processes. We have seen both kinds of motivation. Often, external motivation leads to the formation of groups that are focused on a single issue with a well-defined decision point. An example of this is a group working on an application for a license for a hydropower project. Legislation, and regulations of the Federal Energy Regulatory Commission (FERC), require some level of shared decision-making. Nelson points out that some mandated processes are made more open and participatory in an effort to diminish conflict. This seems to be a trend in FERC relicensing processes, so that license applicants more fully engage the public in the licensing process than was done in the past. While these efforts have been somewhat successful, the difficulty is moving out of old patterns of behavior and decision-making. Participants need to be realistic about the fact that the balance of power really does not change simply because the process appears to be more participatory.

Conclusions

The trend toward public involvement in environmental decision-making is certain to continue. While many networks work in earnest to find common ground and explore mutually agreeable solutions, networks often fall apart. The reason for this is that some parties leave networks when it becomes clear to them that the range of alternatives presented by the group will not encompass their preferences. Some groups never join the network at all, leaving open questions of representativeness. Further research should address the questions of defining conflicts amenable to solution by networks; the problems of identification and involvement of a full range of actors; and linking network processes with network products.

16

Empowering Communities Through the Use of Place Management

Illana Halliday

IN EARLY 1998, THE COUNCILLORS of the Fairfield City Council decided to take time out to review their performance and assess the environment in which they were operating. This is not a common activity in local government, the least sophisticated or recognized of the three tiers of government in Australia.

As a result of their strategic thinking, the council has had a major overhaul of its direction. A clear and achievable vision is driving the planning and budgeting system. Place and system management is providing solutions to complex problems. An organizational restructure has improved accountability. A purchaser-provider partnership is increasing our responsiveness to issues and opportunities.

The council is ready to tackle a wide range of complex problems and issues that face the community. New strategies, systems, structures, and staff arrangements provide opportunities that were not possible a year ago. The most innovative and exciting change has been the implementation of place management. Several different forms of place management have been introduced, with a wide variety of boundaries and outcomes that best suit each place.

Some challenges arose when we implemented place management. We learned some valuable lessons about the definition of the place; role clarification

who are accountable for the outcomes and the budget proposals to pro-
 outcomes. This could produce a program versus place-manager con-
each place manager becomes an advocate for his or her "place," which
the place managers in conflict with each other.

two potential conflicts are managed through effective communication
ipation in planning, budgeting, and performance monitoring. All the
nd place managers are part of the City Outcomes team, so there is fre-
nal and informal communication among the staff. The City Outcomes
so the "purchaser" within the council.

ser–provider separations have become common in government. Each
ager will be vying for attention from the service provider in order to
iorities for that place addressed, particularly when budget flexibility
 emerging priorities to be dealt with throughout the year, rather than
 each priority in the formal budget-review process. To some extent, the
etting is addressed when the purchaser (which includes all the place
 working together) negotiates service-level agreements with the pro-
exibility is a very important inclusion in a work program and must be
 business plans and service-level agreements. This process is in the
 of development. A better role-clarification exercise is needed concern-
rocess. At present, we are operating on goodwill and shared goals.
rocess of resource allocation highlights the need to have partnerships
 council. Formal systems are needed to ensure that information flows
nd efficient. No one wants to take on a police role or to be a constant
 complaint. We are developing a client-request system that will be
customer-service standards developed by the service provider. This will
hrough the customer-call center. The staff members offer expert advice
vices that are possible, putting a brake on unrealistic expectations. This
giving the community and its representatives better information about
 of the services the council provides.

king with the Politics

of the areas that has emerged as a concern is the relationship between
 manager and the elected representative. Some accusations have been
t the place manager takes over the legitimate role of the elected mem-
ll levels. The place manager receives a large amount of direct commu-
from the community. Irritating problems are taken to the place manager
ved. The place manager is on the ground and readily available; his or her
an be quite high in the community.

e the potential for competition exists between the place manager and the
ns, the role is really complementary. The place manager can quickly fix
lems that are identified by the elected member. Priority setting and
 allocation are the ultimate responsibility of the elected members. The
anager ensures that the best information is available to assist the elected
 in those decisions.

Cabramatta project addressed this concern by having regular meetings

and resource decisions; working with the politics; and developing partnerships
with the community.

Fairfield City

Fairfield City covers an area of more than 104 square kilometers southwest of the
Sydney central business district (CBD). It incorporates twenty-eight suburbs,
which are predominantly residential and industrial. There are also some rural
expanses of land to the west. There are four business districts, the two largest
being Cabramatta and Fairfield. The city has one of Australia's largest industrial
estates in Smithfield and Wetherill Park.

Fairfield City has a population of approximately 190,000 people and is home
to one of the most culturally rich and diverse communities in Australia, with over
133 different nationalities. English is the second language in over 60 percent of
homes.

The Changing Environment

The environment in which local government operates has changed considerably
over the last four years. In taking stock of these changes, the councillors of the
Fairfield City Council wished to address the following:

- Accountability—structural reform; performance reporting; and IPART
  (Independent Pricing and Regulatory Tribunal of New South Wales) issues.
- National Competition Policy—Trade Practices Act; market testing and competitive tendering; costing methodologies; and business classifications.
- Increased demands and roles as a service provider—customer demands;
  information technology; environmental pressures; social pressures; global
  economy; financial pressures; and expectations for smaller government.
- Increased focus on participatory democracy and achieving outcomes for the
  community—informed communities; more partnerships; improved direction-
  setting; making a sustainable difference for the community.

The Strategy

The councillors worked in unity to develop a clear vision for Fairfield City. To
implement this vision, the councillors decided to introduce an innovative place-
management model that recognizes the unique character of places and systems
within the city. This model is supported by a new organizational structure.

Places and Systems

The Fairfield City Council faces a range of very complex problems that span the
entire range of services provided within the council or, in fact, within govern-

ment. In the past, these problems have been broken down into simplistic actions taken by a "guild," or a small, self-contained unit of officers from one profession. All the staff made a contribution to solving the problem, but no one was accountable for ensuring delivery of a solution. Frequently, problems that needed integrated actions ended up in the "too-hard basket."

With a strong focus on the outcomes determined in the vision statement, the Fairfield City Council has broken that pattern. An alternative way of looking at the problems is that they are usually contained within either a "place" or "system."

Not all of the complex problems the Fairfield City Council faces are in a tightly contained place. In some instances, the problems span an entire system, such as the five creeks of the area or the open-space system. The system, like a place, becomes the prime responsibility of an officer. Accountability for improving that system in line with the vision rests with the officer.

Structures

To drive the new directions and priorities, the councillors restructured the organization, improving responsiveness to issues and opportunities. The new structure provides a partnership between the purchaser of outcomes for the city and the providers of services. It also increases the scope for partnerships with external agencies and other levels of government.

The program and place managers work together to ensure that the council's activities focus on the outcomes in the vision. Staff with priority-setting and service-specification responsibility (the purchasers) are part of the new City Outcomes Department.

The place managers are all based in the City Outcomes Department. They have a role that is strong in influence to help them in problem recognition and resolution. The power of their positions comes from the strength of their relationships with the community and the councillors.

Challenges and Lessons in Implementing Place Management

Several challenges faced us in terms of implementing place management. Key issues surrounded the definition of the place; role clarification and resource decisions; working with the politics; and developing partnerships with the community. Many of these issues have been resolved; some solutions are still evolving.

Defining Place Management

There are many possible ways to define place management. It can be described in geographic terms, system terms, or in relation to shared issues or opportunities. The management function varies in level of intensity, with one end of a continuum being coordination and the other being a model of full control of all resources and priority setting given to the manager and/or the community.

In the Fairfield City Council, five types of place management are being used.

There are two Mainstreet programs in oper[...] Fairfield. These have clear geographic boun[...] set of issues (economic development, impro[...] tion, and tourism), and the coordinators in [...] control on a day-to-day basis, allocated by [...] mendations from the respective town-center [...]

Cabramatta is the focus of another very in[...] The Cabramatta Place Management project i[...] cil and premiers department. It is focused o[...] lines around the geographic place when it ta[...] ment. Other issues such as drug-related behav[...] place, problems of safety and security, econo[...] ment are being tackled by the state governm[...] way. To some extent, there is a lot of coordi[...] other areas, the budget for some council-fund[...] center manager and committee. This partnersh[...] community.

The local government area has also been [...] include the Cabramatta and Fairfield CBDs. Th[...] lines of suburbs but more closely align to com[...] boundaries produces places that need a differe[...] manager for each of these places is accountabl[...] seeing that problems are solved, ensuring that th[...] gic-planning process, and providing a single p[...] for opportunities or issues about the place. At [...] structured community participation are minimal[...]

The last form of place management that we [...] urb support officer." Each member of staff withi[...] has "adopted" a suburb. These staffers visit "the[...] tion about their appearance and feel, gathering[...] that need attention. They participate in strategic[...] works they believe are important. They work cl[...] ager. They do not have budget delegation and at[...] community consultation. The exceptions to this [...] dinators, who are also the suburb support office[...]

The fact that five different forms of place [...] mented illustrates that there is no one "right" d[...] Rather, a conscious decision is needed about how[...] intensity of management is desired.

Role Clarification and Resource Decisions

The place-management system introduces a [...] and budget processes. No matter what level of [...] when setting up the place-management model, th[...] If you are using program or outcome budgets, [...]

managers [...]
duce those [...]
flict. And [...]
could put [...]

These [...]
and partic[...]
program a[...]
quent for[...]
team is al[...]

Purch[...]
place mar[...]
get the p[...]
allows fo[...]
addressin[...]
priority s[...]
managers[...]
viders. Fl[...]
built into[...]
early day[...]
ing this p[...]

The [...]
within th[...]
are fast a[...]
source o[...]
linked to [...]
operate t[...]
about ser[...]
includes [...]
the cost [...]

Wor[...]

One [...]
the plac[...]
made th[...]
bers at a[...]
nication [...]
to be sol[...]
profile [...]

Whi[...]
politicia[...]
the pro[...]
resource[...]
place m[...]
member[...]
The [...]

with the elected members (predominantly with the councillors, but also other elected members) to ensure that they were fully informed about what matters were current in the community and what responses were taking place. All opportunities for new projects were communicated so that early the elected members could be involved.

The recruitment and selection process for the Mainstreet coordinators includes a meeting with representatives of the elected members and the town-center committee to ensure that an effective working relationship is possible.

Yet again, this potential pitfall is handled with good communication and understanding of the role of each participant. Place managers have to be strongly focused on the result to be achieved and driven to achieve that result without public recognition. They operate in the community but actually are public servants implementing the directions of the elected members.

Developing Partnerships with the Community

One area that is emerging as an exciting opportunity is the more active participation of the community. Community ownership and democracy have an increased role in decision-making. Several of the "places" have active community committees or discussion groups. Although these committees do not have delegated powers, their recommendations are put to the council, and in most cases these recommendations are adopted.

The level of debate in these committees is encouraging to observe. They battle out their own conflicts over priorities or decisions that they are forwarding to the council. As more accurate information is able to be provided about competing priorities, true costs of services, and future opportunities for services, these debates will become even more important.

This is an area of place management that has yet to be fully explored. Empowerment through the provision of information and opportunity to make decisions about their place will allow people to take on an active role in government. It also increases the potential for increased demands for more information or greater levels of participation.

It is worthwhile to examine the different types of format and composition used in the consultative forums supporting place management. Structurally, we have groups that comprise key stakeholders and councillors. In two of these groups, this includes the local state member of parliament providing direct access to the next tier of government. Bureaucrats from the state government, however, are not included, because their inclusion could obscure the community debate. Occasionally state government bureaucrats are invited to attend meetings to provide information on specific items (such as crime rates or health issues). They do not have voting rights. These two consultative groups have been operating for some time and are made up of very informed and empowered people. These people know the system and how to use it and are not fearful of government. The members of these groups were appointed in a top-down process by nominations from the council.

A new group that is being established has taken a bottom-up approach.

Council staffers have been working on the ground with local opinion leaders and people who are viewed as being important by some very disempowered people. This is a sensitive community where many of the people are very fearful of government, and they do not know the system. A conscious decision has been made to work with this community, develop leadership skills, and prepare them to take an active role in a consultative forum. No state government representatives are involved. (Council staffers take valuable data to their state government colleagues, so that actions can be better informed.)

The group dynamics remain tentative as individuals get to know each other and accept this new role. They are building a relationship around a common goal, with a real opportunity to build something for their local community. Government (in this case local government staff) will assist them but does not dominate the process. Over time, it is expected that this group will be self-sustaining, since it will have worked together, with government not being the lead player, to provide local solutions to local problems. Time will tell if the partnerships being forged this way can survive beyond the achievement of the first goal.

Where to Go from Here?

The Fairfield City Council is implementing several different forms of place management. They are not mutually exclusive, and the deliberate overlaps require good communication. We are a learning organization, and as such we are prepared to try the different approaches. Constant reflection on the results we are obtaining helps us fine-tune the models and adjust our systems. This flexible approach is letting us be innovative in how we respond to opportunities or threats.

We have a staff committed to excellence for the community and willing to attempt new things. Many of our internal systems need to be reviewed and enhanced, and the timing of this is ideal.

The old systems are being replaced by new ones that are designed to focus on outcomes, results, and accountability. We have good information-technology resources and staff trained in its use. This is helping us to overcome some traditional communication barriers.

Place management in its many forms will be an important part of our future. We are avoiding the trap of setting too many rigid rules around the concept. Key issues that need to be faced in successfully implementing place management are to ensure that good communication exists, to set a clear shared vision for the organization, and to keep the systems as flexible as possible. Places will change over time, howsoever one has defined them. Place management is about being responsive to emerging opportunities and needs, and as such requires a flexible approach to management.

17

Getting Things Done
Through Networks

Shayne Walker & Catherine Goodyear

Kia ora, Kia orana, Talofa, Hi, Welcome
Nga mihi aroha kia koutou,
Ko te kaupapa, he tino whakahira kia tatou katoa
No reira tena koutou tena koutou tena koutou katoa
Nau te rourou, naku te rourou,
ka ora te manuhiri;
Nau te rakau, naku te rakau,
ka mate te hoariri.

(Your food basket and my food basket
will satisfy the guest;
Your weapon and my weapon
will dispose of the enemy.)

THE MAORI *WHAKATAUKI*, OR INDIGENOUS PROVERB, above is an excellent illustration of the philosophy of getting results by working through networks. When people come together to share whatever they have in their baskets, they can get things done. An urgent need, a program opportunity, or just a good idea could be the catalyst. The words "Why don't we work together on this?" trip off the tongue. It sounds great, and there are warm fuzzies all around, *aroha* (love), and smiles. But months down the track, are people all still smiling, or has the project crashed?

Both of us are committed to the development of our respective networks through joint projects both across cultural lines and within our own cultural sectors. Recently in New Zealand, or Aotearoa (land of the long white cloud), an environment that has encouraged supposedly "healthy competition" through New Right (economic rationalism) management and funding processes, we have tended to become competitors. However, collaboration, cooperation, and looking out for one another have not only remained core values, but have been and still constitute a valid and necessary survival and development strategy, to which groups of people have remained committed. But networks can be used to empower and disempower. The use of networks to prop up a reduction in the provision of core services has meant that they themselves have become commodities that are traded politically to suit those in power in their pursuit of cost saving and further control. In other words, networks are factored in as part of the solution without adequate funding or voice.

We both have experienced *aroha*, and we both have experienced disappointments while working in networks and trying to develop cooperative ventures. We offer two examples of this. One is a project where two groups combined to manage and support the placement of a community worker in a school. This endeavor was planned for months and had written goals but no shared policy understanding; we said what we wanted to do, not how we would do it. It fell apart after six weeks, when one of the groups decided that the contracted worker was not appropriate, and we had no shared understanding about how to deal with the situation.

The other is a coalition of three groups that contracted jointly to provide a service to support families that had babies up to three years old that were at risk. After two years, this continues to work well for the families involved, but the project has struggled more recently because of management issues—how the accountability requirements of a particular funding body would be undertaken, and who was accountable. Here again, there was inadequate shared understanding, which inhibited our ability to manage this project as a group and strained relationships with one another. Better planning and process in the initial stages would have saved us time in the long run.

Our experience tells us that any collaborative project requires well-thought-through processes at its inception, a detailed agreement of shared understandings, clear and simple written policy that underpins this, and in particular making sure that all involved know who is responsible for what and when. The first rule: Never assume that people have read and absorbed policies or agreements of shared understandings on specific issues. Often, a few weeks down the track, and certainly a few *months* down the track, the fact that "there is policy" tends to be forgotten; the excitement and energy over the new program take on a life of their own. However, as two eternal optimists, we continue to seek chances for our networks to work cooperatively, effectively, and safely.

Two Cross-Cultural Ventures

Recently, we have combined our networks to work together on two cross-cultural ventures, with successful outcomes so far. The first was an agreement to use our respective networks to provide joint training for foster parents on an ongoing basis. Over a period of two years, we trained about fifty caregivers together.

The caregivers were Maori and Pakeha (non-Maori people)—strangers to each other, and for some, strangers to each other's culture. In the planning process, we looked at the following:

- Treaty of Waitangi[1] issues for both groups.
- *Whanau*[2] (family and extended family) issues for Maori and Pakeha.
- Legal issues for both around the Children, Young Persons and Their Families Act 1989.
- Legal issues, particularly for Maori, over guardianship.
- Cultural issues for Pakeha caregivers concerning caring for Maori and Pacific Island children.
- Other issues relating to children generally.

The first meeting of each group started in a culturally appropriate way, with a modern-day urban interpretation of the traditional greeting forms: *whaikorero* (formal speech-making), *waiata* (to sing and songs), *mihimihi* (greetings), and *kai* (to eat or food), in the rituals of encounter. The involvement and guidance of *kuia* and *koroua* (female and male elders, esteemed, the repositories of knowledge) were essential, as this linked the past, present, and future for the representative cultures of the participants. The joining together with food, an often overlooked aspect of bicultural collaboration, is one that plays an important part in the development of understanding and togetherness. This is more than just hospitality and eating, as it has elements of learning and growing together that are physical, emotional, and spiritual. There are symbols and meanings that are implicit in the sharing of *kai* (food), such as "let's start with building relationships, lets work on our own processes with each other."

When we got together for food, it meant we were open, we were sharing. It was not just about the *kaupapa* (project, agenda, plan), business, or money, but it was about making an effort and making sure the process was right. During the development of one specific program, we worked through the meetings with food. Each time, the meal was prepared by a manager of a large community agency who usually had staff that would undertake this task. When we discussed this, she said she felt that it was important for her to prepare the food. As the discussion progressed, it became apparent that this was an opportunity to serve one another. For her, this was about philosophy, process, and action.

In the second, more recent venture, we have been involved in a multicultural endeavor to work together to tender for a new parent-support program. This is a partnership among Maori, Pakeha, and Pacific Island networks and is an attempt to use the strengths of all three cultural sectors to ensure that the children and families entering the service will have access to appropriate people and programs.

When we met together for the first time, with varying understandings of what the project was about, some were quite familiar with the concept of the new program, and others knew very little. This meeting was difficult at times, because people were feeling uncertain about the program, but what we did share was that all the participants were committed to the well-being of families, so we decided to meet again.

At the second meeting over a shared meal, everything started to come together, and over the next few hours we developed a mission statement, a concept of how it could work, using a three-partied network approach, goals, and vision. At the third meeting, we started to look at specific policy to underpin this. Since then, the group has won a large contract and has submitted another tender on the basis of the group working together again. We continue to be protective of the process so that Maori, Pakeha, and Pacific Island peoples can continue to work together effectively.

The molding together of these three groups and their networks has proven to be a joyful, but at times difficult, task. The three groups represent three quite distinct constituencies; in fact, the Pacific Island group represents seven Pacific Island nations: Samoa, Tokelau, Tonga, Niue, Cook Islands, Fiji, and Tuvalu. The process for choosing two representatives for each of the three groups is unique to each and requires the utilization of different networking and diplomacy skills that have their own time frames. While there is a timetable to develop this project, being representative, accountable, and sharing the information with our respective communities are integral parts of the process. We have spent several sessions developing our commonalties around several issues, including process. This, combined with a strong commitment to work together in a collaborative way, has allowed us to grow in relationship to the point where we are now developing policies that do not rely on that relationship being intact. We have matured in the way we deal with each other and have accepted that we will not always get along, and we need written policies to cover those times. When we meet, we are pleased to see one another, and we are able to work together by being honest about the issue or *kaupapa* and protective of the process of how we work together. Becoming familiar has not been taken for granted, and working out how we can work together is an ongoing process that we all contribute to. The *kaupapa* for which we gather is one that is close to our hearts, and we are committed to it and each other. An understanding and acceptance of one another's cultural imperatives and how they operate within our respective networks is critical to achieving good results.

When working cross-culturally, the same issues arise, but the process for working may be different. In New Zealand/Aotearoa, it is very easy for Pakeha culture to be dominant, and often, in an effort to be businesslike, it can override the cultural components of, for example, Maori, who have their own ways of conducting business. Minority groups and their networks have their own strategies and resistance initiatives for dealing with the dominant cultures, such as withdrawing or nonparticipation. These become built into the networking practices of indigenous peoples. Projects have fallen apart spectacularly when one party to an agreement forgets the *tikanga* (custom or correct way of doing something) of one of the partners.

When working with Maori, networking through *Iwi* (tribe), *Hapu* (subtribe), and *Whanau* is usually implicit. The implementation may differ between urban and rural environments, but the networking principles are still the same. Accountability is through *runanga* (assembly) structures, *kuia*, and *koroua*. Kaupapa Maori is described as "the philosophy and practice of being and acting Maori" (Smith, 1992, p. 1). It assumes the taken-for-granted social, political, historical, intellectual, and cultural legitimacy of the Maori, "in that it is a position where Maori language, culture, knowledge and values are accepted in their own right" (Smith, 1992, p. 12). The acceptance of Kaupapa Maori is imperative when working with and through Maori networks. Maori have been able to survive because, against all odds, their traditional networks have continued to flourish.

Achieving Results Through Networks

The opportunities and constraints of working through networks to achieve results can be either positives or negatives, but both are necessary to develop an in-depth dialogue, depending on the circumstances.

Opportunities

• Sharing in the process of responsibility.
• The ability to react quickly to local needs and develop solutions quickly.
• Relying on network feedback to develop proactive programs.
• Sustainable community growth that can be owned by the participants.
• Sharing of power to the lowest level possible.
• More involvement of a broader cross-section of people in decision-making.
• Understanding and utilization of different cultural ways of working with each other.
• Growth of individual and group skills and confidence.
• Relationship enhancement and growth.
• "Conscientisation"[3] (Freire, 1970, p. 17) of a larger group of people.
• More integration of issues or problems rather than fragmented solutions.
• The likelihood that consumers or clients have more say and can eventually own the program or *kaupapa* for themselves.

Constraints

• Acceptance and interweaving of ways of doing things of individuals, groups, and cultures can be frustrating but are absolutely essential; the lack of doing so may lead to the downfall of the *kaupapa*.
• The personal cost of changing to accommodate others.

- Longer time frames; decision-making processes seem to take longer because of the consultation within networks that is often necessary and results in more meetings.
- Meeting the needs of all the participants.
- Maintaining the crucial relationships that underpin networks, and having to work with people one may not like but still remaining committed to the process.

Conclusions

It is a simple concept to agree to work together for a common cause, but there has to be a will to work in a collaborative and cooperative way. As in any negotiated process, there has to be real give and take. At a time when so much of what we and our children are exposed to revolves around individual achievement, working collaboratively through networks is food for the heart, the mind, and the soul. There is so much to be done, and with your food basket and my food basket, we will get the job done and be better human beings for it. The weapons we have are our combined abilities and skills and our commitment to making networks achieve useful results.

Na maua noa.
(From both of us.)

Notes

1. Signed in 1840, the Treaty of Waitangi was an agreement between the British crown and the indigenous people for the annexation of New Zealand/Aotearoa.

2. *Whanau* has been interpreted as "extended family" but also means "to give birth." Instead of tribe, subtribe, and extended family, you have bones, pregnant, and giving birth creating a network effect.

3. "Conscientisation," from "*conscientizacao*," refers to learning to perceive social, political, and economic contradictions and to take action against the oppressive elements of that reality.

References

Freire, P. (1970). *The pedagogy of the oppressed.* Auckland, NZ: Penguin Books.
Smith, G. H. (1992). *Tane-Nui-a-Rangi's legacy . . . Propping up the sky: Kaupapa Maori resistance and intervention.* Paper presented at the New Zealand Association for Research in Education/Australian Association for Reseach in Education Joint Conference, Deakin University, Australia.

18

Integrated Systems for Knowledge Management

A Participatory Framework to Help Communities Identify and Adopt More Sustainable Resource-Management Practices

Will Allen, Ockie Bosch, & Margaret Kilvington

A COLLABORATIVE APPROACH to decision-making is essential if we are to achieve more sustainable land and water use, and will require the obtaining and improved use of high-quality information. The need for participatory or collaborative approaches to meet environmental challenges is especially important in communities where human and financial resources may be limited. By focusing on improving information use within a collaborative approach, people can broaden the scope of their actions and solve problems previously beyond their capacity.

Integrated Systems for Knowledge Management (ISKM) provides a framework for guiding our actions as we manage problem situations (e.g., Allen et al., 1998; Bosch et al., 1996). It builds on principles of community participation, experiential learning, and systems thinking, and is applicable to developing the knowledge and actions needed to change situations constructively.

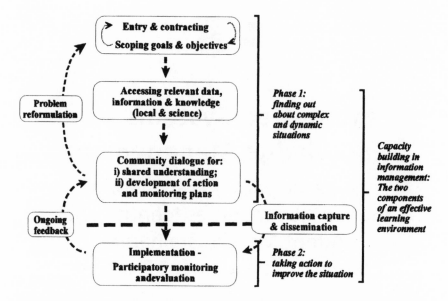

FIGURE 18.1 ISKM—a participatory research framework to facilitate the identification and introduction of more sustainable resource-management practices. The two phases interact to create an effective learning environment.

The ISKM framework has been applied to a range of environmental issues: developing improved management practices to preserve conservation values; weed and pest control in New Zealand; ectoparasite control on sheep in Australia; and rangeland management in Turkey. We have used lessons learned from these projects to develop and refine supporting participatory approaches. Software applications developed include computerized management-information systems (easily operated stand-alone systems, but also designed for the Internet); a condition-assessment and -interpretation module; a computerized herbarium to assist with the identification of indicator plant species; and a model to assess grazing capacity. The three last applications have been combined in a single user-friendly package through a system (REDIS) to help users interpret resource and environmental data (Gibson and Bosch, 1999).

ISKM

The contribution of the ISKM framework (figure 18.1) is in strengthening and enhancing the application of methods to promote participation and self-help in natural-resource-management projects. This encourages the formation of multidisciplinary projects, which involve not only technical experts, but also personnel with complementary skills in the management of participation and conflict, and the integration of biophysical and social aspects of problem solving (Allen and Kilvington, forthcoming).

As such, ISKM is not a new project type or innovative development concept, but rather a specific approach that emphasizes a number of key actions applicable to developing the knowledge and action needed to change problem situations constructively. The ISKM framework consists of familiar processes used in other fields of cooperation, and was designed around five basic management actions: identify the problem and set a management target; search for information on how to achieve the target; implement the best management practice available; evaluate the outcome; and adapt the management if required.

To encourage people to carry out these steps when managing natural resources, ISKM provides a framework to do the following:

- Encourage the development of appropriate processes for community participation.
- Bring people together to share their knowledge (local and science) and jointly develop best-management practices and/or action plans.
- Monitor action plans to assess and interpret the outcomes of management actions within a management-information system, with potential benefits to all those that did not have the opportunity to be directly involved.
- Develop feedback loops to maximize the benefits from monitoring and evaluation, and hence develop a collaborative-learning and self-improving environment.

Phase 1: Finding Out about Complex and Dynamic Situations

Entry and Contracting

The first phase of the approach involves stakeholders in the identification of the problem and its relevant aspects. Both client participants and the researchers enter a learning process, and a community dialogue is facilitated to develop a common understanding of any perceived issue or problem. The establishment of such a dialogue first requires an initial scoping process to define the nature of the system under consideration and the needs and opportunities facing the different interest groups involved. It also addresses who should be involved and what can or should be changed. Because this provides an opportunity to involve the interested parties in the research process from the outset, it is more likely to lead to the development of opportunities and outcomes relevant to community needs.

Accessing Relevant Information and Knowledge

The emphasis on problem formulation ensures a focus on the collation and development of relevant information and knowledge. It provides a basis for the design of appropriate processes (such as interviews, focus groups, questionnaires) to find and access the relevant existing data and information from both local and research communities. The problem is often not that we do not have enough information to address an issue, but rather that information and knowledge are fragmented among professional disciplines, economic sectors (public, private), levels of government, agencies, organizations, and different end-user groups. Years of "experimentation" with different management strategies to achieve different goals have provided resource users with much knowledge about their local systems. Unfortunately, this knowledge is not available to the community on a collective basis. Similarly, much of the valuable-knowledge scientists have accumulated is fragmented (held in different databases, filing cabinets, and offices) and is consequently not always readily available, even to other scientists or land managers.

Community Dialogue

Given the complexity and different social perceptions within many agricultural and environmental situations, the process actively supports improved communication among all those involved in order to build up the "useful knowledge" needed to develop "best-management practices" and provide practical decision support. Facilitated-workshop formats can be used to provide a learning environment within which participants develop a shared understanding of how others see the world and how that shapes the way they act in it (manage their land, carry out their research, develop policy). These workshops should challenge participants to seek areas of disagreement and to debate why these might be. This makes it less likely that useful information will be dismissed out of hand and acts to minimize unnecessary conflict over the value and relevance of information supplied by different sources.

These forums provide those who participate in the process with immediate access to new ideas and perspectives, which may help them reevaluate their current management practices. The use of appropriate structured processes automatically helps identify new and relevant research initiatives as knowledge gaps are revealed (Bosch et al., 1996). Importantly, these activities also provide the community with the opportunity to prioritize their information and technical needs as they work more closely with researchers. At the same time, it helps develop a shared understanding of resource-management issues. The desired outcomes are action plans (for management and monitoring) that provide clear goals, objectives, and guidelines.

Information Capture and Dissemination

The use of ISKM and similar processes provides all those directly involved with a learning environment in which "useful knowledge" is developed through a participatory process. However, there is a need to capture this knowledge to benefit potentially all those who have not had the opportunity to be directly involved. These forums also provide many of the information resources necessary to develop information/decision-support systems (for monitoring, interpretation, and management) that are relevant to the needs of decision-makers and are consequently more likely to gain their acceptance. There is likely to be not only greater commitment on the part of users to a system they have codeveloped, but also a greater understanding of any changes needed to make it work. Here, the Internet is emerging as a new, complex information-management system that allows people to create, annotate, link together, and share information from a variety of media, including text, graphics, images, audio, and video (Bosch et al., forthcoming).

Phase 2: Taking Action to Improve the Situation

For such a socially inquiring information system to advance natural-resource management successfully in the long term, however, it needs to evolve as society and the environment change. Thus the strength of iterative processes, such as ISKM, is that they allow for the substance and context of the required information flows to be updated as more knowledge becomes available and different goals are set. As natural-resource end users (such as land managers and policy makers) adopt new strategies and measure the results of their actions (formally adopting the linked concepts of monitoring and adaptive management), they will continually develop new information, which can be brought into successive iterations of the process. In a similar way, the process can take advantage of a continued flow of new data and information from more formal science activities. Accordingly, the nature of work undertaken by individual scientists will not change, the only difference being that the starting point for scientific experimentation is more firmly embedded, or institutionalized, within the community of practice.

The process is thus iterative, with each cycle serving to maximize the knowledge available to support decision-making by those in the community at any time. The addition of different modules and issues will arise from the need to meet a community objective, which may be financial, ecological, social, or some combination of these. As all the different groups involved cooperate to develop the necessary knowledge and knowledge-based tools, new issues will be raised and the process expanded.

Conclusions

Collaborative approaches such as ISKM should not be seen as the development and strict application of a plan or set of rules; rather, they are processes that require ongoing review and improvement. Their most important result is not a "plan" or a "problem solution," but a working partnership, capable of responding to changing needs in an effective way. It is important to provide opportunities and resources to evaluate progress on an ongoing basis. Constant reevaluation is particularly important in long-term projects, not only to ensure that the project stays on track, but also to help reinforce to all parties that continued involvement is worthwhile.

Finally, it must be remembered that these collaborative initiatives should be flexible and designed to grow. There is no need to involve reluctant stakeholders in the beginning, and in some cases it may be that new stakeholders only get identified along the way. What is important is that those working together can change to accommodate this growth. Community involvement helps create ownership and, accordingly, a feeling of accomplishment in working together to solve a problem. This group dynamic will, in turn, encourage other individuals to participate—from the community, as well as research and other government agencies.

References

Allen, W. J., Bosch, O. J. H., Gibson, R. G., & Jopp, A. J. (1998). Co-learning our way to sustainability: An integrated and community-based research approach to support natural resource management decision-making. In S. A. El-Swaify & D. S. Yakowitz (Eds.), *Multiple objective decision making for land, water and environmental management* (pp. 51–59). Boston: Lewis Publishers.

Allen, W. J., & Kilvington, M. J. (Forthcoming). Why involving people is important: The forgotten part of environmental information-system management. *Proceedings: 2nd International Conference on Multiple Objective Decision Support Systems for Land, Water and Environmental Management (MODSS '99)*, Brisbane, Australia, August 1–6, 1999.

Bosch, O. J. H., Allen, W. J., McLeish, W., & Knights, G. (Forthcoming). Integrating research and practice through information management and collaborative learning. *Proceedings: 2nd International Conference on Multiple Objective Decision Support Systems for Land, Water and Environmental Management (MODSS '99)*, Brisbane, Australia, August 1–6, 1999.

Bosch, O. J. H., Allen, W. J., Williams, J. M., & Ensor, A. (1996). An integrated system for maximising community knowledge: Integrating community-based monitoring into the adaptive management process in the New Zealand high country. *Rangeland Journal, 18*(1), 23–32.

Gibson, R. G., and Bosch, O. J. H. (1999). REDIS <http://www.landcare.cri.nz/redis/>.

Index

About the Editor and Contributors

ROBERT AGRANOFF is a professor in the School of Public and Environmental Affairs at Indiana University, Bloomington where he specializes in federalism, intergovernmental relations and management, community and economic development, and social policy. His writings include *Dimensions of Human Services Integration, Intergovernmental Management: Human Services Problem Solving in Six Metropolitan Areas*, and *New Governance for Rural America: Creating Intergovernmental Partnerships* as well as many contributions to several journals.

WILL ALLEN is an action researcher with more than fifteen years experience in natural-resource management. He has developed a number of Internet-based information and networking systems (e.g., http://nrm.massey.ac.nz/change links/) and is currently looking at the potential for International Communication Technologies (ICTs) to support improved environmental management.

OCKIE BOSCH is a professor of natural systems management in the Faculty of Natural Resources, Agriculture and Veterinary Science at the University of Queensland in Australia. His main interests are quantitative rangelands ecology, complex environmental systems, development of user-friendly software tools for rangeland monitoring, and development of processes and mechanisms for linking science and management through collaborative learning, adaptive management, and information systems.

DERICK W. BRINKERHOFF, a senior social scientist with Abt Associates, Inc., is research director for USAID's Implementing Policy Change Project. He is also a professorial lecturer at The Johns Hopkins University's School of Advanced International Studies. Previously, he spent ten years on the faculty of the University of Maryland, College Park, at the International Development Management Center.

JENNIFER M. BRINKERHOFF is an assistant professor in the Department of Public Administration, The George Washington University, Washington, DC. She has consulted on civil society, training methodologies, and development management for USAID and the World Bank, including regional and country-specific work in Africa, China, Mongolia, and the NIS.

NICOLE AYERS BRUNSON is completing her graduate studies at the University of South Florida, Tampa.

NINA BURKARDT is a social science analyst in the Social, Economic, and Institutional Analysis Section at a U.S. Geological Survey Science Center. Her current research projects focus on analysis of the institutional factors that drive land, water, and wildlife management decisions. She is also involved in ongoing studies of natural-resource-negotiation practices. Her published articles have appeared in many scientific journals. Ms. Burkardt is active in several professional societies and is currently the president-elect of the Western Social Science Association.

TERRY BUSSON is a professor of political science and public administration and director of graduate programs for the Department of Government at Eastern Kentucky University. His areas of teaching include community and economic development, employment policy, and budget and finance. He has published in numerous journals, including a policy-studies book titled *Policy Evaluation for Local Communities*. His current work involves an examination of linkages for employment and training programs.

RUPERT F. CHISHOLM is a professor of management in the School of Public Affairs at the Pennsylvania State University, Harrisburg. His recent publications include the book *Developing Network Organizations: Learning from Practice and Theory* (1998), two chapters in the *Handbook of Organizational Consultation* (2nd ed., 2000), "Action Research to Develop an Interorganizational Network" in *The Handbook of Action Research* (2000), and several journal articles.

BEVERLY A. CIGLER is a professor of public policy and administration at the School of Public Affairs at the Pennsylvania State University, Harrisburg. Her work focuses on state and local politics, policy, and management. She has published over a hundred academic and a hundred practitioner articles and book chapters in various public administration, political science, and policy journals. Her current work involves state–local relations and multicommunity collaborations.

MARDIA COLEMAN is a principal in the urban community research consultancy of Coleman and Ross. Working with Laurie Ross, she has been instrumental in adapting Participatory Rural Appraisal (PRA) for use in the United States and copublished, with Laurie Ross, the article "Urban Community Action Planning Inspires Teenagers to Transform Their Community and Their Identity" in the *Journal of Community Practice* (2000). She serves as a field researcher and analyst in the University of Massachusetts Medical School's program in community-based health planning.

RICHARD ECKENROD is director of the Tampa Bay Estuary Program (TBEP), overseeing a unique federal, state, and local partnership dedicated to the preservation and restoration of Florida's largest open-water estuary. He manages TBEP's varied technical and public-outreach efforts, and serves as the chief liaison between the program and the elected officials, scientists, regulators, and citizens that serve on its various committees.

MICHAEL FINE teaches sociology at Macquarie University, Sydney, Australia. He was previously senior research fellow at the Social Policy Research Center, University of New South Wales, where he was responsible for research into aged and community care, and the finance and delivery of community services.

RICHARD FORD is active in developing community-based methods for planning and action in twenty-five African countries, with special emphasis on the development of the Participatory Rural Appraisal (PRA). His publications include books, case studies, articles, and handbooks focused on enhancing local participation and include, with Hussein Adam, *Mending Rips in the Sky: Options for Somali Communities in the 21st Century* (1997), and, with Barbara Thomas-Slayter, *Alternatives to Anarchy: Africa's Transition from Agricultural to Industrial Societies, Progress in Planning* (2000).

ROBERT W. GAGE is a professor of public affairs in the Graduate School of Public Affairs, University of Colorado, Denver. He specializes in intergovernmental management, with an emphasis on networking and strategy. He is coeditor, with Myrna P. Mandell, of *Strategies for Managing Intergovernmental Policies and Networks* (Praeger, 1990) and wrote numerous articles and reports on intergovernmental management. His current emphasis is on regionalism and the dynamics of regional networks in China.

CATHERINE GOODYEAR is a graduate of the University of Otago in New Zealand. She has been director of the Anglican-Methodist Family Care Center, a family-focused social-work agency, for the past fifteen years. She was awarded a Winston Churchill Fellowship, was a coauthor and produced the *NZ Baby and Child Care Manual*, a health and parenting resource book, and "Our Lives in Their Hands," a report of research into the lives of some of Dunedin (New Zealand) beneficiaries.

ILLANA HALLIDAY is the executive manager of the City Outcomes Department, Fairfield City Council (Australia). She has spent many years in the health industry, covering bedside nursing, education, and administration. She has presented numerous papers and speeches at a variety of conferences in Australia. Her most recent work is "Managing for Outcomes" (*IMM—Local Government Management Journal*, vol. 33 [1999]).

RENU KHATOR is the director of the Environmental Science and Policy Program and professor of government and international affairs at the University of South Florida (USF). A native of India, she is a widely published researcher in the area of environmental policy and politics. Her most recent book, *Public Administra-*

tion in the Global Village, is used as course material by many universities. She is also the author of *Environment Development and Politics in India*.

MARGARET KILVINGTON is a social researcher with ten years' experience in resource management, in both New Zealand and England, specializing in community participation, research planning, and management. She has worked with local and regional authorities to provide analysis and expertise in community involvement in resource management. Recent research includes determining public attitudes toward vegetation in the urban environment, and public attitudes toward natural heritage, to contribute to the understanding of opportunities for biodiversity conservation in productive landscapes.

MYRNA P. MANDELL is a professor at California State University, Northridge, in the School of Business Administration and Economics, Department of Management. She is recognized as a researcher and consultant in the fields of networks and network structures. She has written several journal articles and chapters in books. She recently spent a year doing research and consulting in Australia and New Zealand, where she consulted for the Ministry of Social Policy. As part of her work, she has developed a training program for the development and management of collaborative efforts.

MICHAEL MCGUIRE is an assistant professor of public administration at the University of North Texas. His research on interorganizational networks, collaborative public management, and economic development has been published in numerous public administration and policy journals. He is currently examining how public administration in metropolitan areas copes with the increasingly collaborative aspect of governing.

MATTHEW S. MINGUS is an assistant professor in the School of Public Affairs and Administration, Western Michigan University. His dissertation added to the field of comparative network theory through extensive field research on the networks used by Pacific Salmon Treaty negotiating teams in Alaska, British Columbia, Washington, and Oregon. He managed nonprofit, community-partnership projects for five years. He has published articles in several journals, and has a chapter in *The New Sciences and Public Administration and Policy* (1999).

LISA S. NELSON is an associate professor and graduate coordinator in the Department of Political Science at California State Polytechnic University, Pomona. Her teaching and research interests lie in the areas of public administration and environmental policy. Her recent work has appeared in *Administrative Theory and Praxis*, *International Journal of Organization Theory and Behavior*, and *Social Science Journal*.

GLENN W. RAINEY, JR. is a professor of public administration and director of the Institute of Government at Eastern Kentucky University. His previously published works have appeared in a number of journals and in various anthologies and reports. His experience with networked programs includes over ten years of applied research on job training and career-preparation programs.

LAURIE ROSS is completing her dissertation in community planning at the University of Massachusetts, Boston. She has worked on themes of gender and community-based natural-resources management in the Dominican Republic, and more recently has become an active presence in community planning and organizing in Worcester (Massachusetts). Working with Mardia Coleman, she has adapted methods of Participatory Rural Appraisal (PRA) for use in U.S. urban settings.

SHAYNE WALKER is a member of the Maori community and a lecturer in community studies at the University of Otago, Dunedin, New Zealand. His involvement in network processes is part of his upbringing as Maori. He has worked in community-based social-service provision for twenty years, in several roles. His research interests include Maori social-service development, alternative care, and adolescent development.